# SPIRITUALITY
## THE AWARENESS OF REALITY

HOW TO *SEE* THE UNSEEN AND BREAK FREE
FROM SUFFERING CAUSED BY A NARROW
PERCEPTION OF REALITY.

By

José Alberto Luzardo, Ph.D.

ෲ ❈ ෲ

*Ardent Light Inc.*

Editing by Mike Valentino
Cover and Interior design by José Alberto Luzardo

Library of Congress Control Number: 2012909928
ISBN 978-0-9856958-1-1

Printed in the U.S.A.

10 9 8 7 6 5 4 3 2 1

# THE AWARENESS OF REALITY...

*"[Dr. Luzardos's] book did not disappoint me. The originality of [his] ideas was more than refreshing, and that's not an easy thing when look around this busy field of copycat and near copycat book ideas. The power of his book doesn't stop there... What distinguishes 'Spirituality: The Awareness of Reality' is its reliance on real research into historical antecedents and by a reasoned approach to the evidence. That's right. Dr. Luzardo counts heavily on making sense. Refreshing... The core of his argument, as you might gather from the title, is that spirituality is not some detached corner of reality into which initiates escape the mundane. Spirituality he argues, and I agree, is an ingrained element in every bit of reality, not something that holds us above it."* ~ **David Stone**, author of *'Amazing: Truths about Conscious Awareness— Discovering Ultimate Reality'*, *'A Million Different Things: Meditations of the World's Happiest Man'*. (http://the13theedge.blogspot.com/2013/02/spirituality-awareness-of-reality-by.html)

*"This book, 'Spirituality: The Awareness of Reality' seeks to broaden our perception of what is real in order to be free from all suffering. It is a champion of both the western and eastern traditions of meditation, suggesting a completely holistic understanding of life."* ~ **Reverend Leo Booth**, MTh, a Unity minister and author of *'The Happy Heretic'*, *'Say Yes to Your Life'*, *'Say Yes to Your Spirit'*, *'Spirituality and Recovery'*.(fatherleo@fatherleo.com)

*"In his honest and thought provoking way JAL takes us through a journey of opening to and understanding our own human nature as we open to the idea that there is much more to be revealed as our perception widens. JAL opens his heart as he offers a tender look at parts of his own life. At the same time he uses his scientific background to take us through Quantum Spirituality."* ~ **Reverend Glenda Knox**, co-founder of Common Ground Interfaith Spiritual Center, Tustin, California. (http://www.embracehumanity.com/),.

CR80✻CR80

To my wife, Ngoc, and my three children, Allegra, Renzi and Max. Without them this book would still be waiting to germinate...

CR80✻CR80

# CONTENTS

# FOREWORD

Modern science has opened up a window on exciting new worlds for us. The wonders of Astronomy have exhibited the vastness of the cosmos, and Molecular Biology has unveiled the striking complexity of even the tiniest of life forms. Yet even these jaw-dropping discoveries only expose the physical realm of reality. In other words, one aspect of reality. But not all of it. Not even close.

The truth is, reality is a stunning yet simple composite of the seen (i.e., the physical universe) and the unseen (the realm of spirituality). Genuine spirituality is both everywhere and nowhere at that same time. In fact, it exists outside of time, or we might say that time is merely a way of measuring physical phenomena, all of which ultimately are manifestations of the unseen spiritual realm.

It is through a recognition of this profound and eternal underpinning of reality, that we find meaning and purpose in everything, including our human lives. This book is an exploration of the unseen portion of reality, and how each one of us can gain deeper insight into the oneness and sameness of everything. It challenges us to lay aside self-limiting belief systems based on fear and negative thoughts. In stark contrast, we look at the totality of reality—both the seen and the unseen—as it really is, bigger, better and more beautiful than we had ever imagined.

Within these pages we go far beyond merely esoteric renderings or philosophical speculation. You will be introduced to a practical approach for incorporating into your own life the spiritual truths revealed in each new chapter. Your everyday life, no matter who you are, what you do, or where you live, will be infused with meaning and purpose like never before. "The Awareness of Reality" is a voyage of self-discovery that will enlighten your mind and enrapture your soul.

Mike Valentino
Editor of numerous spiritual books, including several for Christian publishing houses Baker Books and Deep River Books

# PREFACE

When I told my boss I needed to quit my job to finish a book and spend some time for self-growth, I had the impression he was not surprised. He already knew that I was writing a book as I continued on my path of self-discovery. Utilizing my abilities and intellect to serve the corporate world from Monday to Friday (and some weekends) during most of my waking hours contravened this powerful desire to take something out from deep inside me and share it with the world. Abandoning a well-paid job and the financial security that comes with it was not straightforward. It took decades, a wife, three children, a mother, siblings, friends, coworkers, a church, a *kriya* yoga practice, heavens, hell, Earth; it took everything, it took 15 billion of years of universal evolution (and I am still not quite done yet). But once I made the decision during one weekend, I was serene, peaceful and content.

I always knew I was going to write a book. I first believed the book would be related to engineering, science, control systems, firmware, or real time embedded systems. After so many years of academia and direct application in the industry, what else could I expect? I thought that only after writing a technical book would I write a second book about "life and its vicissitudes." I confided in Gail Minogue, the well-known numerologist, telling her my plan while she was reading my numerology chart. She candidly told me that my "first book" had to wait because it was not what I was really being called to do. I interpreted her observation as if she had told me "do not waste your effort and energy on that venue; there is something much bigger within you." She mentioned that my numerology chart indicates that my life path and destiny numbers are both six, the number that characterizes the need to help and serve others,[1] and that this "healing quality" of mine will show up no matter what. At that time, immersed in my own small world, I dismissed that advice somehow and continued focusing on making money the way I knew to support my family.

A couple months later, after this consultation, I was laid off, and then I realized that there was definitely something wrong with my small world. Reality became more defined. I started, thus, writing my "second book" which is now my first book. But when my wife was laid off herself, I returned to the work force and lost my compass again until one day in the fall of 2010 when I had that talk with my boss.

I wrote many chapters and developed many ideas during these past years. I wrote so much that my editor told me that sometimes it seemed to him that he was reading two different books. And he was right. In a dream, I saw how I could split the material into two books, of which this is the first. The organization of the written material was not easy but was concise and well defined. This book is about spirituality as it must be first approached, from the individual point of view. The second book is about spirituality within the social context, that is, how spirituality manifests itself in society.

My major challenge writing this book was two-fold: (a) how to convey the idea that spirituality is universal, that it is not a belief of a particular tradition or culture, and (b) how to convince readers about the necessity of being spiritual regardless of their current circumstances. Throughout the book I try to get rid of the ideas that spirituality is an accessory of life that we may not choose and that spirituality belongs to only New Age people inclined towards the Eastern philosophies and religions. Anyone, regardless of their condition, can find spirituality. For some it will be harder than for others, perhaps, but we all are capable of appreciating and experiencing it in its entire splendor.

---

[1] *Divine Design* by Gail Minogue, Academy Road Teachings, Tarzana, CA, Second Edition, 2004, pp. 50-51 and 81-82.

I tried to impregnate this book with "common sense"–a term that I define only at the end of the book in Chapter 9–and a "direct style." I believe that spirituality is simple and basic. When spirituality is hard to comprehend it is so not because it is complex but because we are confused. This is why common sense and a direct style can help to dissipate the confusion. I hope this book helps you to get rid of whatever confusion you might have and, thus, when you look around you, you can appreciate reality as it is.

I want to thank my precious wife, Ngoc Luzardo, partner in life and business, whose feedback and contributions were invaluable; my mother, Ana Teresa Flores, for always asking me, 'how is the book going?'; my editor, Mike Valentino, for his corrections and observations; my proofreader, Peter Crabb, for detecting those hard-to-find mistakes in the final manuscript; Rev. Judy DePrete, Rev. Glenda Knox and Common Ground's community in Tustin, California, for their moral support; Sadhguru Jaggi Vasudev and Isha Foundation for the Inner Engineering program, and the 15 billion years of evolution for taking me where I am now.

JAL

# 1
# INTRODUCTION

On the subject of spirituality we can scarcely say anything fundamentally new. The Truth never changes and has already been exposed over thousands of years through universal spiritual teachings from ancient to modern masters. Today more than ever we have a vast number of sources at our fingertips to learn about spirituality such as spiritual communities and organizations, books, films, documentaries, and the wonderful "source-for-everything" called the Internet. I am very grateful for these sources. How fortunate we are that humankind has managed to preserve for thousands of years the unraveling wisdom of ancient texts such as *The Tao Te Ching*, *The Bhagavad Gita*, *The Sutras of Patanjali*, *The Bible* and many other ancient texts that plumb the depths of our reality.

Of course, spirituality is more than knowledge about the Truth. It is a deep personal experience that cannot be taught or instructed. We can indirectly perceive the spirituality that emanates from the blessed ones as their words match their impeccable actions, but only our personal experience of spirituality can clearly and absolutely unravel its utmost profound meaning for us. Therefore, the novelty of spirituality lies not in the content of the Truth, which never changes, but in the myriad ways through which human beings realize the Truth. The authentic experience of spirituality stems from within and flows outward as the spiritual individual connects and communicates with others at the most essential level, not with the purpose of converting people, but with the purpose of understanding and comprehending them. Thus the spiritually motivated individual attempts to go beyond people's circumstances in order to raise the fundamental union that exists among all of us but that we cannot see. Buried under many layers of deception, we have forgotten and neglected our essential union with all. The time has come to place spirituality above our delusions so love and compassion will always flourish.

But, why do we need spirituality? To answer this question we need more questions. When was the last time you thought you were happy? What happened to that feeling? How long did it last until you became angry, frustrated, or depressed again? And when you felt those uneasy feelings, did it matter to you that you felt "happy" before? Most of the time, our "happiness" is attached to material, physical or emotional comfort whose nature is external (coming from outside the individual) and ephemeral. To maintain this "happiness" we would require comfort from the external world quite frequently, but this is impossible to attain. In trying to achieve such "happiness," we go to extremes and excesses, sacrificing our own well-being and that of those around us. Isn't this a paradox? By seeking happiness we end up miserable. In reality what seems a paradoxical situation is not. If we look closer we can appreciate the misconception here: We seek happiness by chasing after things that are unrelated to happiness. Spirituality, instead, does not make us chase after anything. It makes us realize that everything we need to be happy lies within.

Only through spirituality can we achieve the state of transcendental happiness,[1] the happiness that we all long for. Spirituality leads us to happiness because spirituality is the awareness of *reality*–the *seen* and the *unseen*, concepts we expound on in Chapter 2. Without the awareness of our whole reality, how can we know we are living our full potential? How can we experience contentment and peace? Without spirituality, we live our existence constrained and limited to the small portion of reality that we happen to know. This small portion of reality will never tell us the Truth; it will always tell us that it contains everything we need, that we don't have to look somewhere else. In this limited situation, we will never experience the transcendental happiness that every single

---

[1] The word "transcendental" in this context means "surpassing all others; superior" (*The American English Dictionary of the English Language*). Transcendental happiness surpasses any other "happiness" that does not come from the wholeness of reality.

human is entitled to. Conversely, as we open the doors to spirituality, unknown aspects of reality start unfolding in front of our eyes revealing to us the full extent of our capabilities and the enormous prospects of happiness lying just ahead. Only then, the fog vanishes and the path to the most wonderful state of existence appears clear and certain to us. In this sense, the process towards spirituality—the complete and absolute awareness of reality—has traditionally been depicted as a journey on the spiritual path. This spiritual journey is detailed in Chapter 4 to highlight the necessity for us to travel on the path of spiritual realization. In this journey every single step towards increasing our awareness of reality counts as we improve our well-being and increase our joy.

Notwithstanding its benefits, the spiritual journey has its own challenges. We can appreciate that the spiritual path does not constitute the rule but the exception, although some signs indicating otherwise are becoming more visible. The strength and the persistence with which we hold onto the small portion of reality that we happen to know represent the main deterrents to our spiritual journey. Namely, the more we believe that our small portion of reality is the whole reality, the more we contend with others trying to defend our belief, and the more agitated we become. With this in mind, it seems clear that people defending their individual "small realities" cause their own suffering and, thereby, the current collective havoc in the world.

The belief in a "small reality," referred to as "belief system" in Chapter 3, works as a program that operates in our minds and strives for self-preservation by dictating our behavioral responses, thoughts, feelings and emotions. The mind constitutes the origin of all these responses as humans interact with each other in the world; for this reason, the understanding of the human mind becomes paramount from the spiritual point of view. In Chapter 6, I elaborate on the obstacles that hamper the spiritual progress of the human mind. The spiritual journey, then, involves the underlying process of making the mind reach its fullest spiritual capability, that is to say, making the mind increase its receptivity to the whole of reality—especially the unseen. I call this process the Seven Pillars of Spirituality, which are described in Chapter 7. The application of the Seven Pillars of Spirituality leads to a practice specified in Chapter 8. This practice contains aspects of several disciplines holistically assembled together. The holistic approach to the spiritual journey is fundamental inasmuch as only a holistic approach can consider each of us as an inseparable part of a whole called reality.

Spirituality has been with us since time immemorial; in fact, spirituality ascended as the first sign of our consciousness long before any form of writing was created. I believe that spirituality is very human and encompasses all the other aspects of human existence. If spirituality finds fertile soil to sprout and grow, it will take care of our daily emotional and physical needs including all those problems that plague our world today. If spirituality does not find fertile soil the current trend will persist, but the seed will remain, waiting for the right conditions to germinate.

Your spiritual experience awaits you. You will be reminded from time to time about the little seed in your soil. Every reminder will be like an alarm clock that tries to waken you out of your snooze. "Hey, have you taken a look at this little seed inside you? It seems that it pertains to you," that alarm clock might sound like. How would you respond? When the soil is not prepared for sowing, a typical response would be to press the snooze button: "Oh really? Nah, but that's O.K. Besides, I have no time for it right now. An important matter requires my attention." Later on, immersed in your daily activities you forget all about your little seed until the alarm clock sounds again, and then you will have another opportunity. Will you press the snooze button once more? As my own stories show in Chapter 5, I was reminded many times of my own seed until the day I decided to let it grow.

Spirituality is subtle, for not everybody is sensitive enough to appreciate it, though all are potentially capable simply by virtue of being human. Spirituality is also strong, for it profoundly transmutes those who experience it. And most of all, spirituality, unlike belief systems, is absolute and true as explained in Chapter 9. Spirituality provides us with the true individual fulfillment that spreads out in the world. No war has been or will ever be fought in the name of spirituality[2] but its strength can conquer an entire civilization through its subtle ways of individual transformation.

---

[2] Unlike some religious beliefs that are used to justify wars, spirituality excludes any war or confrontation as a way to establish itself.

# 2
# THE ESSENTIALS OF SPIRITUALITY

In Chapter 1 we define spirituality as the awareness of reality. Reality is the seen and the unseen. The seen represents our entire physical world, the universe; it can be perceived with our five senses and explained through science. The unseen cannot be explained with science nor perceived with our five senses, but it can be experienced nonetheless. In order to *see* the unseen we possess a special sense that works only when we purposely turn it on.

## Understanding the Seen and the Unseen

The seen and the unseen constitute our reality. Spirituality attempts to strengthen our perception of the unseen (commonly neglected because of our attachments to the physical world) in order to have a better, more refined appreciation for the seen. Namely, authentic spirituality does not make us disregard the physical aspects of our reality in order to pursue the non-physical; it essentially makes us perceive the intimate relationship between these two realms. Merging into the unseen makes us appreciate and experience the seen—the physical world—in its rightful way.

The unseen can also be called the unmanifest since it is prior to all physical manifestation—the manifest—and has none of its attributes. The unmanifest cannot be detected using any physical means or explained using science because if it could, it would be manifest. The *Tao Te Ching* states it more elegantly: "The Tao that can be followed is not the eternal Tao/ The name that can be named is not the eternal name."[1] The unmanifest is immutable, eternal, same single source. The manifest is mutable, always-changing, temporary, diverse. By feeling the unmanifest and the manifest together, I attempt to write about God:

---

### GOD

*God does not change.*
*God is immutable because God does not need to evolve:*
*God is the absolute perfection.*
❄
*God does not move.*
*God is still because God is already everywhere:*
*God permeates everything and lives in everything.*
❄
*God has no origin, no end.*
*God is eternal because time relates to changes.*
*If there are no changes, then there is no time,*
*for time, by definition, has to change with the changes.*
❄
*God is the unseen prior to the seen,*
*the void before the existence,*
*the unmanifest preceding the manifest.*
*But, how can we know the void without the existence?*
*How can we know God without the universe?*
*For the same reason we need darkness to know light and cold to know hot,*
*we need the existence to know the void,*
*we need the universe to know God.*
❄
*For light and darkness, or hot and cold,*
*constitute nothing but the opposites of the same essence,*
*existence and void constitute the two opposites of God,*
*both equally good, both equally magnificent.*
❄
*The existence and the void are interchangeable:*

---

[1] *Tao Te Ching* by Lao Tzu, Translated by Charles Muller, Chapter 1, Barnes and Noble Classics, New York, 2005.

*by feeling the void one feels the existence,*
*by feeling the existence one feels the void.*
*From the powerful and indescribable void,*
*the existence emerges and*
*from the myriad forms of the existence, the void will prevail:*
*all in the eternal cycle of God.*
*What we call existence is just an instant of no duration*
*in the timeless eternity of the void.*
*And our greatest purpose ever is to know God while we exist.*
❅ ❅ ❅

There are no definite borders between the seen and the unseen.[2] They form part of an indivisible whole. To believe they are
separate is detrimental to spirituality itself and, therefore, to our
realization of happiness. Happiness is the experience of oneness,
the non-dualistic state of being united with all.

## The Seen and Its Differences

Based on what we can see and sense all around us, we can
conclude one important thing: this physical world is thoroughly
diverse. More specifically, we cannot find two objects, two people, two cells, two atoms completely identical in this physical universe. Quantum Physics establishes that no two subatomic particles can have exactly the same quantum state, which means that
the sheer foundation of matter and energy enforces physical diversity. We must realize that there is no use fighting against or escap-
ing the diversity and differences that this physical universe floods
us with, and instead we should embrace the beautiful infinite heterogeneity of everything around us, including precious human beings.

This physical diversity also applies to the human mind, our
mind, which processes the information that comes to us through
our five senses. As objects and events are presented to us differently since the moment of our birth,[3] and as each of us has unique

---

[2] The transition between the unseen and the seen is referred to as the *quantum realm* in Chapter 6 on the occasion of expounding on the human mind.
[3] And very likely, even before birth during our womb days.

ways of processing the information coming from those objects and events, we end up having distinct individual perceptions of our physical realm. The perception that each of us has of our physical world, with its events and objects, constitutes a subjective image constructed from the association between current sensorial stimuli and past experiences as shown in Figure 1.

Because the mind is such an important tool for our spiritual endeavors we dedicate an entire chapter, Chapter 6, to elaborate on it. But at this point in which we discuss the differences we continuously encounter in our daily lives, it becomes pertinent to highlight how the mind perceives our heterogeneous physical world. Figure 1 depicts the perception of the seen, the physical world, through our mind. The planet Earth represents the seen. As for the unseen, it is of course impossible to depict, but I chose the sunlight to symbolize it. In Chapter 6 we will talk about how the seen and the unseen interact through the *quantum realm* to unfold the Creation.

In Figure 1 the mind has been split into three parts according to its basic functions. The mind records (recording component), analyzes (analytic component) and composes (composing component) information. The recording component consists of all our past memories and experiences and includes also the learning, conditioning and beliefs we have acquired previously. The memories in our mind are stored with attributes that define the type of memories they are: good, bad, dangerous, pleasant, etc. They are classified according to these attributes as we classify files in a file folder. Because this past information is presented together with the five-sense information to the analytic component of the mind, we also call this recording component the sixth sense.

Most of this past recorded information started once as stimuli that our five senses detected from the outside world. However, as mentioned previously, the information from the sixth sense has been classified and labeled according to how we perceived the outside world stimuli for the first time. This explains the feedback mechanism through which the perceived reality composed by the mind conditions the memories stored by the

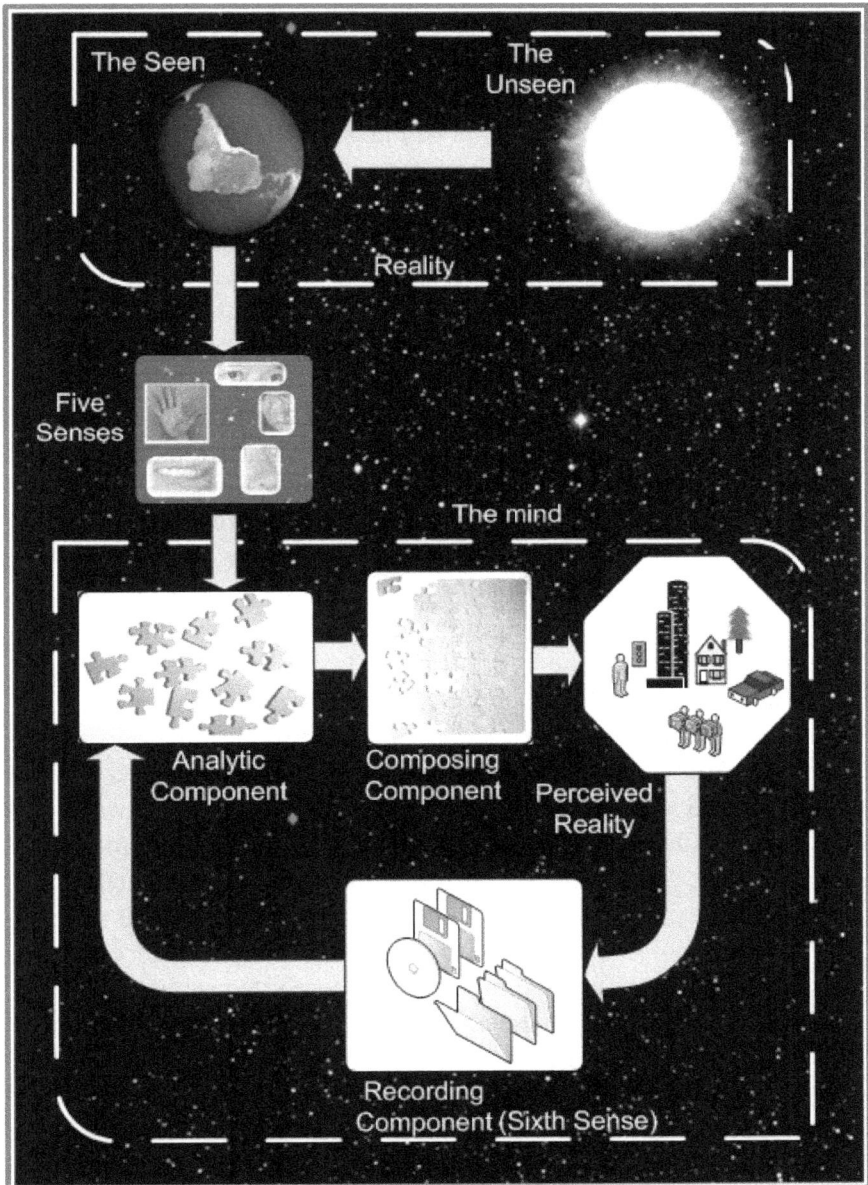

**Figure 1. Perceiving the seen through the mind**

recording component (see Figure 1). For example, the first time we burned ourselves with fire we perceived such experience as painful. Therefore, fire was stored in our memory with the attribute of being harmful. Notice here that the recording component of the mind also contains the memories of our evolutionary past wherein all our instincts for self-preservation developed. In conclusion, the recording component of the mind, called also the sixth sense henceforth, consists of classified recorded information from our evolution and all the experiences we have lived until the present moment.

The analytic component of the mind receives and processes the information coming from the five senses and the sixth sense. Its job is to separate every single object, strand of information or sensation received by the five senses in order to associate it with information from the sixth sense. This explains why, for example, we know the object chair is a 'chair' when we see it and the word 'chair' refers to that object when somebody mentions it. In other words, the analytic component analyzes, separates and discriminates in order to determine the associations between the objects and the events of the current situation and the objects and the events of past situations. These associations are passed to the mind's composing component which puts them together to compose the individual's perception of reality. The composing aspect of the mind then projects such perception internally as awareness. The awareness thus created makes the individual react and act accordingly. For example, you see fire that can burn you but the fire is in a pit and you are sitting on the ground several feet away from it. You are outdoors; it's a cold night and the warmth from the fire actually feels good. You are surrounded by friends who are talking and laughing. All these sensations and many more, which the analytic component identifies very efficiently for you, are compiled by your mind in order to compose your perceived reality; next you have the awareness that the fire is a campground fire completely safe; you relax and enjoy your camping trip. The closer our perceived reality is to reality, the larger our awareness and the more beneficial our actions.

Summarizing, based on our physical components and the way we perceive the world in our mind, we all are very different. We, the human race, can be depicted only by a collage of extreme discrepancy and heterogeneity. As we walk on this planet, expect nothing but diversity from anyone, from any culture, from any religion. The diversity of our beliefs is the result of our growing up

THE ESSENTIALS OF SPIRITUALITY

in different settings; namely, it represents the distinct responses to the different external conditions that this world, this physical realm, imposes on each of us. In Chapter 3, as we elaborate further on belief systems, we describe how harmful it is to uphold them as absolute and real. When we come to the awareness that physical diversity constitutes a fundamental aspect of our human lives and that as such it has no permanent attribute, we will find how absurd it is to quarrel over our differences. Respecting life, embracing diversity, creating harmony, living a prosperous coexistence are all essential qualities to walk on this diverse planet and appreciate its heterogeneous intrinsic beauty; otherwise, we will be discontent and unhappy because differences are always all around us.

## The Unseen and Its Sameness

The second paragraph of the Declaration of Independence of the United States of America states: "We hold these truths to be self-evident, that all men are created equal, that they are endowed by their Creator with certain inalienable Rights, that among these are Life, Liberty and the pursuit of Happiness." How is the expression "all men are created equal" a self-evident truth? On the contrary, based on the previous section, we can affirm that all men are different, physically different, that is. We all are different not only by appearance but also by thinking as we hold our dissimilar belief systems as true. Then, what makes us created equal? Moreover, what are these inalienable rights, Life, Liberty and the pursuit of Happiness? Are these the rights that cannot be taken away from anyone? If so, then they are inconsistent. If I want to exercise my inalienable right of Liberty in the pursuit of my Happiness, I might need to dispossess some people of their Liberty, or, perhaps, I would like to rob some other people of their land. After all, they are very different from me. Wasn't this how slavery existed for so many years in the U.S. and other countries, and expansion and colonialism were and are still the trademarks of powerful nations? And to protect my Life, shouldn't I be allowed to organize preemptive attacks against those I perceive as my enemies, thereby, taking their "inalienable" Right of Life away from them before they take mine?

Playing the role of the devil's advocate is not pleasant, but the above paragraph has two special purposes. First, humankind has recognized the notion that human beings are equal and entitled to the same inalienable rights despite the fact that we are all physically different and have different belief systems. The U.S. Declaration of Independence in 1776 and the French Declaration of the Rights of Man and the Citizen in 1789 constitute evidences of this assertion. Indeed, all political movements in one way or the other use this notion of "all men are created equal" to attract a large number of followers. And second, despite the "all" in "all men are created equal," the equality concept has been absurdly employed to set boundaries among human beings. The application of the equality concept has been local, not universal as the word "all" should indicate.

The white men of European descent in the American colonies declared their equality to the white men in Europe whose status they wanted to attain as they had no need to "lift up" others with "lower" status than theirs. The French Revolution with its Declaration of the Rights of Man and the Citizen in 1789 opened the doors for the new political and economic classes to rise in replacement of the privilege-based nobility while denying the women, the poor and the slaves those same "Rights of Man and Citizen." Similarly, the Bolshevik Revolution intended to alleviate the proletariat penuries and give workers real opportunities within the economic machinery, but instead created an oppressive regime class that stymied the advancement of individual rights. Thus, human civilization at times has realized that humans are equal, despite their obvious differences, but has failed miserably putting theory into practice.

What went wrong? What went wrong (and is still going wrong in many instances) was the lack of understanding of "equality." When we say all human beings are equal we need to find the reason for this assertion because if we look around us we see nothing but differences in the physical realm. What makes us equal? Where is it? How do we perceive our "sameness"? Whatever makes us the same cannot be found in the heterogeneous physical realm; we must search for our sameness in a realm other than the physical: the unseen. Our non-physical real essence is the same always. It does not change, it is immutable, because no physical attribute, no knowledge, no life experience can ever affect it; otherwise, it would belong to the physical realm. Our sameness is eternal, it transcends our birth and death, because birth and death are physical phenomena and, as just said, no physical phenomenon can alter our sameness. Our sameness is universal; it includes everyone regardless of their condition. Therefore our immutable eternal sameness has always been there; hence equality among all human beings has always been there, and we just need to realize it at the individual level. No revolution, no law, no regulation, no society can impose sameness or equality on anyone, for true sameness is a personal experience.

If sameness is not experienced by the individual, equality is just a narrow term colored by the individual's beliefs. In an historical context, equality has been understood as merely the need of a group to enjoy the privileges of another group considered to be in a "better" position. This has achieved only replacement of one privileged group by another privileged group, which merely perpetuates the inequality as reflected in the above historical examples.

Thus the U.S. Declaration of Independence, the French Declaration of the Rights of Man and the Citizen, and any other similar documents that declare equality among human beings implicitly acknowledge the existence of a non-physical realm—the unseen—in which we all are the same. More than a political or economic assessment, these documents essentially entail a spiritual connotation because they recognize precisely the part of our reality that is not physically accessible. Terms such as "self-evident truth of men's equality," "Creator" and "natural or inalienable rights" cannot be explained using logical physical explanations from the seen, but can be accepted only if we believe in the unseen.

Humans have always had the innate capability to sense reality in its entire splendor, but many times they don't believe in or are unaware of such capability. For instance, do you remember the times when you felt that you were not the same as other people? Perhaps you felt above others and thought you had the right to judge them, or maybe you felt inferior, not worthy of their attention and interest. In either case, as you probably remember now, you were not happy and content at those times. When we fail to see the spiritual implications in the word "equality," which goes beyond economic and political connotations, we start putting boundaries on its application and interpret it within our own narrow perception of reality. Thus an individual validates their anger, frustration, depression and any other excess, and the social collective[4] justifies slavery, segregation, sexism, poverty, economic exploitation, war and environmental destruction. Only when humans, individually, come to the awareness that their sameness in the non-physical realm is absolute, and that this non-physical realm, the unseen, is as real as the air they breathe, will they never be distracted by physical circumstances. They will look at themselves and *see* the eternal and immutable essence whose perfection escapes words. They will then be able to bring peace to themselves and then to all human beings, in the totality of humankind, for spirituality is forever all encompassing.

## The Seventh Sense

Our transcendental and absolute sameness in the non-physical realm cannot be perceived through the information received by our five senses and the beliefs that originated from our interaction with the physical world. Our five senses provide information from the always-changing and heterogeneous physical world, and our mind distinguishes, sorts, classifies and stores said information. In this physical diversity, during our evolution, the mind had no choice but to evolve into a very efficient machine that not only classifies and stores but also associates current situations, events and objects with the information that has been stored and classified previously (see Figure 1). Thus the mind assesses current situations versus a set of beliefs or values previously created. Are they good? Are they bad? Am I in danger? Are they gratifying? What should I do?

If we allow ourselves to be driven only by the sensations of the physical world, we will become hypersensitive to differences and insensitive to the transcendental and absolute sameness of the unseen, in which discerning is not needed. The 'sense' that perceives the absolute sameness of our non-physical realm then atrophies. But if we accept the "self-evident truth" that all human beings are

---

[4] Collective beliefs are considered in Chapter 3.

equal, as betokened by the U.S. Declaration of Independence, then we have hope that this 'other sense' is still working. This is why we are still capable of sensing "self-evident truths" that contradict the information received by the typical five senses. This 'sense', the seventh sense,[5] is better known as intuition. Intuition constitutes the art of immediate cognition in which no sensorial or past information intervenes and that traditionally relates to the heart—as the Spanish word *corazonada*[6] indicates—and, thereby, to our noblest feelings (see Figure 2).

In Figure 2, we can see how the seventh sense contributes directly to the individual's perceived reality bypassing the five senses and the analytic component of the mind. The operation of the composing component is also not required since the unseen has no parts to compile; it is perceived as a whole, all at once. The unseen cannot be perceived otherwise.

Notice that since the information from the past and the information from the five senses do not play a role while perceiving the unseen, the perception of the unseen is (a) universally the same and (b) free of contention because the information received through the seventh sense does not need to be scrutinized and weighed against old beliefs and conditioning. The experience of perceiving the unseen through the seventh sense stays with us and will be stored and classified in our mind (through the sixth sense) as with any other experience. This fact is very important because it denotes that perceiving the unseen has the benefit of cleaning and healing dysfunctional belief systems and traumatic memories.

In order to develop our intuition, the seventh sense, we must first be open to its possibility. Openness to our immutable and eternal essence constitutes the necessary first step that frees our intuition; once liberated, our intuition can grow and with it our transcendental possibilities. When doors are closed there is no possibility of coming into the awareness of our permanent essence. Skeptics cannot go beyond their own beliefs. If the doors

---

[5] We will revisit the sixth and the seventh senses again in Chapter 6 as we elaborate on the mind and its spiritual capabilities.

[6] The word *corazonada* in Spanish is used for hunch, premonition, and generally is indicative of intuition. It comes from the word *corazón* (heart).

are open, intuition will lead us to the awareness of our absolute sameness in the wonderful eternal realm of the unseen.

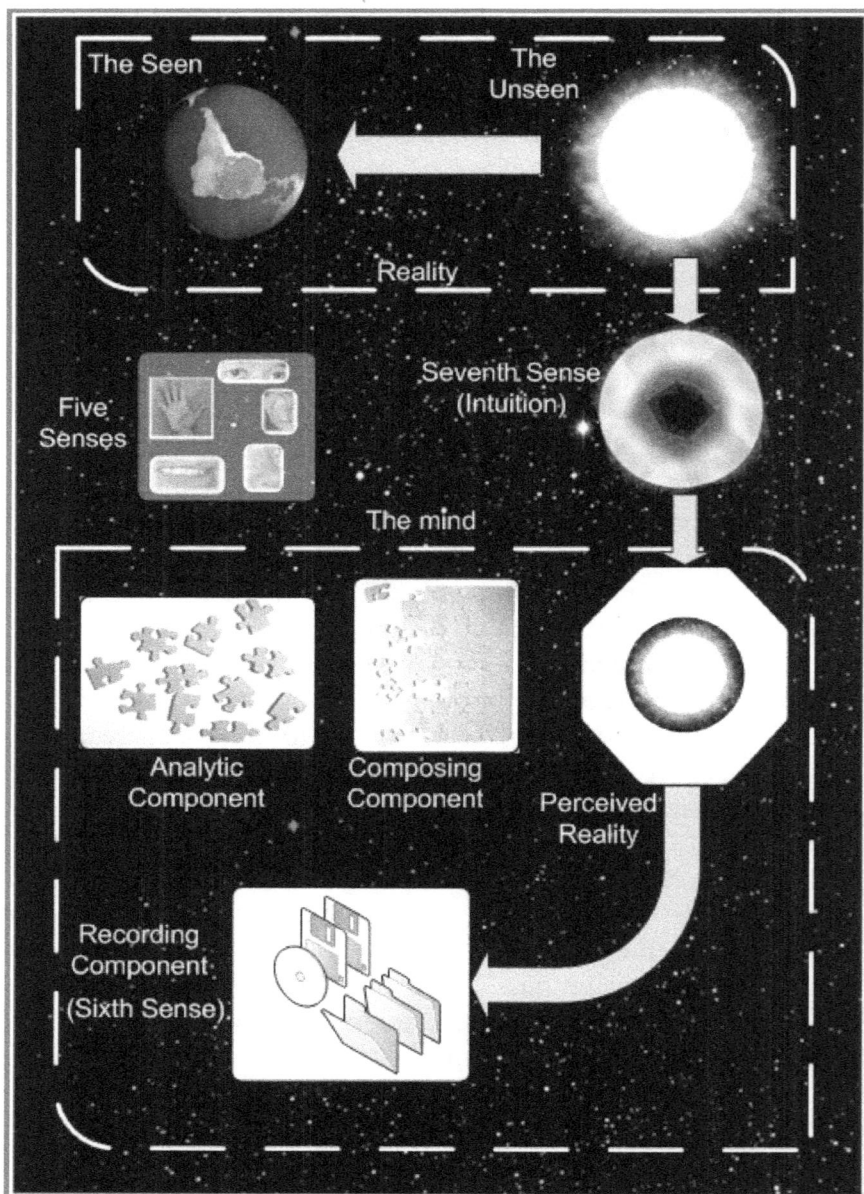

**Figure 2. Perceiving the unseen through the mind**

Being open to the possibility of the existence of this immutable and eternal realm represents the indispensable first step to becoming spiritual. Nonetheless, spirituality—the ultimate and complete awareness of reality—involves much more than this crucial initial step. Becoming spiritual is usually presented as a spiritual journey, which is described in Chapter 4. This journey is in reality a process that gradually develops our spiritual capabilities. As we progress in this journey, we will notice that our joy and peace increases, and our fear diminishes; we trust more and lack less. Spirituality creates transcendental peace and happiness from deep within; it entails the final and permanent state of total clarity, which obliterates all confusion and fear. Consequently, it behooves us to conduct our lives on the spiritual path in order to experience true happiness.

## Summary

This chapter reviewed the essentials of spirituality. Spirituality is the awareness of reality as comprised of two realms: the seen and the unseen. The seen and the unseen are indivisible and inseparable. Lacking spiritual vision, humans tend to separate them as opposing poles in a dualistic view of reality, which generally creates their personal discontent and agitation.

The seen is characterized as heterogeneous, always changing, always different. The unseen is always still, always the same. Despite our apparent physical diversity, human beings have recognized equality among humans as an indication that we are able to sense the unseen through a special sense. This sense is our intuition which we rename the seventh sense.

The idea of equality that humans recognize is the physical manifestation of our sameness. Our sameness, the unseen, is the underlying aspect of our reality that binds all of us together as one; our sameness makes love and compassion possible. Buddha said, "All sentient beings posses the Buddha Nature; all can become Buddhas."[7] Our sameness is this Buddha Nature, it is the *Atman* and the Christ that we all are. Jesus said it too: "The Kingdom of

---

[7] *On Buddhist Democracy, Freedom, and Equality* by Venerable Master Hsing Yun, translated by Dr. John Balcom, Buddha's Light Publishing, 2002, p. 3.

God is within you" (Luke 17:21). Experiencing our sameness takes care of our well-being and physical needs. Therefore, developing our seventh sense constitutes a primordial aspect of the spiritual journey and the spiritual practice described in the following chapters. But first we need to understand how the sixth sense with its belief systems hinders the development of the seventh sense as discussed in the next chapter.

# 3
# BELIEF SYSTEMS:
# THE HUMAN RESTRICTIVE CHAINS

The number of possibilities for a human life is infinite. At any time, life is presented to each of us as evolving circumstances in which we make decisions. Every time we do, the law of cause and effect—also known as Karma[1]—makes us face new circumstances and then again we make decisions to choose a new possibility out of an infinite number of possibilities. We make a choice and life continues on the road we just opened. We cannot undo our decisions, we cannot go back on the path we have paved with past choices, but we can change paths anytime. Life seems a one-way continuum, a non-stop flow full of detours and turns at every single moment. The detours and turns are up to us because we have free will and the power to choose; circumstances and events, however, might seem to be out of our control.

We did not choose our parents or the place of our birth (the law of Karma did it for us). As children, we did not pick the words we were told, including those not so nice words coming from our parents; we did not ask for abuse or lack of love, or for the many rules, dogmas, stereotypes and any other kind of doctrines we were subjected to. And yet we are still paying the price today for those things we did not ask for when we were children and adolescents as we carry the burden of the seemingly insurmountable debt of our upbringing. We can see this in ourselves as well as in others. Perhaps we can see it in the story that Andre Agassi told

---

[1] The law of Karma is considered again in Chapter 4, p. 54.

about himself during an interview broadcast on public radio.[2] The tennis Grand Slam champion and Olympic gold medalist said that he hated tennis because he was forced to play it and practice it for endless hours as he grew up. I could perceive from the interview that he felt imprisoned for living a life that he did not choose, or at least a life that was presented to him as his only available choice. His life was selected by his father, Mike Agassi, an Iranian-Armenian immigrant who went through his own penuries and hardships during childhood. Mike decided that tennis was the path for Andre to succeed in life and to enjoy the American dream, which had been denied to Mike in the streets of Tehran.

Mike Agassi achieved his goal inasmuch as Andre became wealthy and famous thanks to tennis, but perhaps at the expense of Andre's emotional and personal balance, as it can be inferred through his accounts of his insecurities, divorce, and drug consumption. What is remarkable about this story is the fact that Andre Agassi made the decision to reconcile himself with his father; at some time in his life, he decided to face his past and to acknowledge his feelings about his father. He, in other words, opted to transform his life. Such decisions are the only way for us to start resolving our emotional issues. As we can appreciate from Andre Agassi's story, we pay our debt with emotional distress—an unfair situation for anyone...so why should we keep on paying it?

## Belief Systems

The belief system of an individual is a set of beliefs that operate together to identify the role of said individual within a social context. This role sets the individual apart and dictates what he or she does or doesn't do in order to create a sense of separation and distinction. This sense of separation derives from an evolutionary trait that the mind has developed to protect our physical integrity. In order to survive, we needed to separate ourselves from other living creatures, those that threatened us and those that we killed to eat.

---

[2] "Fresh Air" with Terry Gross, National Public Radio, broadcast on November 11, 2009, http://www.npr.org/templates/story/story.php?storyId= 120248809.

Belief systems determine the way we answer these two questions: Are we the mere result of chance and fortuity as life unfolds the circumstances and events before us? Or, are we the result of our decisions in life? Those who attribute their success to their vision, intelligence and will, taking most of the credit for their achievements in life, are playing a role dictated by a belief system of importance and recognition. They want to separate themselves from the rest by being above. They do not realize that nobody reaches a specific situation in life without the participation of other human beings, a society, a system, the entire Universe and its laws. Just the fact of being born in a particular family, country or culture, or even in a particular era, can make all the difference in the world. We all are connected yet some deny that connection, as they do not feel connected to others. They lack the humility to recognize that they are the same as everyone. They do not feel the profound gratitude of being one with our marvelous Creation; they separate themselves from all as they hold onto their pretensions.

Conversely, those who accept their hardship in life as due to fate are also playing a role dictated by a belief system. In this case, it is a role of powerlessness and inaction. They blame their penuries on their circumstances as being completely out of their control and do not realize that their own decisions have contributed to their situation. They play the victim role to draw the attention they desperately need. They also feel disconnected. But in this case, their disconnection is mainly from themselves since they are ignorant of their creative power within and they assume that they have no control over their lives.

How we experience the breakup of a relationship is another example of how a belief system determines one's role in life. Those whose belief systems considerably highlight their personal inadequacies, defects or imperfections choose to blame themselves for the breakup as they fall into depression as a victim of circumstances. In contrast, those whose belief systems stress the deficiencies of others rather than their own choose to blame their former partners as they search for a "better" companion in order to "move on," away from their current feelings of frustration and dissatisfaction—feelings that in most cases have to do more with themselves than with their partners.

The truth is that our lives are actually the result of a complex interaction between our circumstances and the decisions we make and that we can never assume that only our decisions or only our circumstances molded us. In this complex interaction, circumstances and the decisions we make feed each other in an apparent unbreakable cycle in which past circumstances seem to bias our decisions now and our current decisions seem to determine our circumstances in the future—the classic what-came-first-chicken-or-egg conundrum.

All our past experiences, previous circumstances, past decisions and all the events of this evolving universe since its beginning combine to create our present circumstances according to the law of Karma. The circumstances we face right now must be taken as they are because we cannot do anything to change them. We cannot control them; they are the result of the immovable past. At this present moment, however, we possess the free will to make a new decision that will impact ourselves and others around us. At this precise moment, we can exercise our free will to change our lives forever by realizing that even though these present circumstances are unavoidable we can still move on towards happiness and fulfillment. Will our decision be the right one right now? The answer to this question is crucial and has profound implications. We make decisions that contravene our desire for happiness because of the limited pool of choices we think we have, even though, in reality, the set of choices for a human life is infinitely open. This limited pool of choices that we think we have to choose from represents the core of our belief systems.

In many situations, we fail to realize that the right choices lie outside our belief systems. What are right choices? The right choices are the ones that lead to transcendental happiness. A right choice foments universal connection and togetherness; a right choice makes you a creator. A creator is one who keeps or reestablishes, when disrupted, the harmony in the universe. If you make a choice that distances yourself from your own potential, or separates you from others, or causes you to disregard nature,[3] then you

---

[3] All kinds of separation are always interrelated. If you start separating from others, you will end up being separated from your well-being, and from nature itself. If you separate from your own potential and capabilities, you will be

should know that your choice is not a right choice and that you are indeed disconnected from your eternal essence. You are unable to *see* the unseen, the eternal and immutable essence that permeates the entire Creation. Furthermore, you are actually disrupting Creation's harmony and consequently hurting, directly or indirectly, those around you as well as yourself because you have taken a detour away from the path towards happiness. In this context, you need to step out of your box and look again. Remember that, for better or for worse, you are what you believe. In this precise moment, you are nothing more than what your current individual belief system says of you—and therein lie your constraints.

## Collective Beliefs

We may notice that some of our beliefs originate from family, culture, country, religion, teachings, education, and so on, all of which intend to impose values and behavioral responses on the individual. This imposition is carried out through the human conditioning that we receive since the moment of our birth. Human conditioning, as its name indicates, is a process through which humans try to force values and behavioral responses on other humans using consistent repetition and reinforcement.[4]

Typically, human conditioning is generated within what we call the collective, which represents any group of people that as a whole has values accepted to be above those of the individual. In

---

disconnected from others and nature. Likewise, if you disregard nature you are disregarding yourself as well as others.

[4] Classical conditioning is based preliminarily on the work of Ivan Pavlov (1849-1936) who conditioned the salivation response of a dog with the sound of a bell, thus the dog anticipated the forthcoming food. Later, John Watson (1878-1958), developing Pavlov's findings further, established the Behaviorist School of Psychology with the goal of studying the prediction and control of human behavior. Then, Burrhus Frederic Skinner (1904-1990), a behaviorist, developed the idea of "operant conditioning" or "shaping behavior." He explained that under operant conditions a specific behavior can be either rewarded or punished. Rewards will reinforce the behavior, punishments will weaken the behavior, and thus a desired behavior can be shaped. The main premise of human conditioning is that we behave as we learn to behave and for that matter persistence and consistence of the conditions that reinforce the desired behavior become paramount.

this sense, the collective protects its social cohesiveness by persistently imposing its distinctive values, stereotypes and dogmas on the individual. To implement its cohesiveness, the collective relies on some sort of authority system—parents, school, law and government, church, workplace—established traditions, customs and social habits, and, in these modern days, mass communication media. As the individual is repeatedly exposed to the same behavioral patterns that the majority exercises or the authority imposes, these behavioral patterns are reinforced with rewards (such as collective acceptance) and punishments (such as ejection from the social group). Over time the individual ends up adopting the values and behavior of the collective.

*****

To illustrate the previous point I would like to describe two seminal experiments in the field of social psychology. The first of them is known as the Asch Conformity Experiment performed by Solomon Asch in the 1950s. In his experiment, the experimenter displayed a card on a table for all the participants to see. On the card, there was a single bar on the left and a group of dissimilar bars on the right. The experimenter then asked each participant to say aloud which bar from the right has the same length as the single bar on the left. The lengths were easy to discern and the answer was always the obvious one. But in this experiment, all the participants but one were confederates (actors) who were assigned to pick unanimously a wrong answer at certain times. The real subject of the experiment (the only one who was not an actor) had to say his or her answer after hearing the actors' answers. Stunningly, Asch reported that a high percentage of the subjects picked the same erroneous bar as the confederates at least once. At the beginning, the subject picked the correct bar as it was easily distinguishable and despite the fact that the actors unanimously selected another one. Nevertheless, as the group kept on agreeing on a given wrong answer, the subject finally joined the group and started selecting the group's erroneous answer too. This experiment shows how individuals conform to the collective regardless of what the collective advocates for. It demonstrates that individuals want to be like the others within a collective.

The other experiment was carried out by Stanley Milgram in the 1960s—the Milgram's Obedience-to-Authority Experiment. The purpose of this experiment was to explain some of the atrocities inflicted on prisoners in the Nazi concentration camps during World War II. Many war-criminals argued that they were just following orders and they couldn't be held responsible for their actions. The question to be answered with this experiment was: For how long will a person inflict pain on somebody if they are told to do so by an authority? The experiment was done under the auspices of Yale University and advertised to the public as a "Study of Memory." In the typical Milgram experiment, the subject was the "teacher" and a confederate was the "learner." The assignment of the teacher consisted of asking the learner different questions to test the learner's memory, and for each wrong answer the teacher had to apply an electric shock to the learner in increments of 15 volts from 30 volts to 450 volts. The teacher and the learner were in different rooms so the teacher couldn't see but only hear the learner. The experimenter, the scientific authority, the professor in white coat, was in the room with the teacher all the time imparting commands and directions. The electric shocks were phony and the confederate, that is, the learner, played a tape recorder synchronized with the selected voltage. The higher the "voltage" the louder the expression of "pain" from the tape recorder, except for the highest voltages in which there was only silence. Most of the subjects became distraught and anxious about the pain of the learner, but once the experimenter told them they had to continue with the experiment, they just went on increasing the voltages despite the fact that they believed they were inflicting pain on another human being. This experiment shows that human beings tend to submit to authority regardless of moral and ethical values. Authority constitutes the maximum manifestation of a collective. The institution of science, the collective in this case, supported by the prestige of Yale University, provided an ordinary man wearing a white coat with enough power to override compassion in the heart of the subjects of this experiment.

These two experiments are representative of how individuals behave in order to fit in society. From an objective point of view we wonder how people could act this way. Moreover, most of us would claim that we would never do something like that, but the fact is that many of us do. Under pressing circumstances, we might choose to conform to a group and forget our conscience if we are not spiritually present.

*****

The need for a human to join a group under the same flag, cause or dogma derives from our social nature. As a social creature, a human joins the collective as a sheep joins the herd; both of them developed an evolutionary trait to act collectively in order to preserve the species. Conforming to the collective, therefore, is a defense mechanism for self-preservation. However, more than for physical preservation, due to their complex nature, humans join the herd for "emotional preservation," more specifically for acceptance, validation, and identification with the group. This group could be small; it could be your parents, friends, coworkers, or significant other. The group could also be large such as your country, culture, religion, or race; it could even expand to cover our entire society, or perhaps humankind.

Humans have an instinct to mimic others as they become indoctrinated by whatever social environment that befalls them. Early in life, they are shaped by their families and they believe, consciously or not, what they are told during childhood as they try to identify themselves with the family group. This could explain why people who were told repeatedly during childhood that they sang terribly deny themselves the joy of singing, and could explain as well why somebody who does not even like tennis is a tennis player as mentioned previously. Later on, society takes the dominant role and sets expectations for them that they instinctively fulfill in order to be accepted and recognized. This is why sometimes they believe that their culture, race, religion, political party or country is above all, and this is also why they become unhappy if they do not receive acceptance and recognition from others.

The human conditioning we have been undergoing since birth has found its way to our psyche and has forged collective beliefs. Notwithstanding their relative nature, collective beliefs are often perceived as being absolute, leaving no room for different collective beliefs; those who do not believe their truth become outsiders, aliens, and quite frequently enemies. Collective beliefs establish borders that separate one group from another, setting up differences and hierarchies among groups, and as history has shown us these beliefs can supply the justifications to deny others their own humanity–resulting in racism, classism, sexism, slavery, genocide, war, terrorism and other diseases of human psyche. As an example of these justifications, Inquisitors believed they were destroying evil when they burned people to death at the stake, people whose only fault was being a "witch" or "heretic." Certainly we learned and we no longer burn witches anymore, yet we can find so many examples, both past and present, of collective beliefs taken to the extremes of human wretchedness that we cannot help but wonder if we have learned enough.

## Individual Beliefs and Collective Beliefs

Individual beliefs are those beliefs that are not derived from human conditioning. Distinguishing collective beliefs from individual beliefs is quite important to fully understand the spiritual limitations of belief systems. The following examples could help to tell them apart and to highlight their respective importance. Assume that I believe that singing will never bring me any joy because I am extremely self-conscious about the quality of my voice. Is this a collective or an individual belief of mine? It depends. We mentioned this example in the previous section above. If, as in that case, when I was little, I was frequently reminded of my singing skills every time I sang by being the object of jokes and laughter, then we need to conclude that my external social group consistently and persistently conditioned[5] me not to sing. Consequently, in order to conform to said group I stopped singing. In this case, my belief is a collective belief. Nonetheless, if my family never cared, one way or the other, how I sang and I kept on singing for many years until one single moment when I heard for the first time a rude comment on my singing, then we need to conclude that the external factor that led me to stop singing was a single event. That is, it was not persistent conditioning. In this particular case my belief is an individual belief.

---

[5] The word "conditioning" already involves persistence and consistency. "Consistent and persistent conditioning" might be redundant but it creates more emphasis.

Notice that even if one has been conditioned to adopt some particular beliefs by only one person, these beliefs are still collective beliefs; the collective, in this case, consists only of the person who conditions with their authority or influence. For example, assume you make your child take piano lessons for hours and hours each week because you want to draw people's attention and admiration for her so she can succeed in life. She learns that "playing piano is important in life" because of you, and that is the only reason for which she plays. As piano actually does not mean much to her, she would rather spend the piano practice time with you. Since she spends more time with the piano than playing with you, she could have mixed feelings about your love for her and could harbor resentment towards you. "Playing piano is important in life" is a collective belief because you imposed it on her. But her resentment towards you, manifested perhaps by her believing that you don't care about her, is her own individual belief because nobody conditioned her to accept such belief—she made it up by her own interpretation of her circumstances.

In a sense, individual beliefs have to do with the individual's personal experiences[6] and the unique way the individual processes them, all of which contribute to the uniqueness of each belief system. This uniqueness constitutes a special human capability that I mentioned in the preceding chapter. A belief system is analogous to a living organism that changes dynamically through the interaction between collective and individual beliefs. When an individual belief validates and strengthens a collective belief, a constructive interaction between individual and collective beliefs occurs. For example, the pianist girl of the example above has the collective belief that "playing piano is important in life." Now, as she notices that her mother praises her more when she practices for hours and hours, she draws the conclusion that "my mother loves me more when I play piano." The individual belief "my mother loves me more when I play piano" validates and strengthens the collective belief "playing piano is important in life" indicating a constructive interaction between these two beliefs.

By the same token, status-quo preservers have individual beliefs that make them feverishly defend collective beliefs. The

---

[6] Which includes those as a result of previous human conditioning.

reasons for somebody to strongly defend a pernicious collective belief are manifold. Among them we can mention: the need for recognition, the desire to become a leader, the urge to identify with a group, and the common fears that force people to seek protection from the collective. In this case we can remember those who defended the collective belief of segregation as if they were defending their own lives such as Alabama's Governor George C. Wallace. He said on January 14, 1963, "…I say segregation today, segregation tomorrow, segregation forever."

On the other hand, when an individual belief is at odds with a collective belief, a destructive interaction (a conflict of values) between individual and collective beliefs occurs. For example, assume that our young pianist instead feels resentment against her mother for not spending time with her as practicing piano keeps the daughter and the mother apart. In this case, her individual belief "my mother does not care about me" goes against the collective belief "playing piano is important in life." For the little girl, life is all about spending time with her mother, and naturally she starts questioning why playing piano is so important in life. Questioning and then openly opposing collective beliefs constitute the main characteristics of status-quo dissenters.

Looking in our recent history, we can find many status-quo dissenters. After centuries of slavery, segregation and poverty, most black people collectively accepted, subconsciously or consciously, the "fate" of being discriminated against and considered it too strong to fight back. They identified their herd and conformed to it. It took some special individuals within the black community to overcome this stigma and bravely launch the Civil Rights movement. Their opposing individual beliefs made this possible as they became status-quo dissenters, such as Dr. Martin Luther King, Jr. His "I have a dream" speech on August 28, 1963, poetically stated his dissent: "…I have a dream that my four little children will one day live in a nation where they will not be judged by the color of their skin, but by the content of their character." Similarly, a subject who questions the experimenter and decides to stop the application of the electric shocks in the Milgram's Obedience-to-Authority Experiment is also a dissenter.

As a person matures the interaction between individual and collective beliefs changes over time in response to new conditioning or experiences. Due to this dynamic and complex nature of belief systems, preservers and dissenters of the status-quo are not exclusive roles. Sometimes we behave as preservers defending and strengthening the collective beliefs and sometimes we behave as dissenters antagonizing and fighting the collective beliefs. The interaction between collective and individual beliefs drives human lives. It has placed each human being in a seemingly eternal contention: "to be or not to be." In other words, to follow their own inclinations or to abide by the collective—whatever that collective happens to be, e.g., parents, friends, coworkers, significant other, country, society, etc.

The elaborated interaction between collective and individual beliefs explain as well why humans are the only social creatures that can transform the entire collective into a new structure with new values and stereotypes; they can go from followers to leaders and impose their own beliefs on the entire collective. Political leaders, including some dictators, can knock down the old establishment and build up a new one. Religious leaders are also good examples of this exclusive human characteristic as betokened by the fact that most religions originate from the teachings of a few individuals. What a single human being adopts as their particular belief system will affect other people and definitely the possessor of such beliefs. Only spirituality will ensure that we interrelate harmoniously with all.

## Belief Rationalizations

In either case, following the herd or leading it, human nature exposes itself as a tangle of complexities. It is natural to see why trying to untangle human nature becomes a thorny task. How to explain the coexistence of aggression and compassion side-by-side in this world? How to explain human opulence feeding upon human misery? How can you explain your anger, frustration and depression, all of which constitute the antithesis of happiness? There is no doubt that the only way to answer these questions is to convulse the foundations of most belief systems, and not everyone is prepared to be shaken to the core of their values. All the people of this planet have explanations and justifications for their actions; many rationalize their belief systems.

The subjects in the Milgram's Obedience-to-Authority Experiment believed that it was okay to continue inflicting pain on somebody because the experimenter in a white coat requested it. They rationalized that the experimenter—the scientific authority, the collective—had the knowledge to determine the safety of an electric shock despite the expressions of excruciating pain that such electric shock caused in a person. The subjects above all wanted to conform to and be accepted by the collective. Therefore they decided to engage in their assigned role and rationalized why they were inflicting pain on others. Likewise, the Inquisitors mentioned previously rationalized their burning of people at the stake. They surely rationalized their actions based on the fact that the institution of the Catholic Church (the collective) accepted and validated torture and death as part of religious dogmas. One always wonders where their conscience was before the suffering of a fellow human being. How did they, when left alone, face their own values and virtues? Why did they allow the collective to rid them of their conscience? They rationalized their actions. Erich Fromm called rationalization the counterfeit of reason because it looks like reasoning but actually opposes it. In his book *Psychoanalysis and Religion*, he wrote:

...Indeed, the power of rationalization, this counterfeit of reason, is one of the most puzzling human phenomena. If we were not so accustomed to it, man's rationalizing effort would clearly appear to us as similar to a paranoid system. The paranoid person can be very intelligent, make excellent use of his reason in all areas of life except in the isolated part where his paranoid system is involved. The rationalizing person does exactly the same. We talk to an intelligent Stalinist who exhibits a great capacity to make use of his reason in many areas of thought. When we come to discuss Stalinism with him, however, we are suddenly confronted with a closed system of thought...He will deny certain obvious facts, distort others, or, inasmuch as he agrees to certain facts and statements, he will explain his attitude as logical and consistent. He will at the same time declare that the fascist cult of the leader is one of the most obnoxious features of authoritarianism and claim that the Stalinist cult of the leader is something entirely different, that is the genuine expression of the people's love for Stalin...He will find a thousand and one reasons why Russian nationalism is not nationalism, why authoritarianism is democracy, why slave labor is designed to educate and improve anti-social elements. [7]

To a lesser or greater degree we are all paranoid about our belief systems, and within each belief system there are aspects that are touchier than others, all with the powerful capability to trigger in us very strong reactions. Analogous to the Stalinist in the excerpt above, we can find a faithful adherent of a particular religion completely convinced that people who do not accept and follow the creed of their religion will go to hell and that is why conversion becomes an imperious necessity for the infidel's salvation. This salvation most frequently means soul salvation, but sometimes can mean physical salvation when humans, based on their religion beliefs, take the liberty to judge and condemn others, the infidels, to capital punishment. What our religious, faithful person has not realized yet is that our religious beliefs are conditioned by external agents—family, culture, society, etc. For most people, the religion they practice has been a product of chance; they just happened to be born into a particular religious belief system. Our devotee could have grown up in the middle of the Amazon since birth without exposure to any mainstream religion. Naturally, he would worship the jaguar and the river, and he would never suspect that he has already been condemned as an infidel. Obviously claiming the absolute rights of the Truth from a dogmatic religious point of view is against the idea of a benevolent, compassionate and fair God, about Whom every major religion preaches. Why would a benevolent, compassionate and universal God limit His reach only to certain people who happen to have fixed dogmas on how to know Him? Yet it is very common to find this kind of disturbing inconsistency in most belief system defenders.

---

[7] *Psychoanalysis and Religion* by Erich Fromm, Bantam Matrix Editions, New York, Toronto, London, 1967, pp. 55-56.

## Intuition and Spirituality

Rationalizations lead us to contradictions that we can detect in our daily lives. When you find a contradiction of yourself, you have found a piece of information that tells you that you are deviating from your happiness. You should take advantage of this moment and veer back to your spiritual path. For example, when you find yourself loving and protecting those very close to you but despising others because they don't think or look like you, then you are contradicting yourself as love is universal. This contradiction shows that you are not happy. Getting annoyed, disturbed or angered by others constitutes a sign of discontent—a discontent that may adversely affect the ones you say you love.

An open intuition, or seventh sense, helps us to *see* our entire reality and our absolute sameness. An open intuition will tell us immediately about our rationalizations and contradictions, and more importantly it will make us veer in the right direction towards our path to happiness. On the contrary, a closed intuition makes us strengthen our belief systems and their rationalizations leading to all kinds of problems. In this case, we are admitting that our essence, what we really are, constitutes nothing more but what we have learned and acquired from our experiences in the physical realm. Each of us would be just a bunch of traditions, rituals, customs, knowledge, dogmas, habits, and social mannerisms, all of which have no absolute and permanent attribute. Either we declare that we are not permanent and absolute, therefore not having an immutable and eternal essence that makes us all "be created equal" as discussed in Chapter 2, or that our real essence, the absolute and permanent sameness, escapes whatever belief system we have adopted.

What does your common sense tell you about it? As you try to find an answer to this question, think about those times when you felt deeply connected to someone for no particular reason. Think about those moments when human compassion moved across despair and hopelessness. Think about those humans who sacrificed their lives for the common good of the entire human race. Above all, think that those who have triggered your anger or depression, or have disagreed with you, or have pushed your buttons, could have been a different representation of yourself mirroring your own weaknesses as if you had lived their circumstances. If, after thinking, you comprehend why sometimes you help others expecting nothing in return or why you are compassionately able to put yourself in someone else's shoes, then you have found out that your intuition is as wide open as your heart. You've also discovered that what helps you to bond together with others constitutes the realization, to a lesser or greater degree, of our sameness, or equivalently, of our immutable and eternal realm. As this realization intensifies, it becomes evident that belief systems are an accessory of this physical life. Going beyond them is an exercise to comprehend the totality of our real selves, a totality that expands infinitely beyond our limited temporary physical nature and that embodies a magnificent unbounded reality. This can be fully appreciated in the wonderful children's book *The Little Soul and the Sun*:

> "Well, there is nothing else but the Light. You see, I created nothing but what you are; and so, there is no easy way for you to experience yourself as Who You Are, since there is nothing that you are not."
>
> "Huh?" said the Little Soul, who was now a little confused.
>
> "Think of it this way," said God. "You are like a candle in the Sun. Oh, you're there all right. Along with a million, ka-gillion other candles who make up the Sun. And the Sun would not be the Sun without you. Nay, it would be a Sun without one of its candles...and that would not shine as brightly. Yet, how to know yourself as the Light when you are amidst the Light–that is the question."[8]

Doubtlessly, we are here to get to know our own light because everything around us does not look like our own light. We are just living a play on this life stage; everybody plays their roles and we all should know that we are not the roles we are playing. As we do when we act in a play, let us enjoy our unique and distinct roles, especially since each of us writes their own individual script.

---

[8] *The Little Soul and the Sun* by Neale Donald Walsch, Hampton Roads Publishing Company, Inc., Charlottesville, VA, pp. 6-7.

# Summary

Belief systems behave like chains that forcefully constrain humans from perceiving reality as it is. In this chapter, we dug into this idea of belief systems and exposed their characteristics with the purpose of understanding why they are so powerfully restrictive. We distinguished two kinds of beliefs: collective and individual beliefs. Collective beliefs result from human conditioning in which humans indoctrinate other humans; individual beliefs derive mainly from the individual's unique interpretation of their life experiences.

The major obstacle to freedom from belief systems lies in human rationalization. Nonetheless, we all are able to detect the inconsistencies of our rationalizations if we start opening our seventh sense to embark on our spiritual journey, which is presented in the next chapter.

Physical diversity creates belief system diversity. Despite the apparent physical and belief system diversity, human societies have realized the "equality among humans" and many individuals, including you and me, have felt a deep and profound connection with other humans in such a way that differences no longer matter. The chapter ends suggesting that these realizations are indications of our real profound nature that may surface every now and then—a nature that we must embrace to finally perceive reality as it truly is.

# 4
## IT'S A JOURNEY. SHALL WE SET SAIL?

Realizing the full meaning of our sameness does not come easily if our intuition—the seventh sense—shuts down. Most people trust only their five senses and belief systems in order to assess any possibility, any turn, any detour, they might proceed with. Any possible decision is evaluated against the immediate physical comfort and security that the decision in question would bring to us. This is very understandable inasmuch as we must attend our physical needs to fit into this physical world. Troubles originate, however, when we dilute our feeling of sameness in pursuit of some exaggerated notion of security and physical comfort. Then "to fit in" becomes "to stand out." The more I stand out from everyone, the safer I feel, or more precisely, the more I think that I feel safer. Standing out symbolizes the antithesis of our immutable sameness. In this context, standing out does not mean to exercise our differences but to impose them; it does not mean to share our differences but to deny the value and beauty that exists in those who don't look, think or act like us. If our intuition shuts down, we will fall into the trap of this delusional physical world, thereby, compromising our happiness, bringing desolation to ourselves, and remaining unaware of our universal capabilities. By so doing, we would miss the opportunity to transcend into the peace and stillness of our essence.

## The Spiritual Realization of the Individual

Nonetheless, we can never completely close our intuition to the eternal and immutable realm from which everything emerges. No hermetic seal can achieve such a purpose, not even in the greatest of the skeptics, and not even in the most delusional. Spiritual real-ization is always possible. There will always be fissures in those tight belief systems through which specks of deeply universal connection will find their way into the individual. We all are ca-pable of having moments in our lives when we approach, in one way or another, the beauty of being deeply connected to all. Some-times life wakes us up through pain and suffering. Other times a moment of inspiration and awareness arises and guides us, or a conscious effort or practice helps us to experience our always-existing union with the source of creation–the one we call God, Great Spirit, *Allah*, *Brahman* and many other names that convey the same meaning of union as love, and connection as compassion. These moments could have a profound and lasting effect on us. They could represent the awareness shift that we need to break with the physical world delusions and finally engage our real and universal nature. On the other hand, they could just pass by as any other memory if we do not appreciate their true significance and again close our intuition with intellectual and logical justifications.

There are many examples of lives marked forever by these awakening moments, lives of people who left behind a transcen-dental legacy for all to share. As an example of this kind of tran-scendence, I would like to cite the song "Let there be peace on earth." The first time I heard this song, which happened late in my life, I deeply felt the simple message of its lyrics and music and I experienced the everlasting truth of brotherhood among us. I im-mediately knew that this song was inspired from the elevated source, from that immutable and eternal realm to which we will be able to return someday, and as such this song transcended its orig-inal purposes. This fact motivated me to learn more about this song and its authors. I found what I wanted to know from an inter-view with Jill Jackson Miller, one of its authors,[1] in the show "Humankind," program #35, distributed by Public Radio Interna-tional.[2]

"Let there be peace on earth" was composed in the summer of 1955, and since that moment this song propagated very quickly all

---

[1] The other author was her husband Seymour "Sy" Miller.

[2] Visit http://www.humanmedia.org/catalog/program.php?products_id=66 for the interview.

over the United States and overseas. The most startling aspect of how "Let there be peace on earth" grew popular was the people's enthusiasm to share it and take it with them to as many different places as possible in a time without Internet and mass media; essentially, it spread by word of mouth. Many religious congregations and choirs have sung this song; in fact, it is a song with which all religious faiths identify. It has become an unofficial anthem of the United Nations and has been sung on very special occasions to remind us that, even amid despair and turmoil, there is always a chance for peace.

To receive an inspiration of this magnitude, one must be completely open, and one's intuition—this knowing by just knowing from within—must be quite free. Jill Jackson Miller had her seventh sense open. The circumstances that drove her to her spiritual realization were by no means happy ones. Her accounts of her troubled childhood and adolescence are very eloquent: "The story is that I was an orphan at three, a rejected step child at five, a ward of the court at nine, adopted at twelve, a runaway at nineteen, and then a little while after that I committed suicide... And when I attempted suicide and I didn't succeed, I knew for the first time unconditional love, which God is. God is unconditional love. You are totally loved, totally accepted, just the way you are. In that moment I was not allowed to die and something happened to me, which is very difficult to explain. I had an eternal moment of truth, in which I knew I was loved, and knew I was here for a purpose."

The abandonment and rejection that Jill felt could escape our full comprehension as she recounts her vicissitudes in a very natural and detached manner during this Internet audio clip. Comprehending her situation, going beyond the intellectual and rational understanding of the feelings of a three-year-old who loses her parents requires digging very deep in a hard soil—a soil hardened by our belief systems—to uncover past memories of the forgotten child that we once were. Only so can we remember how vulnerable we were, how malleable we were, how disoriented we were, always yearning for guidance and looking upon others to get a sense of self. The wonderful childhood innocence, always open and ready to receive, does not know how to differentiate. A child's openness has room for everything. Children accept everything because they want to be accepted and, above all, because they want to be loved. A child who does not feel acceptance and love is a child crying out loud in the middle of a crowded street as people walk by with ears deaf to her crying.

Jill might have been this child. She did not know what an authentic family signified; she, very likely, never felt warmth emanating from a comfortable and emotionally secure home; she felt loved by absolutely no one as she grew up. To cope with her situation, Jill Jackson Miller elaborated a belief system in which she took the blame for her troubled childhood and adolescence by accepting the notion that there was something wrong with her.[3] The compelling need to commit suicide followed in the midst of hopelessness; with no purpose in life, suicide seemed the ultimate solution. But her attempt to kill herself failed with transforming consequences for her. An "eternal moment of truth" came to her. She had the revelation that she was loved very deeply. She *saw* beyond the delusions and knew that everyone was capable of loving her, and they did so up to the extent of their understanding. When we appreciate at the deepest level, as Jill did, that people do what they do because of their understanding, then we *see* the connection among all of us; we *see* that this connection sustains our real selves irrespective of our individual belief systems. We are all connected; moreover, we are all one. If we can *see* the sameness in each of us, then we can experience the "eternal moment of truth" that Jill Jackson Miller experienced more than half a century ago.

Stories like this make one wonder. What actually makes some people with traumatic experiences overcome their penuries as they shift their awareness to the universality of all human beings? In contrast, others with similar troubled experiences sink deeper and deeper into their traumas which seem to have no expiration date.

---

[3] I have noticed that people who go through a problematic childhood usually adopt typical defense mechanisms to cope with the lack of love and acceptance and to deal with the imposition that social groups in general exercised and still exercise on them. On one hand they blame themselves, getting easily depressed and lacking confidence in some aspects of their lives. On the other hand, they blame others as they become hostile and contentious with excessive confidence in some aspects of their lives. These defense mechanisms are not mutually exclusive as we all apply both of them up to a degree depending on our own past and present circumstances, in other words, depending on our belief systems.

How can we be sensitive to the signs that lead us to the realization of our wholeness? Those signs could be right now in front of our eyes and yet we fail to see them because our intuition remains closed by our beliefs. In order to set our intuition free we need first to express our clear desire to open ourselves to the possibilities from the realm of the eternal, immutable and absolute. We need to walk to the *window* and open it in order to see the splendid *outdoors*. If we believe that our room, this material world framed by walls of beliefs, comprises the only possible reality, the *window* will remain shut and the beautiful *landscape* will never be seen. We individually can initiate this awareness process by closing our eyes and saying with words or thoughts this noble wish:

> *I want to know my true essence which
> has remained unknown to me.
> I want to perceive the realm of the sacred, the realm of
> peace and harmony.
> I want to open myself to my spirit and my union with all.*

By simply expressing this wish as a prayer, meaningful changes in your perception will occur. If you do not recognize the need to see the *outdoors* at the *window* because you think that this room in which you are is all that you need, then life in one way or another will always try to remind you about the *window*. When you feel anger, depression, frustration and any other feeling of inadequacy as circumstances are not exactly the way you want them to be, you could find yourself carried away by a torrential stream that sweeps away the soil, the plants and the trees, and erodes a vibrant valley to render it bare and empty. If this is your situation, you must realize that this torrential stream constitutes the manifestation of your own internal troubled "reality" that your belief system makes you perceive. This counterfeit reality not only disrupts your life, but also the lives of those who happen to be exposed to you. In these moments when you don't find ease in your life, it is good to remember that the *window* is still there, and you may approach it. As long as you stand by the open *window*, namely, as long as your intention intensifies in sincerity and faith, you become sensitive to the signs that lead to your spiritual realization, and at its due time your wholeness will be revealed to you in a "moment of truth."[4] This is the event wherein you experience that you are everything and everything is you, or said in different words, this is the event when you experience God, and a transformation within you begins to unfold toward your highest and noblest purposes. Everything begins with making the individual simple choice of walking to the *window*, because, in fact, a *window* exists in each of us.

"Let there be peace on earth" also unveils that sheer peace starts with an individual decision. Nobody needs to wait for others to do what only one must do. No one will walk you to your *window* and make you stay there to enjoy the peace and harmony of the *outdoors*. "Let there be peace on earth" says it in a meaningful way; these are its lyrics as I recall them:

> *Let there be peace on earth,*
> *and let it begin with me.*
> *Let there be peace on earth;*
> *the peace that was meant to be.*
> *With God as our father,*
> *brothers all are we.*
> *Let's walk with each other*
> *in perfect harmony.*
> *Let peace begin with me.*
> *Let this be the moment now.*
> *With every step I take,*
> *let this be my solemn vow:*
> *to take each moment*
> *and live each moment*
> *with peace eternally.*
> *Let there be peace on earth,*
> *and let it begin with me.*

Most people associate peace with the absence of wars. This general connotation encompasses the uttermost consequence of the lack of peace. But peace actually starts much closer, from within.

---

[4] Death has been for many a "moment of truth" as it was for Jill Miller with her suicide attempt. Being close to death during near-death experiences has brought the realization of God to many.

Put differently, peace does not start by fixing humankind but by fixing oneself. Peace constitutes an internal state of balance and harmony regardless of the disturbing havoc outside. It holds no contention for anything in life. Peace is an absolute and sacred state. "Peace… comes within the souls of men when they realize their relationship, their oneness, with the universe and all its powers, and when they realize that at the center of the Universe dwells *Wakan-Tanka* [Great Spirit] and that this center is really everywhere, it is within each of us."[5] Of course, when we realize our oneness with God, we realize that there are no transcending differences among us. Peace begins to manifest when "I let it begin" within me, not when anybody else lets it begin. This is the reason you, and I, and everybody else must let "this moment now" be the right moment to "vow" to open ourselves to "peace eternally."

## The Journey in a Poem

I have been invited to follow the spiritual path many times in my life. I have had moments and have let many of them pass by without apparently major consequences in my spiritual development. These invitations came through deep feelings that originated from within me, sometimes with no apparent explanations; they came through dreams, visions and inspirations. I particularly remember one moment when I wrote, out of inspiration, something that has to do with the need of making the individual choice of opening oneself to the invisible, to the unknown goodness of our permanent essence. Years ago, precisely on the night of the 28th of June, 1982, I suddenly felt so absolutely happy for nothing in particular. As I was by myself lying down on a bed, a sense of joy came to me so strong and clear that I felt an irresistible urge to write. I didn't know exactly what I was going to write about. I took the closest pen and sheets of paper and I started to write, facing down, chin on the edge of the mattress, arms hanging out, and sheets of paper on the floor. I wrote and wrote, and I never stopped until done. After many years, I came to read again what I

---

[5] These words were said by Black Elk, a spiritual American Indian quoted by Joseph Epes Brown in his book *The Spiritual Legacy of the American Indian*, The Crossroad Publishing Company, New York, 1992, p. 39.

had written that night, and now, after the maturity that comes with years and in the light of my own realizations, I can see that a spark of my inner self resurrected that night amid the personal struggles of a single young man without a stable emotional relationship.[6] As any spark, it didn't last very long, but at least a written record of that joyful moment is still alive and for the first time I share it in English, translated from Spanish:

---

### WHAT MATTERS TO ME

❋

*What matters to me are the small things, the little details, those ones that are unappreciated by most people. Yes, little things, small details, they do matter to me.*

❋

*Seeing the rain falling down around me is what matters to me. How she gets everything wet: the plants, the trees, the soil... But not me! The rain doesn't get me wet because I'm under a roof that I made by myself. I thatched my roof with all the nice things I found around: straws, tweaks, branches, dry leaves. My refuge might look fragile and weak to some. But, it's not. It is the strongest and safest refuge of all simply because I made it with my own hands, my own effort, and above all my own Love. My refuge is the perfect refuge that protects me against the rain without isolating me from her. It still allows me to appreciate her, to feel her. It's the one that allows me to say: seeing the rain falling down is what matters to me.*

❋

*Feeling the heat from a fireplace in a cold night is what matters to me. How a few of logs burn to ashes providing me with the light and heat I need! I know that a little bit farther, a few yards away, it is cold and dark; but I instead have this little fire that illuminates and heats up my life. It's a fire that makes me feel well, but it also reminds me that a little bit farther, a few yards away, it's cold and dark.*

❋

*Looking up and seeing all the myriad stars that sparkle and shine in the sky like a luminous concert is what matters to me.*

---

[6] Not that I knew what a stable emotional relationship was about at that time.

*It's to realize the magnitude of the Universe, and suddenly feeling small and unnoticeable before such a great magnificence... before the perfect masterpiece of the Creation. But then I understand. The Universe is the perfect masterpiece, and I am a part of such a masterpiece, I play a role in the perfection, I contribute to the perfection. Then it comes to me: how important it is to be small and unnoticeable!*

*❄*

*Walking bare-foot at the beach in an unremarkable night, feeling how the wet sand sinks under my feet, listening to the sea stories as each wave comes and goes, they are all the things that matter to me. It's sitting down in front of the ocean and talking to him. It's seeing very far where the ocean blends with the sky in the horizon of my life. It is there, in that horizon, where my great destination is. I know that even though I might not get there, I need to sail that way because I know that in the journey many of my dreams will come true and most especially I will be able to love and appreciate the small things, the little details.*

*❄❄❄*

## Openness

This poem constitutes the vivid visualization of my own journey, which in many respects resembles everyone's journey. As every journey, the spiritual journey is characterized by stages. Consequently, there must be an initial step. As the old adage says, a one thousand-mile journey always begins with one small, simple, initial step. In this initial step, as I have mentioned before, we willingly and consciously open ourselves to our intuition to know what cannot come to us otherwise. It is like having eyes for the "small details." In order to see the "details" and the "little things" that underlie the general physical forms we need willingly to look closer.

Although the general physical forms represent just one miniscule aspect of our reality, they monopolize most of our attention. As a curator does not get fooled by the general appearance of a piece of art and needs to look into its details to assess it, we cannot get fooled by the physical world. We need to have "eyes" for the "details," for the absolute eternal aspects of our existence. It is the act of willingly setting the intention to become intimate with our eternal essence—that vast and still unknown part of us—that gets our feet on the road of our spiritual journey.

## Faith

If the first stage above is *openness*, then the second stage is *trust* or *faith*. We cannot start an enterprise thinking that we are going to fail and derail somewhere along the way. We need to have faith in the Universe's resources as a tree in autumn knows that new leaves and flowers will sprout again, and definitely we must have faith in our capabilities from within, in our internal strength to start and finish the endeavor of realizing spirituality. Faith provides us with the energy to travel the long journey; without it, we could default with unpredictable consequences. How do you build up your faith and trust for this journey? You do by tapping into the inexhaustible source of energy called God, the Universe, or the Creation.[7] A way to do this is through the practice described in Chapter 8 but, preliminarily, I would like to offer you this prayer I composed to set the intention that starts building up one's faith:

*FAITH*
❀
*I have faith.*
❀
*I have no fears.*
❀
*There is nothing in God's Creation to be afraid of.*
❀
*I feel my faith flowing through me.*
❀
*I cooperate with God's universe in
an effortless flow of radiant energy.*
❀
*And with my faith I construct my own reality
in the light, so my happiness is assured.*

---

[7] In this book God, Creation and Universe are entirely equivalent.

❊

*My abundance then overflows and overflows creating*
*abundance beyond my own self to others.*

❊

*I am in God's light. I am God's light.*

❊

*I am in love. I am love.*

❊

*Light and love are the solid foundations of my invincible*
*spiritual strength.*

❊

*So it is. Amen.*

❊❊❊

This prayer starts by establishing a fact: God provides you with the resources you need to achieve your noblest goals. For your spiritual journey you want your noblest goals to be in perfect harmony with God's creation as you become an instrument of the universal order: *I cooperate with God's Universe in an effortless flow of radiant energy.* Keep in mind that selfish goals disrupt Creation's perfect balance. In this sense, the poem indicates that as you build up your own faith, you will not need to break Creation's harmony by cutting trees or their branches. You will find everything you need, "the straws, tweaks and branches," around you so you can thatch your own roof. Under this roof, you will always be safe as your roof turns into the most beautiful and secure sanctuary of all: *And with my faith I construct my own reality in the light so my happiness is assured.* Amazingly, as you build your roof using what Creation—your faith—can manifest, you will always notice that the more you shelter yourself within, the more you feel the without. You will feel the rain and the wind, that gentle sensation of moist and fresh air caressing your face, when you settle under your roof. Paradoxically, you will feel deeply connected to others as you go deeper and deeper inside of you.

Consequently, abundance surely will overflow through you to reach others and help them in their own realization: *My abundance then overflows and overflows creating abundance beyond my own self to others.* This constitutes the uttermost expression of our own real essence—*light and love*—that has no similarity to the way most people approach the physical world. A refuge in the physical world means isolation, like a fortress. In the physical world, we shelter ourselves out of fear and we do so by strengthening the differences among us. If you fall into this trap, you will find yourself following the path of fear which consequently leads to suffering and constant contention.

Nevertheless, you have the capacity to perceive the signs that indicate you are heading toward true happiness as they become more evident. Just look at how connected you feel to others including those whose beliefs are so different from yours; look at how comfortable you feel living the present moment without anticipating the problems of tomorrow or reacting according to the events of a lifeless past; look at how much you are willing to share without feeling unsafe and, above all, look inside of you and if you find unconditional love, then your faith is allowing you to build the "strongest and safest refuge of all."

## Purification and Renewal

In many traditions, fire symbolizes the destruction that clears the path to new possibilities. After a fire, the forest seems dead with scorched trees and ashes all over, but vegetation will emerge again sustained by those ashes. Similarly, one's *purification and renewal* is achieved through the fire that burns the old self to ashes; thus the new self can surge and thrive.

The process of *purification and renewal* is painful and hard inasmuch as most of our habits, beliefs and dogmas (belief systems) developed so encrusted in our psyche as emotional defense mechanisms that, metaphorically speaking, only fire can get rid of them. As explained in Chapter 6, many of these defense mechanisms entail automatic responses that are produced by our instinctive mind when fear arises in us. As a result, we apply the "fight-or-flight" reactive response to both life-threatening situations and reminiscences of past traumas indistinctively.

Discovering why many of our habits, beliefs and dogmas became instinctive reactions of anger, frustration or depression[8] constitutes the major purification process of our spiritual journey.

---

[8] Instinctive reactions are considered in detail in Chapter 6.

Only when we are aware of the reasons for our uneasy reactions can we start steering our lives to true fulfillment as our spiritual realization unfolds. Fire hurts and so does healing ourselves. Identifying our traumas and insecurities will take us to the painful events that we have blocked for so many years and to the realization that our pure essence nevertheless has remained unaltered. Be assured, therefore, that when those unnecessary emotional defense mechanisms burn like the logs in your fireplace, a nice warm sensation will overtake you. This warmth will bestow the comfort of freedom on you as well as the sensibility to feel sympathy for the others that remain there where you once dwelled, just a few yards away where "it's cold and dark."

## Expansion

*Expansion* is the natural stage that results from the stages described above. In this stage we perceive our infinite and perfect nature in mystic moments in which we feel that the entire universe is in us and that our wholeness is contained in everything and in everyone. During the expansion stage in the spiritual journey we transmute into God's essence, our true nature, for brief times. As we expand we trust more and lack less. Then, we start appreciating that eternal enlightenment becomes less of a fantasy utopia and more of a reality. We start comprehending that we have a place, a purpose in God's creation, and we come to the awareness of our active role in the perfection. As this awareness permeates every single cell of our essence, an overwhelming and profound feeling of humility sweeps over us and a flood of happiness makes us feel blessed and fortunate. We perceive an enormous sense of gratitude, for feeling "small and unnoticeable" is the most wonderful indication that we are *expanding*.

## Ultimate Realization

As we evolve through the above stages of spirituality, we *realize* that those spiritual stages are not sequentially delimited, but that they actually overlap and positively influence each other and grow indefinitely. Our openness will make building up our faith easier, and faith will make us open ourselves even more. As our openness and faith grow feeding one another, facing our imperfections and past traumatic experiences inevitably becomes easier and more natural during the purification stage. The elimination of traumas and fears will get rid of unnecessary defense mechanisms that tie us up. Therefore, we will grow even more open and secure with absolute faith in our own capabilities to work according to the natural universal order. As our existence role transforms into a universal role, we expand more and more, experiencing more and longer mystic moments of oneness, which confirm to us that we are on the right path. Thereby, we continue opening, having faith, purifying and expanding even more and more in a cycle that gradually increases bliss and joy. Finally, we come to the *realization* that our infinite essence—with no limits, no tight belief systems, and definitely with none of the limitations that are so characteristic of the physical realm—is real and safe. We can even *see* it, we can even appreciate it, and we can even experience it each time we expand to be one with God.

Notwithstanding its magnificence, the "great destination" of our journey never becomes an obsession or the anxiously desired goal of our endeavors. The final destination is a reality, it's already there, it's unmovable and will always wait for us, and this is the only thing we need to know about it. It is the small or big day-to-day steps we take in our spiritual path that constitute the essence of our endeavors. We focus on the journey not the end destination. It is like driving from Los Angeles to San Francisco following GPS directions. San Francisco is a real known place that will not disappear; our mission, therefore, consists only in making the right turns at the right intersections as directed by the GPS, and we will be there in due time. In our spiritual path, we take care only to make the right turns at the right bifurcations and at the right time by following our "internal GPS" guidance, that is, following our intuition, our seventh sense, our heart—after all, our final destination exists and is immovable.

The "horizon" of one's life, the "great destination," is nothing but God's pure essence within that we have always had and always will have because, in fact, we are that divine essence. We all are, we are the same. This constitutes the grand paradox in one's life: the spiritual journey always leads us to right here right now for us to rediscover our real human nature, the nature of innocence and purity.

Our spiritual journey is a wonderful sail to a magnificent place through the most beautiful ocean and open blue sky. This trip is not a departure but a return: a return to our innocence and purity. Why then should we delay it?

## Is There a Need to Be Spiritual?

I could convince you to initiate your spiritual opening by telling you about all the wonderful events ahead in your spiritual path. Or, I could talk to you about the "damnation and punishment" you might face if you don't step on your own spiritual journey. In the latter case I would be employing an unfortunate tactic so well exploited in our society. Our parents raised us under the premise that punishment will deter us from what they considered "bad" behavior; society tries to prevent crime and corruption by promising those who trespass on the law a well-administered sentence. But crime, law and punishment can be so relative that they are almost cultural subjects. It becomes very easy to divide "good" from "evil" according to cultural perspectives. There is no evil in not following a spiritual path and essentially there is no evil in living a self-centered life of excesses.

Excesses are compensation mechanisms for emotional needs. A normal behavior becomes an excess when it tries to compensate for an emotional or psychological need that is not directly related to it. It is like trying to eliminate hunger with water; even though water could temporarily calm down the hunger sensation because it dilutes the gastric juices, it will never compensate for the nutrients that a starving body needs. A starving person who drinks too much water in the false belief that water is the remedy for hunger might have serious health complications due to water intoxication.[9] Yes, water, too, as any other substance, is a poison when consumed in excess. Using a more practical example, money is necessary to cover our physical needs, but it becomes an excess when we subconsciously try to solve our emotional issues by

---

[9] Water intoxication happens when a large amount of water is consumed in a short time not allowing the body to take time to naturally dispose of it.

hoarding money beyond any plausible physical need. Likewise, anger is a human feeling that makes us act (react) against something that might threaten us. When the perceived threat fails to materialize, any expression of rage to defend ourselves from the "threat" becomes excessive. These examples show that false belief systems always create excesses.

Society establishes lawful boundaries within which you are entitled to dedicate yourself to your excesses. But as you engage in the fulfillment of your emotional needs following false belief systems, you need to observe the totality of outcomes caused by your endeavors. You must answer typical questions such as: am I happy? Are the means I'm using harmoniously balanced so their legality will never be questioned in the future?

The first question can be answered only if you know what happiness really means. In my personal experience, the time when I felt the happiest was not related to any material possession, social recognition or any kind of sensorial pleasure. It didn't happen when I got my best job or when I purchased my home. Although I felt financially secure and content, none of these experiences made me transcend my own self-centered perspective. It also did not happen when I married my beautiful wife, nor did it when I had my three precious children. Even though these moments, no doubt, brought me profound spiritual realizations that paved the way for my subsequent spiritual journey, none of them made me experience the universal union with the totality of the Creation. The time I felt the happiest occurred in a dream in which I saw my wife[10] standing at a window. She was extending her arms at this glorious window as a gesture to draw my attention towards it. The light that emanated from the window was the most magnificent thing I ever saw. I can't describe its beauty. It was not of this world. Its brightness, an indescribable white, was thousands of times more intense than the sun, and yet my eyes were not hurt when I, completely mesmerized, stared at it. As I was drawn to the light I felt I was abandoning my body; I heard a sound very much like my breathing becoming accelerated as my heart seemed to emanate through

---

[10] Undoubtedly, my wife has represented the major motivation in my life for my spiritual awakening. Her indications for the window are meaningful in this respect.

my chest as a light of its own. And so it did. I left my body behind and in an instant I experienced the greatest feeling ever. I knew who I was because my real nature was uncovered by the light that I became, and that as such all the knowledge of the Universe was accessible to me with no effort. I felt that I was everywhere and that I belonged to everything, I felt connected with everything that the Universe entails. I could be anywhere I wanted to go and then I chose to go to the place of my dreams: a gorgeous valley with hills and mountains covered by luxuriant greens unseen on Earth. As I emerged from the light, I found myself flying in the blue radiant sky of this beautiful valley, and next to me I saw an angelic being that accompanied me crossing the sky. Then I realized that my enjoyment was so great that if I stayed there longer, I was never going to go back. This thought did not bother me at first; however, for some reason that I did not understand, I felt I had to go back.[11] I made the intention to return, and so I did. Last thing I knew was me suddenly lying on the bed with wide open eyes looking at the ceiling and still very happy.

Thanks to this dream I experienced God and realized that true happiness occurs when we expand to everything that exists in the divine light. Here on Earth, we can start our expansion when we go beyond the perceptions of our individuality to transcend to all human beings and to other living creatures, plants or animals that inhabit this planet. We experience true happiness when we see the world through the eyes of others; we grow happier when we feel with the hearts of others; we are really happy when we lend our hand to give others what they need, and also we are really happy when we open our hearts to receive from others. Thus we extend ourselves to experience fully our sameness among all of us.

Love, compassion, understanding, wisdom, all of them constitute the main exchange among the people who experience real happiness and radiate God's light. Real happiness derives from the harmony within us according to the natural universal order. A truly happy person strives to forgive, heal and reach others to expand their own harmony as much as possible. Excesses created by false belief systems have an intrinsic individualistic connotation. They

---

[11] Now I understand that this angel who accompanied me was there to care for me and make sure I came back. I was not ready yet, I had to come back.

have a limited perspective that over-satisfies our physical needs as a compensation mechanism for emotional lack. As we overindulge ourselves in one area, we deplete another area destroying our balance and harmony.

The answer to the second question (*Are the means I'm using harmoniously balanced so their legality will never be questioned in the future?*) has the purpose of enticing you to revisit the justification or rationalization of your actions. Do you justify (rationalize) your actions because your social group, culture or country deems them to be legal or acceptable? If you think so, then you need to transcend your own belief system. We know that the rules we follow are relative to our particular society, culture or country, and most of all they change through time. What was legal or commonly accepted in the past can be illegal or completely aberrant today. We can find many examples of this phenomenon in history: conquest and domination, slavery, child labor, segregation, pollution, smoking, etc. Noticing this trend creates interesting reflections in us: Would you own slaves if a time machine transported you to an era when slavery was permitted? And if the same time machine transported you to the future and after some time knowing about the future you came back to the present, would you do right now something legal but so harmful that the future society will have to ban it and you know it? This is the sort of dilemma where we stand alone on the edge of the abyss: either we fall due to a defective belief or we stand erect thanks to the innate universal conscience present in all of us.

Therefore, how do you know that what you are doing is harmonious to all, including yourself, and that as such it will remain accepted by any future, more consciously advanced, society? The law or your currently accepted social practices do not necessarily determine the fairness or harmony of your actions; after all, law and accepted cultural rules represent a human invention, and they do change. Spirituality is absolute, it applies universally to all; it is not a human invention, it is a human attribute. The harmony and fairness of what you do go beyond human inventions. Perhaps, if you are open enough, you can feel your connection with all as your conscience, in this precise moment, tells you how fair and harmonious you are when you engage in your endeavors. Are you listening?

\*\*\*\*\*

Since there is no "good" or "evil" in not following a spiritual path (should this be your choice), you will only have to experience life without spiritual guidance. How detrimental could this be? The law of cause-and-effect, also known as Karma, answers this question. Whatever you do affects the Universe and correspondingly will affect you. You will experience the consequences of your actions not because a god is punishing you but because a natural universal law is being applied to you, and in fact is being applied to everyone without discrimination. God is not inflicting any sort of punishment on that one who jumps off the cliff unaware of the law of gravity. Therefore, the most obvious consequence of living a life without spiritual guidance is that spirituality will remain unknown to you and you will simply carry out an existence without it. Imagine a treasure buried in your backyard and you are oblivious to its existence; it is a treasure so valuable that it would solve all your financial problems and assure your future for life. But how can you take advantage of such treasure if it remains unknown to you?

Consider the story of the bodybuilder who lifted weights to keep his body muscular and strong. He thought that his body was nothing but the outside part of it, that is, his physique. He didn't believe he had internal organs like the heart, the liver, the kidneys, and other anatomic pieces that a normal body has inside. He knew that a good-looking and strong physique opened the doors for instant gratification from the external world: attention, respect, women, probably a career in Hollywood. The only problem with instant gratification, he thought, is that it doesn't last, it is actually very brief: attention doesn't last as people lose interest in you, women come and go, and those acting roles in Hollywood do not go beyond small parts to fill in some scenes of cheap movies.

As he stood in front of a mirror to see the reflection of his body, he saw what he cared about, he saw his entire reality; he saw nothing else but his physique. Then he concluded that the briefness of instant gratification could be compensated by more and more of it, but he could get only so much with his current physique, and thus he tried to get a stronger and even better looking physique. Anabolic steroids sounded promising, and he took them. He noticed in front of a mirror how his muscles grew bigger and bigger as he lifted heavier and heavier weights. He knew the steroids were working beyond all expectation and he never stopped taking them until the day when an ambulance rushed him to the emergency room with a cardiac arrest.

For the bodybuilder, who didn't know he had internal organs that he had to take care of, it was too late. His heart malfunctioned because of the steroids' side effects and the lack of cardiovascular exercises. The bodybuilder's muscle hypertrophy contrasted particularly with the weakness of his heart. This contrast characterized the imbalance and disharmony that existed between the outside and inside of his body: the gain on one side was at the expense of the other side.

Notwithstanding previous signs indicating that there was something wrong within his body, the bodybuilder never really made any serious attempt to check on his health because every time he stood in front of the mirror, he never saw his heart. If he had seen it, he would have done something to improve its condition; his heart just did not exist in his reality. Spirituality is our reality; it is unbounded and timeless and, most of all, experiencing it has no harmful side effects. On the contrary, authentic spirituality brings you to a state of bliss and happiness in which all your physical and emotional needs are taken care of. You will then have the time and disposition to spread your light to all around you. If our spirituality remains unacknowledged and neglected, we will never know the magnitude and splendor of our full potential.

## Spirituality Is an Individual Endeavor

Stepping on our spiritual path is an individual duty. Our spiritual journey is a personal endeavor. We could count on help from others, but ultimately it is a solo journey inasmuch as it's a journey to within, it's the return to our innocence, to our essence, to our source which is God.

In his book *Siddhartha*, first published in 1922, Hermann Hesse precisely stresses the urge of a special man to assume such a personal journey. Hesse narrates the fictional odyssey of a young *Brahmin* in search of his most elevated self in which he would be released from suffering and attain communion with the absolute divine essence. Siddhartha, the young *Brahmin*, after many vicissitudes finally meets the fully enlightened Gautama,[12] the Buddha, the Exalted One. He is overwhelmed by His presence, His radiance, His immutable peace and calmness. His teachings help Siddhartha to perceive "the world as perfectly coherent, unbroken, clear as crystal, not dependent on chance, not dependent on the gods."[13] But Siddhartha is still struggling within; he still has no peace, and so he utters his conflicts to the Buddha:

> You have found deliverance from death. It has come to you out of your own seeking, on your own path, through thinking, through meditation, through knowledge, through enlightenment. It has not come to you through teaching! And–such is my thinking, o Exalted One–no one attains deliverance through teaching! To no one, o most Venerable One, will you be able to speak and convey in words what happened in the hour of your enlightenment! ...This is the reason on account of which I intend to continue my journey–not to seek out some other, better instructions, for I know there is none, rather to leave all teachings and all teachers and alone attain my goal or else die. Oftentimes, however, I shall remember of this day, o Exalted One, and of this hour, when my eyes beheld a holy man.[14]

As Siddhartha internalizes the need for a self-reliant quest inasmuch as enlightenment can't be taught, he neglects the fact that as a *Brahmin* first, then an ascetic *yogi*, then finally a recipient of the Buddha's teachings, he developed an advanced spiritual practice and acquired an enormous amount of knowledge from all his teachers. From Hindu traditions to Buddhist teachings, he grew wiser to a self-realization: His own experience of enlightenment was up to him from the day, from the hour, when his eyes beheld a holy man, and he decided not to follow him. In your own journey, you follow no one but your inner self. You can educate yourself, you can discipline yourself into spiritual practice, you can learn

---

[12] Gautama is the family name of the Buddha.

[13] *Siddhartha* by Herman Hesse translated by Rika Lesser, Barnes and Noble Books, New York 2007, p. 28.

[14] *Ibid.*, p. 29-30.

from spiritual leaders and their exemplary roles, and you can join spiritual communities and churches, all of which will help you in your spiritual venture, but the ultimate journey is up to you and will be realized through your own personal experience of enlightenment. Spirituality manifests individually within each person according to their own circumstances and needs.

In our journey, very likely, we will encounter some setbacks due to our attachments to this physical world. These attachments derive from mental constructions of doubtful usefulness—our belief systems. Ultimately, our spiritual journey embodies the undoing of belief systems as expressed in the beautiful lyrics of the song "Unbecoming" by Daniel Nahmod:

> ...Now that I know I can take my own road
> I feel a freedom that I have never known
> (It's about)
> Unbecoming
> What I never was (It's about)
> Unlearning
> What was never true (It's about)
> Unbelieving
> All the lies that I've been told
> Unbecoming is the story of my soul...[15]

In the next chapter I will talk in more detail about these limitations that impede our spiritual evolution, but this time I will do so through my own life experience of unbecoming.

Let's not wait any longer and set sail right away.

---

[15] See http://www.danielnahmodlyrics.com/hm-unbecoming.html for the entire lyrics of the song.

# 5
# STORIES OF A LIFE

I feel I should write about my stories if I want to convey a message of spirituality. My own spiritual journey has led me to the words I put on the pages of this book. Therefore, I think it is very appropriate that I share some of my stories and how I started the process to accept them in peace.

## A Story of Healing

What does a mother or a father feel while holding a little soul that could depart? What deep anguish torrentially floods heart and mind before the possibility that the unimaginable might happen? What terrible despair strongly controls reason and emotions when nothing can be done to end the child's suffering as he clings to life? And how incapable and worthless would we feel in that situation? Wouldn't we strongly embrace the child tightly in our heart in a desperate attempt to allow ourselves to finally depart with him? Or yet, we could see a light of hope...

For this particular mother there was no rest. Her four-month-old baby was sick and her mind struggled with fear that his condition might worsen beyond return. One thought after another, all of them morose, tormented her mind. Her baby was such a wonderful being, so pure, so clear. He was the hope of many dreams. Witnessing her baby growing up as he discovered and learned the surrounding world was her deepest desire at that critical moment; it was the joy expected by any human being blessed with parenthood. But her fears made her doubt that she would ever experience that joy. Seeing the baby's precious little soul depart was a frightening thought she simply couldn't abide.

The baby was critically ill with high fever and diarrhea. He also had vomited his last breast milk. He was so weak that he did not have the energy to suck from his mother's breast. He stopped eating. He stopped crying. He was unusually sleepy. Dehydration was taking a heavy toll. His mother worried even more.

Holding him in her arms, she tried to figure out what to do. Her options were limited. In her poverty, in this poor neighborhood of Maracaibo, she had no means to take the baby to a doctor or hospital. Moreover, she was a single mother completely alone who had to take care of nine children including the baby. Phones did not exist nearby, and if she could have gotten to one, whom to call? Her neighbors were as poor as she was, and as busy with their own problems as she was with hers. It was an excruciatingly difficult situation for her because the possibility of losing the baby was very real.

But in the darkest moment, there is always a bright light. She knew about a doctor who helped poor people for free. He was called "the doctor of the poor" and his kindness and compassion was legendary. It was common for him to buy the medicines for his patients using his own money when he was alive. Dr. José Gregorio Hernández died in 1919 after being hit by a car in Caracas. But death did not stop him from healing and curing people according to countless testimonies of his miracles in Venezuela and many other countries. He was her hope.

She went to a little altar in a corner of her impoverished home. The altar consisted of a few things: a crucifix with a dying Jesus hung on the wall, a Virgin Mary statue, the typical Dr. José Gregorio Hernández statue with his black suit and hat, and some wild flowers in a glass bottle. But she didn't have a candle. She needed to light a candle for Dr. Hernández and place it in front of his statue. She called upon her oldest child and gave him a coin to buy a candle from one of her neighbors who operated an improvised store at her home four-houses down the dirt road. Cradling her baby in her arms, she waited with the same expectation as somebody waiting for the arrival of a powerful medicine that saves lives.

Once the boy returned home with the candle, she wasted no time to light it and place it near the Dr. José Gregorio Hernández's little statue. She prayed to him with absolute faith and devotion. She implored him to heal the baby, and to make the child completely healthy. She invited him to be the baby's spiritual father, and promised that the baby's first name would be José as a way to show her gratitude and to honor him. Then she prayed.

While she was completely immersed in her prayer, she felt a presence and heard a voice saying, "give the baby a small spoon of lemon juice and cooking oil." Nobody was nearby. For her, Dr. Hernández had spoken giving her instructions to treat the baby. She did not hesitate and followed the instructions as she was told.

The mother blessed the improvised medicine with the sign of the cross: in the name of the Father, the Son and the Holy Spirit, and gave it to the baby using a small spoon. As she made the baby swallow the lemon and oil mix, she looked for any sign of discomfort in her infant. Fortunately, the baby swallowed the required amount without major problems before his little eyes closed into a deep sleep.

It was nighttime, the rest of the children were ready for bed, and their weary mother was exhausted. She desperately needed rest, as she would have to check on the baby later. It didn't take too long until she fell asleep next to her baby-as she was still praying.

## A Story of Death

Little José woke up sweaty and frightened from a terrifying nightmare. He looked around and found himself all alone in the room that early evening. He was only six years old and, as expected for a child of his age, he still could not comprehend very well the magnitude of the recent loss that his family had just suffered. He realized, however, what death was all about when he saw his brother's inert body in the coffin and knew he was gone. Hence, finding death again in his nightmare was definitely petrifying. As his anxiety built up, he jumped off the bed and launched a tense search in the small three-bedroom apartment where he lived with his family. He did not want to find in the apartment what he just saw in his nightmare.

The apartment was small for the remaining eight siblings and a single mother who had to work hard to raise all of them. His oldest brother Ernesto had died few days ago when a driver ran the red light and hit his brother's motorcycle in a senseless traffic accident. Ernesto was only eighteen years old when he died. The kid looked up to his oldest brother as his only paternal figure. Ernesto was kind and loved by everyone and helped his mother in many ways, including keeping his problematic brother Jorge under control. Jorge had behavior problems in which he exploded with anger attacks destroying mostly anything he could reach. Jorge was only sixteen years old by then, and he already smoked and drank. Ernesto had to intervene to control Jorge's violence, and it was not unusual that, in order to do so, he had to physically restrain Jorge. As a result, fights were unavoidable for these two brothers. Little José-or Joseito, as his mother and siblings called him- nervously hid away when violence erupted hoping that his "good brother" could defeat his "bad brother," but his greatest hope was always for peace at home rather than a victorious brother. With Ernesto gone, the kid dreaded that peace would be more remote than ever.

Joseito went to the other bedrooms; in each bedroom he first looked up to the ceiling and then around. He saw two of his sisters resting or sleeping in one of the rooms, but the object of his search was still missing. He was worried and even more scared because he realized he was reenacting his own nightmare in which he was going from room to room and in each room he always saw the same shocking image. Then his pace picked up a little faster as he was heading to the living room. He again checked the ceiling first; then he looked around to find no one in there. He most certainly did not want to see the persistent image of his nightmare. He ran into the kitchen and found it empty too with its ceiling clear. With his heart racing faster than his little legs, he prayed a little prayer, "Dear God, I want to find Mamá," as he ran to the balcony.

He stopped suddenly and an enormous wave of relief washed over him when he saw his mother standing right there on the balcony. During his search he feared he would find his mother hanging from the ceiling completely inert just like his brother in the coffin. Instead she was standing still, holding the balustrade handrail with both hands, and staring at some invisible point in front of her. Even though he found her safe, Joseito sensed that things were not quite well yet.

Amid the suffering and pain caused by Ernesto's death, everything looked blurry to her. Her first born son had always been a source of happiness for her. His fresh approach to life was an inspiration for her to cope with all that was required to raise nine children and deal with Jorge. Ernesto was already working and helping her with household expenses. She tried to convince him to continue studying, but he insisted on working because more income was needed to sustain the family. The motorcycle was to help him go to work and move around the city. His tragic death was so sudden; one moment he was fully alive, cheerful as always, and the next moment he was gone forever. As she remembered her dear son, she wept and cried.

Life seemed to be cruel to her. She believed her burden was unbearable. She had neither the financial help nor the emotional support of a male companion. What to do now? How can she continue this difficult duty ahead? She lowered her eyes and saw the ground four floors below. "Why do I have to go through this pain? Why me? Why me?" she wondered. Now her eyes were fixed on the ground four floors below. She was sure it was going to be fast and then everything would be over. She believed her children would be fine with their aunts and uncles. She missed Ernesto so much. By now her mind was a sea of confusion with thoughts that changed constantly, but the ground, four floors below, was immutable. A decision was made; she closed her eyes.

Suddenly, out of nothing, she felt the presence of a little figure holding her leg and then a light shone in her mind. It was her youngest child who approached her and embraced her as much as he could reach. She looked at him and noticed his big eyes. The light shone even more and the sea was becoming calm. The ground below disappeared, and then she realized that he probably was hungry. Without thinking twice, she took him to the kitchen and fixed a snack for him.

## A Story of Lust (well, not really)

I didn't care very much that it was not safe standing late at night on that corner in Caracas. I was just staring at the entrance door of that well-known house. Men seemed to be sneaking into it, carefully looking over both shoulders and then quickly scurrying inside making sure that nobody they knew saw them.

From where I stood I couldn't see much of what was behind that door. Every time the door was opened after the typical double knock—a secret pass code, maybe—"knock, knock," there was this overweight lady with a big smile who welcomed the visitors. She opened the door just enough for them to enter. Then I could see the red light. Why such a tacky red light? You could not really appreciate people's faces with that light, I thought. Their physiognomies would be difficult to distinguish; in fact, I concluded to myself, it seemed that the red light provided the masks for everybody to wear as in a night of carnival. I felt very uneasy and wanted to go home, but for some reason I stayed.

The doorwoman was wearing nothing but tight and very short "hot" pants with what looked to me to be the top part of a swimsuit or some kind of colorful bra. They didn't match. The colorful bra and the "hot" pants didn't match. "What the heck," I was telling myself, "these ladies are not there to model in a fashion show." Very likely they were not up to my standards; nevertheless, I needed to make a statement or so I thought.

I was trying to make up my mind: to be or not to be. Oh Hamlet! Your dilemma was nothing in comparison with mine. You should have forgotten everything about your father because neither *being* nor *not being* was going to bring him back alive. You should have done just as I did: regard him as a non-existing entity that never was and never will be. I did it at five years old; you could have done it too.

Coming back to my own dilemma, unlike Hamlet, I was not holding Yorick's skull but my thoughts, which were dense as petrified bones. I was looking forward to a pleasure that had been denied to me. My girlfriend wanted to be a virgin until marriage or until at least, as she once told me, she felt more assured of my feelings for her. At fifteen, either case sounded to me like waiting for an eternity. I needed to rush in because I was getting way behind my friends. Some of them were lucky with their girlfriends (having non-picky girlfriends was such an advantage). Others were taken by their fathers to a place like this because fathers supposedly had to test the manhood of their boys. I could imagine their thoughts: 'No boy of mine is going to become gay under my watch.' If your father didn't take you to a brothel, maybe your big brother or a "more experienced" friend would. Sometimes "good friends" taught you too much stuff to handle at once.

I came by myself. I was all alone standing there and kept on staring at the entrance door of that house. My father was already a non-existing entity (didn't I mention that before?). Not that I was missing him at that time (or was I?). And I didn't want the extra pressure that my friends would have exercised on me, so I didn't tell them. In fact, I didn't tell anyone. This was a personal matter; I had to deal with it all by myself as I usually did with anything I had to face in life.

Sex was such an important matter; even more, it was the matter around which life turned. Who told me that? Maybe I concluded it by myself. I just needed to listen to my friends, watch pornographic movies, look at beautiful women on TV or anywhere I went, in order to be convinced that if I didn't have sex then I was not living life to its fullest. I just wanted to experience it. No strings attached please; I already had my girlfriend. That was why I was there.

I exited my thoughts when I saw the door opening again. The lady with non-matching clothes was there smiling again at the new visitor; she was so friendly and welcoming. "Well I guess I have to meet her. I'm next," I told myself. With my mind still drifting away and with no clear purpose, I started heading towards the door. I didn't know what mysterious force was pushing me in that direction but I could tell that it was not me who was walking to meet the lady. I wished something like an earthquake or perhaps a fire would happen, so I didn't have to double knock at the door. None of those calamities happened, at least on the outside. Inside me a real earthquake was going on and a subsequent fire was consuming the remainder of my innocence and childhood's dreams. In the dichotomy I was in, the external forces were winning and I was little by little becoming numb to my earthquake and fire.

In less than a minute I arrived at the door. I was going to knock at the door when something occurred to me, "I'm not eighteen. They will have to send me home when they find out I'm still a minor." I knocked at the door: "knock, knock." And the first big joke of my life had just started.

"Hi baby," said the lady who had opened the door any number of times that night.

"Hi," I said trying to be polite and courteous. I didn't know what else to say or to do. My eyes moved away from her trying to capture the images beyond the entry point.

"You wanna see?" said the lady noticing my curiosity. "Come in. Standing there you won't get anything." Then she took me by my hand and pulled me inside. She closed the door behind me. My heart was thumping like never before. Then I could see more of the indoor scene. The red light really didn't allow me to appreciate very clearly the faces and furniture details; however I saw people, men and women, talking to each other very closely. They were standing or sitting on the chairs and couches placed against the walls of a living room. The living room had a central space left empty on purpose like a dance floor. The laughter and the sound of many voices cast away the background music; no one was dancing.

My eyes turned to the lady again when I felt her body against mine. Her dense presence surrounded me, increasing my discomfort. My feeling of being misplaced in such a hidden reality was almost unbearable. I just wanted to be squeezed out of it.

"Oh, this little boy is nervous. Is it the first time? Come on, come here," she said holding my arm and taking me to the middle of the living room. "Well, since I'm not your type and, you know, I have to take care of business over here, you can pick the one you really like," she said and then she left me there.

I was now in the empty space in the middle of the living room alone again. Some lost memory of my childhood came to my mind when I was five or six years old, and my big brother Jorge pulled down my pants in some other living room. Like in my childhood memory, there were people laughing around me but, in this living room, I didn't cry.

I tried to pretend that I was in control of the situation and smiled at no one in particular. By then my eyes were used to the scarcity of light and I could appreciate more details of people's physiognomy. My eyes started roaming around the room trying to detail the women by the walls. I was looking so fast that my brain was processing no information whatsoever. Then I made eye contact with two provocative ones. She was a young woman, late teen or early twenties. She was slim and from the way she approached to me, I could tell she was available.

"Do you like what you see?" asked the slim lady. She was wearing tight jeans that enhanced her body and some kind of skimpy top on her small breasts.

"I think so," I automatically answered. I thought she was the kind of girl whom I would have liked to invite to the movies and for some ice cream afterwards.

"Then come with me, kid," said the girl with insinuating hips as she showed me the way to the hall that led to the bedrooms. As I followed her I thought it was not a good idea to invite her to the movies.

\*\*\*\*\*

I looked around the small room. In actuality it was one of the smaller rooms into which a big room had been divided for business convenience surely. A dimmed light was hanging from the ceiling; a twin-size bed with a thin cheap mattress sat in the opposite corner, and a sink was just next to the door on my left hand side. "What is this sink for?" I was trying to figure out as a non-pleasant odor made me doubt the cleanliness of the place.

"Well, what are you waiting for?" said my companion as she extended her hand palm-up towards me, "it's 50 bolívares."

I got the message and driven by the same mysterious force that made me come into this place, I gave her the money that I took from my wallet. She put it in the right front pocket of her tight jeans and closed the door behind me. Then she pulled me over to the sink and, in a quick maneuver, pulled down my pants and then my underwear. At that time I knew what the sink's purpose was. She examined my penis carefully and washed it as I watched the entire process from above. I knew what was coming next, yet I dared to ask, "What are you doing?"

No answer. Once it was clean and dried she started giving me oral sex. Everything was going on so fast that I didn't have time to feel anything pleasurable. The careless mechanical action she was practicing on me was not producing any pleasure; on the contrary, I was becoming more nervous and anxious.

"Come on, baby, get it up!" she said interrupting her performance after a couple of minutes of fruitless effort.

"I wish I could command it or press some magic button," I told myself completely embarrassed. In fact my blood was going all over my body but that area; it was as if my circulatory system had been purposely avoiding it.

"Come to bed. Let's see if the main course gets you hard," she said realizing that her oral efforts so far were futile. Matching actions with words, she took me next to the bed and started taking off her pants. First time I saw a live woman naked. I wanted to detail her female anatomy and most of all I wanted to gently touch her but then again her unkindness struck me.

As she was getting on the bed and noticing that I did not have any initiative whatsoever, she grabbed my wrists and got me on top of her. I withdrew a little from her body to look exactly where I was going to put it. My attempts were no match for her expert skills; she knew exactly what to do and placed me right on the spot and with well mastered maneuvers she managed to get me inside her without my participation. Nevertheless, no excitement came to me; my heart was so busy beating as fast as it could that it forgot to pump blood to the organ on which manhood is based. I realized that I was not really playing a significant role. She was conducting and playing the orchestra at the same time. Her *tempo* was *prestissimo* for the sake of speed rather than harmony. Her instrument was her hips. In these circumstances, the *grand finale* didn't take long and came without the sense of having reached a climax. I didn't know an ejaculation was possible without pleasure.

My one night lover got me off her and walked to the sink and grabbed a bowl, her personal bidet, from beneath the sink. She filled the bowl with water and squatted on it to wash the tool that allowed her a living. As she was washing, her eyes turned to me and her voice commanded me:

"Get out. You are done, little boy." Yes I was done, badly done.

\*\*\*\*\*

When I was in bed later on that night, I felt somehow tired and my mind was travelling to the "once upon a time" land. As I was falling asleep, I remembered that when I was a kid and during some time in my puberty, I always dreamt of a sweetheart with whom I could walk in a beautiful forest for long time. I dreamt of a nice girl who always was nearby so I could talk with her about mostly everything anytime. Kissing and hugging her would have been such a joy, not sure about sex. I didn't understand what role sex had in all of this. But as I was closing my eyes, it seemed to me that sex was taking over and only erections and orgasms mattered. Where was that kid? Soon I fell asleep completely.

## Shaping Life with Stories

Stories. We all are made of stories. Our past molded us to what we have become now. Our belief systems stem from our stories. What we believe now represents the cumulative result of what we have learned from our stories. In Chapter 7, we relate stories to movies, and as such, stories should essentially be neutral, neither bad nor good. They represent past events that cannot hurt or gratify us anymore because they ceased to occur long ago. Nonetheless, the particular interpretations that we create from our stories can significantly affect us.

As mentioned in Chapter 2, what we learned from our previous experiences, or stories, gets accumulated in our sixth sense (memory). This information, along with the current five-sense information, is presented to the mind in order to establish a perceived reality that extends to the anticipation of probable future events. We do this moment by moment. Every moment, we apply what we know to what we do according to our interpretation of the current circumstances as we anticipate some future outcome. This process, which most of the time runs subconsciously,[1] entails the basic evolutionary human trait that made possible our survival as a species. In this process, we seemingly move from the past to the future using the present as the transition between them. Problems, however, arise when we move from the past to the future without an adequate transition in the present. Sometimes the transition is too slow and the past seems still and present, and sometimes it is too quick and the future seems to be happening right now right here.

The way people move from past to future reminds me of the Roman god Janus. In Roman mythology, Janus was the deity of beginnings and endings, transitions and doorways that lead from

---

[1] Chapter 6 includes an entire section that dissects the subconscious and conscious roles of our minds.

one place to another, and was commonly depicted with two heads: one head looking into the past and the other looking into the future (January, the beginning of the year, was named after this god). This Roman deity symbolizes the fact that human nature encompasses both the past and the future. Humans cannot deny their past because it has brought them to where they are now, and they cannot underestimate the future because they have to do the corresponding right actions now for a harmonious future.

The right balance between past and future determines the quality of the transition in the present time. If the quality of your present is not harmonious you are either transitioning too slow or too quick from past to future. Specifically, your particular Janus could be out-of-balance by having an oversized past-looking head. This head looks at the past and makes you stay there as you relive the events that branded you. This head is the state of your mind that dwells in the distant past perhaps because of a trauma or a loss that you suffered. In this case, when the transition from past to future is too slow, the oversized past-looking head brings you into depression as you shelter behind the victim paradigm, the "flight" of the "fight-or-flight" defense mechanism. Conversely, your Janus could instead have an oversized future-looking head. This head, thereby, makes you project everything into the future. You anticipate your troubles and difficulties because you had many of them in your past. You deny your past because your past denied you what you needed; therefore, you make sure that this time you will get what you want and for this reason you take measures and get ready to extremely defend yourself by being in a reactive mode. You behave as if the future were already happening. This is the case when the transition from past to future is too fast, and the oversized future-looking head makes you dwell in the non-existing future causing contention and restlessness. You use this head when you primordially defy circumstances and want to force your will, in other words, when you use the "fight" of the "fight-or-flight" defense mechanism.

The interpretation of our stories has this dual characteristic that potentially makes us swing from one extreme to another, from depression to aggression, from low self-esteem to over confidence, from submission to defiance, all of which stem from our fears and impede us from reaching the harmonious balance distinctive of peace and happiness. Nonetheless, if we shift our perception, if we open ourselves enough, if we let intuition, the seventh sense, flow through us, our stories can show us the truth behind them; they can speak out to let us know their purpose in our journey.[2]

Your own stories, therefore, can make you live an unpleasant present, compromising your future, or can free you from restless contention and disturbing feelings. The good news is that you can opt which way you want your stories to work for you.

## The Impact of My Stories

Because of my healing story, I consider the fact that I grew up to become an adult a miracle. What were the odds for a four month baby to survive gastrointestinal infection in such conditions? How can a simple candle and a home-made remedy save a life? The only answer I possess is the existence of *subtle* forces that stem from our vast spiritual energy that we activate through love, faith and prayer. Furthermore, the manifestation of these subtle forces is as real as the combustion engine force that moves your car. I am very appreciative of my mother who passed on to me such convictions through her example.

I personally keep a little statue of Dr. José Gregorio Hernández in my home altar where a candle or two may be lit. I always pray to him and express my gratitude for the good health he bestows on my family. I have absolute faith in his benevolence and willingness to assist as he did when he was alive and was known as the doctor of the poor. While he became a role model for humankind by the virtue of his integrity and generous dedication as a physician, his spirituality reached high limits leading him to try the austere and pious monk life not once but twice. Many miraculous cures have been attributed to him after his death attracting millions of devotees and faithful in Venezuela and other countries. For these reasons, the Venezuelan Catholic Church started a process for his beatification in 1949, a process whose last word is yet to be finalized by the Vatican; nonetheless, in 1986 Pope John Paul II

---

[2] Chapter 8 describes a spiritual practice that expands our intuition and frees us from the fears caused by our stories.

issued a Decree on Dr. José Gregorio Hernández's virtues granting him the title of "Venerable."

As faith and prayer embody a fundamental pillar in my personal healing belief, natural herbs and remedies represent another pillar that support said belief. After all, why should I take a drug whose list of harmful side effects is longer than the list of its curative properties? I am convinced that chemical drugs are harmful because their main purpose is to produce corporate profit, not to cure people. Instead, lemon (or lime) is a wholesome medicine that I use for cold, flu and other infections, or to give my immune system a boost. I started to appreciate the entire fruit, including the rind and the seeds, once I became acquainted with its properties motivated by my mother's story of how a sip of lemon juice and oil saved my life. I have repeated that same story to my children, and when they do not feel well I bless lemon juice with oil, and administer it to them, just like my mother did (blessing is the expression of the highest intention that directs my love to the enhancement of this powerful home-made medicine) and then, they feel all well later on.

On the spiritual and healing properties of the lemon, the beautiful legend of The Nazarene of Saint Paul[3] tells us much. The Nazarene of Saint Paul is a wooden sculpture of Jesus Christ carrying the cross that was brought to Caracas' Saint Paul Church in the 17th century from Spain. Tradition says that after the sculptor finished the statue he heard Jesus' voice saying, "Where have you seen me that so perfect you have made me?" But it was amidst a terrible epidemic that was devastating Caracas' population in 1696 that the Nazarene's healing legend really started. As a last resort, the populace asked for divine intervention taking the Nazarene for a procession along the narrow streets of the then colonial city. When the statue was being carried, the head and cross of the Nazarene got tangled with the branches of a lemon tree and as the bearers tried to proceed with the procession, some lemons fell to the ground. "Miracle!" a voice was heard from the crowd. "They're medicine, Christians... it's the Lord's lemon tree!"[4] The divine

---

[3] *El Nazareno de San Pablo*, as it is known in Venezuela.

[4] My loose translation of part of Andrés Eloy Blanco's poem *"El Limonero del Señor."*

sign could not be clearer to the people who immediately started to harvest those lemons to obtain the juice that cured the sick, thus saving many lives. The Nazarene of Saint Paul tradition continues today as thousands of Venezuelan devotees accompany the Nazarene along its procession in the streets of Caracas praying and asking for new miracles on the Wednesday of every Holy Week.

My own healing story took me on a path of alternative medicine due to which I became a *Reiki*[5] master, a 500-hour Yoga instructor and an advocate for natural healing. I believe that conventional medicine is disruptive, intrusive, and guided by profit, not by a genuine interest of preventing disease and restoring the body's natural healing mechanisms. Natural healing, instead, relies on the body's natural abilities to fight against and recover from illness. But only a harmonious body can do so; therefore, real healing, the holistic healing, is not about masking the symptoms or containing the damage but about strengthening or restoring the body's harmony with the mind and the spirit—body, mind and spirit, the classical trilogy of our essence. As we practice natural healing on ourselves, we must bring our perfect spirit to play a role because we want its perfection to be projected in our body. We want our mind to set the highest intention with faith, love and kindness to work as a perfect bridge between our spirit and body, and specially to release any low feeling—such as hatred, anger, frustration, and depression—from impeding our healing.

To complete the trilogy of our essence, we must treat our body respectfully by exercising adequately and most importantly by having a proper diet making raw organic vegetables, including fermented vegetables, herbs and fruits our major intake and avoiding sugar, carbohydrates from grains, GMOs,[6] and chemicals and artificial ingredients as much as possible. In this regard, the spiritual practice described in Chapter 8 is very effective for self-healing. On healing others we ought to bring together, as mentioned above, our spirit and mind to work on somebody else's body/mind harmony inasmuch as most diseases have a psychoso-

---

[5] *Reiki* is a Japanese term that means "universal life energy" and can be associated with the *chi* energy of ancient Chinese medicine or the *prana* energy of Indian philosophy. *Reiki* practitioners use their hands to direct this "universal life energy" onto other people for healing purposes.
[6] Genetically modified organism.

matic or emotional origin. We achieve this purpose through powerful intentions and visualizations until the healing is completed. A healing is completed when they physically heal and are able to maintain their spirit-mind-body connection by themselves in such a way that they can take ownership of their own healing. I practice this healing philosophy every time I have a chance in Reiki or Yoga sessions, or with my own children. I ask my children to experience fully what they feel when they are ill, I ask them to talk to their body and say "thank you body for doing such a wonderful job protecting me," and I let them know that what they feel is a natural process due to which they grow stronger. And as they gain awareness of their body and start controlling it, I apply Reiki to them and merge my spirit with their mind and their soul as only love can do; thus, I show them that they are not alone. Finally, without any drug to mask symptoms, they always get better and stronger much faster, and they do it with trust in their own body's healing capabilities.

My healing story as a baby has always been so positive to me. I like it very much and I thank my mother and Dr. Hernández's spirit not only for my healing but also for the fact that this story revealed to me the profound truth of holistic healing in a world where modern medicine, and its drugs, creates more ailments than cures.[7]

---

[7] "A group of researchers meticulously reviewed the statistical evidence and their findings are absolutely shocking. These researchers have authored the following article entitled 'Death by Medicine' that presents compelling evidence that today's healthcare system frequently causes more harm than good...This fully referenced report shows the number of people having in-hospital, adverse reactions to prescribed drugs to be 2.2 million annually. The number of unnecessary antibiotics prescribed for viral infections is 20 million per year. The number of unnecessary medical and surgical procedures performed is 7.5 million per year. The number of people exposed to unnecessary hospitalization is 8.9 million per year...The most stunning statistic, however, is that the total number of deaths caused by conventional medicine is nearly 800,000 per year. It is now evident that the American medical system is the leading cause of death and injury in the US. By contrast, the number of deaths attributable to heart disease in 2001 was 699,697, while the number of deaths attributable to cancer was 553,251." From *LifeExtension Magazine* at http://www.lef.org/magazine/mag2006/aug2006_report_death_01.htm  on the report "Death by Medicine" by Gary Null et al.

*****

Although I survived as a baby thanks to a miracle that cured me physically, do not think that I did not need more healing to make it all the way to adulthood. And this time it was not due to a disease or any other physical condition; this time it was due to something less defined, more concealed. Concealed to me, that is. These constitute the emotional childhood repercussions that most of us deny. My childhood and adolescence were no more remarkable than anyone else's, but they deeply impacted me as everyone is impacted by their own childhood and adolescence. As the youngest child, many times I found myself lonely even though I was surrounded by eight siblings and one caring mother, and yes, no father. Having no father produced a stigma in me due to which I felt shame. I also felt unattended and abandoned. Why wasn't he with me? I never found a good answer for this question. My mother was very busy providing for her children, and my siblings, most of them teenagers, had their own worlds that they cared about. I therefore spent a long time all by myself playing or thinking. I had to survive on my own.

I always longed for that paternal figure and my oldest brother was such a good role model for me. I remembered the day he took me for my first and last ride[8] on the motorcycle he'd just bought a few days before. I sat behind him and held him tightly with my arms around his waist and my cheek pressing against his back as he rode his noisy motorcycle around the block a couple of times. I was looking for a sense of security that I thought I found in him. I lost that security a few days later when he died in a traffic accident with the motorcycle.

My mother lost all hope when Ernesto died. Her suffering was a soul suffering that I witnessed day after day. As I saw her crying in despair, I drew the conclusion that she loved him more than she loved me. This thought bothered me somehow but, for me, the desire to see her well and carrying on with her life held much more importance. The only thing I could do by then was to try to be with her as much as I could. I believe today that I was given this

---

[8] I have not ridden any other motorcycle in my life ever since. I never liked them again after my brother's accident.

mission through my intuitive child awareness.[9] This mission was the reason I had the nightmare in which my mother committed suicide and, therefore, I had to stay with her. But before I could stay with her, I first had to find her. My mother confessed to me later on that she had suicidal thoughts after Ernesto's death and that living on the highest floor of an apartment building made those thoughts more feasible. When I found her on the balcony, those thoughts agitated her mind and when she saw me clinging to her as I was clinging to Ernesto on the motorcycle, she suddenly knew that life must go on and that her mission was to provide for her children; after all, didn't she pray for my life when I was a baby?

Consequently my fears about my mother dissipated. Nevertheless, I still felt insecure because of Jorge. He had a short temper that drove him into anger attacks in which he screamed and yelled, and in frenetic rampages he used to throw and toss anything he could reach destroying the few possessions we had. The sound of the objects crashing into pieces on walls and floor together with the yelling paralyzed me in fear. I remember my mother begging him to stop, but he never listened to her, he never stopped, he never really cared. Ernesto was the only one who could stop him by physically restraining him in fights that made me even more anxious. As a result, I developed an aversion towards Jorge that bordered on hatred. His presence, knowing that he was around, made me feel very uneasy and uncomfortable. I do recall the times when he approached me with affection and I had to bear the cigarette and alcohol smell that surrounded him. His affection was rough and unskilled; I just wanted him to leave me alone. Jorge impacted me so much that for many years, I have to admit, I couldn't feel comfortable with anyone who resembled him somehow. His physical features solidly stayed in my mind, his face was always a clear memory: his nose, his mouth, his wide forehead and scarce hair; even the way he smelled stayed with me forever.

All of these feelings were relieved, or so I thought, when I knew that Jorge had died. He died when I was 11 years old; he was 21. His death was surrounded by strange circumstances. I saw the picture of his shirtless body in the newspaper lying on the

---

[9] This is the intuitive awareness that every child has and that we, the adults, neglect and dismiss altogether.

same ground where I used to play in my early childhood days, close to the apartment that witnessed his anger, his fights with Ernesto and our suffering for his big brother's death. At eleven I felt liberated, I did not cry or feel pity for him; at that time I thought that the nightmare was over.

No, Jorge was not gone. I let him still live in my mind without my conscious consent. He taught me how to solve family disputes with imposition and yelling. I was following his lessons very well when I thought I was rejecting all that he represented: a curious paradox, but very common. Most people end up behaving like those they reject, hate or despise. In my case I enormously dreaded that violence—violence of any kind, physical, verbal, emotional—would find a course in my children. This fear did not allow me to distinguish natural child behavior from a real act of violent sibling rivalry. The path I took to overcome my fear was to be a verbally commanding person, imposing my belief by yelling at them and denying them their treats and allowances as a way to punish them if they did not behave the way I expected. Clearly I behaved as Jorge had behaved when he angrily tried to make sure he was the one in control, the one who decided what we could enjoy because it was up to him to destroy anything we cared about or cherished. My two oldest boys experienced the consequences of my trauma more than my little girl because, at some point in raising my children, I started seeing clearly the suffering I was causing around me, the same suffering I had experienced when I was little even though circumstances were different. It was a shift of perception that helped me to perceive life from my family's perspective, a shift that was created by a conjunction of several events in my life; among these events there was one related to Jorge himself.

My mother told me one day that Jorge used to help homeless kids in a very special way. When he brought them home he explained to my mother that their needs were bigger than ours and they could stay for a couple of days until they felt better. These were hungry kids he found in the streets without parents or any other adult supervision, and Jorge, despite the fact he was only 13 or 14 years old, understood he could do something for them. He shared the food of his own plate with them, and at night he gave up his own hammock so they could have a better sleep than the one they were used to on the street concrete. As I learned about this unknown aspect of Jorge, a realization came to me and I started seeing him with other eyes and learned much more about him. I suddenly knew he had been indeed a very sensitive boy since he was born and later on in life he expressed his sensitivity through music and affability. He loved to sing and dance, activities that made him popular among young women, and he also loved to make new friends regardless of their personalities. He was able to express himself very well through his charm and sociability outside his family. He cared about his friends and his friends cared about him; nevertheless, he couldn't be himself with his family for he knew that there was something wrong that made him feel miserable at home.

"We have never had a father, mamá, because that one who says he is our father and is not here, is a lousy man," so little Jorge told my mother one day. He certainly felt miserable; all his sensitivity was crushed and disintegrated at home by the lack of affection, by the absence of attention, by feelings that were never reciprocated. My mother did what she knew best: to work hard for food, shelter and education for her children. But affection, love, emotional care, all of that was so foreign to her. She knew about discipline and rules, but not how to approach a kid. Once on the verge of tears, she told me, "I wish I had known that Jorge needed affection and love." This is representative of how a child's sensitivity transforms into hopelessness and hopelessness develops into frustration and frustration becomes anger as the child grows up.

I had then the vision of my own children becoming Jorge: I felt what my own children would feel if I neglected them, if I were not there as a caring and loving father. I saw what Jorge went through and asked him to please forgive me. I wanted to tell him that I loved him and that I wished with all my heart that he had had a life filled with joy as every child in this world deserves. As I write this, I would like to tell him: "Jorge, I am very sorry for rejecting you, and I lament your tragic end. I feel the fear and the pain that you felt the day of your death perhaps because I know that you thought of me at that time. We all miss you."

I feel blessed when I can see beyond the appearances, beyond the forms, beyond anyone's actions, because only then am I at peace. Childhood traumas result from looking only at those appearances. As a child, we have no choice but to observe and apprehend from the immediate context that we had when we started our transformation towards adulthood. For most of us, that context entails our family, home and place of our childhood days. Our traumas develop in our subconscious mind[10] and become an integral part of our personality ready to pop out at the least sign of uncomfortable past events being repeated. Many times we are oblivious to their existence, sometimes we deny them, and most of the time we say that we are happy but we keep on reacting with frustration, anger or depression, and we rationalize these mood swings by blaming others and the world around us, or by blaming ourselves. Sometimes we are confrontational and ready to fight. Other times we just simply declare defeat as we believe we don't have any control over our well-being. In this state of mind it is not possible to see beyond the appearances, beyond the forms, beyond anyone's actions; in other words, it is not possible to find real peace.

In order to realize that we are still affected by past events, we need to recall how sensitive children are. Due to their sensitivity, children can learn all the vast information they need from their surroundings to acquire the skills they need to survive. This learning must be done very quickly and instinctively. In many cases, what we learn becomes subconscious traits that are as responsive as those instinctive traits we developed during our evolutionary past (when physical preservation constituted the key to our survival). Furthermore, a child does not necessarily have to go through devastating painful experiences–such as physical or sexual abuse–to be affected deeply; seemingly trivial events can also have profound consequences. A simple word of love or neglect, a spontaneous encouragement or derision, or just a good or bad epithet used to address the child, creates a profound impact on his personality that can last a lifetime.

In this respect, I have much to say. As I mentioned before I was the youngest child of nine siblings, and as such I was always the naive one. My siblings always overrode me. I felt little and insignificant. Figuratively speaking I had always to look up to see everybody but nobody looked down to see me, or so I thought. Most of the time, I had to play by myself and invent my own

---

[10] Chapter 6 deals with the subconscious mind in more detail.

games, and I realized that actually I didn't need anyone in most of what I did. I grew self-sufficient but with a sense of being ignored. As a result, a need grew in me to be recognized and praised all the time. Of course, when I did not receive any praise at all, I became frustrated and easily irritable. This trait of my personality arose very often at school and later on at work, but it could appear in any other context making me contentious and argumentative as I had this urge to raise myself above everyone else, without which I believed that I was not being appreciated in all my worth. Recognizing this unskillful behavior of mine represented a serious challenge in my spiritual path for it was so reactive and instinctive. It embodied years and years of subconsciously developing an inefficient and sophisticated defense mechanism suitable for survival in the jungle of neglect and lack of attention, an imaginary jungle that resided in my mind and nowhere else.

When we feel that we are not appreciated in some context, for instance, the workplace, we could react by imposing our will in some other context over which we exert more control, like home. By seeing how our ideas, beliefs and dispositions condition people around us, we "regain" our self-esteem at the expense of those who happen to be in the particular setting that we control. It constitutes a compensation mechanism that attempts to cope with the lack in one area through the excess in another area. Children are the first victims of this dysfunctional compensation mechanism that parents carry out perpetuating, in an endless vicious cycle, their own traumas. My children were the first victims of my need for attention and recognition; a need that very conveniently disguised itself as "parent knows best."

No doubt that my aforementioned realization about Jorge helped me to rid myself of this compensation mechanism, but also the infinite love in the eyes of my little girl and my two boys helped me to finally come to the realization that I need to learn from them as much as they need to learn from me. They represent my great opportunity to revive the forgotten child that I was once and, thereby, undo my traumas as I grow spiritually by letting love build the indestructible bridges between them and me. This constitutes a process without a foreseeable end in which I fully open myself to my children's wisdom and natural intuition. They don't need much indoctrination, only a lot of space to express their own simple intuition and the love that they always carry with them.

When I realized my real worth within me, I decided that I no longer needed recognition and praise, and consequently I started experiencing freedom in my life; that day my kids found a new Papa, a more caring and less self-centered Papa. Those who feed themselves with recognition and praise from others are susceptible to suffering from starvation as they rely on others for their survival.

*****

Perhaps the need to be accepted and approved by others, the collective, underlies all the suffering that people experience through life. The way we want to be accepted and appreciated by some people is up to us. Sometimes we might want to be the imposer, the leader, the one who decides what's good and what's bad; other times we just want to fit in, to be just like the others so we can identify ourselves with a group. In either case, we try to satisfy the instinctive survival necessity of conforming to the collective (as explained in Chapter 3), and as we do this, we place the object of our happiness in others without realizing that it is from within that happiness really stems. When we gain awareness of our real sameness—the essence of our spiritual realm within—the struggle to lead or follow and the contention to stand out or fit in cease because it is from within that our real connection with others flows naturally, always finding the path of least resistance as a river does when it flows to the ocean.

But it is the initial step of opening our intuition to the wonder of our sameness that most people hesitate to take. We know that if this step is hard for adults, then, what can we expect from a teenage boy eager to be like his peers? My first prostitute experience was terrible and its repercussions were even worse, beyond what anyone could ever foresee, not even me. After that experience I had to prove to myself I was up to the task. It was the same old me showing his self-worth again but now in a different facet. Thereafter, from that time, every intimate relationship turned into a new challenge, a sexual challenge, that is, as I became unable to connect deeply at an emotional level. It is not difficult to understand, therefore, how sex became a sport for me in which I could score as much as I wanted. In this state of unawareness I fell in love and married my wonderful wife without knowing how to express love. It took a painful marriage crisis on the brink of divorce to comprehend how badly affected I was. My extramarital relationships caused enormous pain to my wife; her excruciating pain roused me from my lethargy and opened the doors to the realization that real love constitutes an active expression of care and interest for the loved ones.

Real love is constantly active and proactive; if love can be selflessly expressed to one special person, then real love lives in us and the entire world will benefit from it. How can we love humankind if we are inconsistent loving one person? Conversely, how can we claim we love someone if we express judgmental attitudes and sometimes hatred towards other people? If this sort of inconsistency finds a place in our lives, then real love has yet to mature in our hearts. My wife and I overcame our crisis and a beautiful trust has been born again. And most importantly, we face together the challenges ahead as a beautiful manifestation of love and partnership.


## Summary

In this chapter I have tried to describe some important life experiences that helped me to comprehend and grasp my purpose in life. I am still on my own path and, as my growth continues, I don't think there is an ending to my journey in the foreseeable future; nonetheless, this situation is perfectly fine because my focus lies in my journey's day-to-day process. Regarding this book, I will carry on my purpose of showing how paramount spirituality is for our lives. We have seen, with respect to my life, how our immediate context shaped us. Our parents treated us as they did because that was the way they knew based on their own experiences, or perhaps, regretfully, based on their own traumas caused by their own upbringing.

We can go back to our grandparents to explain our parents' traumas, and then to our great-grandparents, and as far back as we wish. But we must also take into account that our ancestors conformed to a collective as we currently do, if we want to explain the complexity of our lives. Our culture, our society, our customs, all of them stipulate the limits, the expectations and the values for each individual and create an intricate dynamic between collective and individual beliefs as discussed in Chapter 3. This individual-collective dynamic precisely constitutes the source of one's suffering.

The idea is to break this cycle of suffering at some point in our lives, the sooner the better. We have a tool available to us for this purpose. This tool is our mind. We need to understand our mind very well if we want to access its infinite spiritual possibilities. The next chapter is dedicated to the understanding of the mind and its infinite spiritual potential. After all, becoming spiritual is equivalent to making our mind capable of perceiving reality–the seen and the unseen.

# 6
## THE HUMAN MIND

In previous chapters we have mentioned the mind in many of our discussions. In this chapter we formalize the main aspects of the human mind to clarify its role in spirituality. There is no question that we stray from our spiritual path because our mind tends to reinforce our belief systems, but it is also true that manifestation of spirituality is unachievable without our mind.

The expression "monkey mind" is commonly used to refer to a state of mind dominated by thoughts of fear, anxiety and contention. Notwithstanding these kinds of thoughts make us unhappy as we do not engage the present moment, the expression itself derogates the mind. We shouldn't use it as we shouldn't use any words that belittle our human body (we should honor our entire reality, the physical and the non-physical).

As we do not blame our body for drowning if we haven't trained it to swim, we cannot blame our mind for engaging in disturbing thoughts if we haven't trained it to accept the infinite possibilities of the immutable and perennial. After all, the mind can only work with the information it receives; hence, we should become more open to the information coming from the magnificence of the unseen if we want to attain peace and happiness.[1]

The mind protects the individual from anything that it perceives as harmful. All the stress and restlessness that the mind produces is to warn us of a perceived threat or a future necessity that requires our attention. Thanks to its capacity to anticipate and elaborate complex inferences, our mind makes us take the appropriate

---

[1] A spiritual practice, like the one described in Chapter 8, is excellent for this purpose.

actions to satisfy our physical needs. We should honor and respect our mind because our intelligence, the ability to compare, abstract and infer, allowed us to survive as a species despite the limited abilities of the human body to prey upon and fight animals and to withstand the inclemency of the climate.

Our mind is neutral. Most of the time it does its job well based on the information it receives, as mentioned previously. If our lives are characterized by excesses, if we don't find peace, joy or contentment, if depression or anger rises in us frequently, do not blame the mind, blame the information that the mind processes. This information comes from our senses: the typical five senses, the sixth sense and the seventh sense, mentioned in Chapter 2. Among these seven senses, the sixth and the seventh have special significance for our spiritual realization as explained in the next section.

The mind that we all are familiar with resides mainly in the brain and operates our cognition and memory consciously or sub-consciously. But as we progress in the understanding of the mind in this chapter, we will discover that the mind goes way beyond any limited preconception we might have had about it; it is indeed a great ally for our spiritual realization. This Mind, with upper case 'M,' infinitely extends to fuse with God's intelligence in sub-tle ways that we all can develop. The last sections of the chapter are dedicated to the understanding of the Mind through the under-standing of energy and quantum physics.

## The Sixth and the Seventh Senses

The information that the mind receives comes from our five senses and the sixth and seventh senses as explained in Chapter 2. Figure 1 depicts a very simplistic model of the mind's operation. The sixth sense delivers all the past information accumulated throughout a lifetime. It encompasses the individual's belief sys-tem, all learning, conditioning and memory. The sixth sense is part of the mind itself as memory retrieval is a mental process, but we present it as a sense because once something is stored in our memory, it behaves in many circumstances as if it were infor-mation coming from our five senses: absolute and true as the clear blue sky. It becomes, in other words, a dogma, a constituent of a belief system "etched in stone."

The relevance of a single past recollection is colored by how the mind perceived reality at the time the recollection took place. Notice the reinforcing cyclic pattern in Figure 1, where the perceived reality potentially can reinforce the belief system that caused it. Assume that your beloved mother treated you to something sweet (cookie, ice cream, piece of a pie, etc.) every time she expressed her love and care for you. Thus it became natural for you to associate love and care with sweets; hence, the appellatives "honey," "sweetie," and "sweetheart" to refer to a loved one. Eating sweets could become a substitute for love when you feel that you need love. In your perceived reality, sweets entail a connotation of love, which is why you put so much sugar in your bloodstream, thereby damaging your health. Furthermore, you reinforce your own interpretation of reality because every time you eat sweets they taste good and give you pleasure just as they did years ago during your childhood when your mother expressed her love for you. In your mind you are given the same sense of comfort as you were in your childhood; in other words, you are reinforcing the belief that eating sweets equals being loved and comfortable. It is clear that you cannot escape from your perceived reality unless you start expanding your possibilities with new and more comprehensive information to feed your mind.

The seventh sense is the sense that provides information from the unseen—our sameness, our eternal and immutable realm. In Chapter 2 we recognize the seventh sense as our heart-centered intuition: the art of knowing by just knowing. As we can see through the direct path in Figure 2, the information provided by the seventh sense does not need analysis or composition; it directly contributes to our perception of reality. Without the seventh sense our receptiveness is narrow, subjective, and driven by our particular belief system. In contrast, with the seventh sense we become more universal and boundless. As we can perceive our eternal sameness more directly through the seventh sense, our acuity of reality increases unveiling our infinite potential.

Note that the sixth sense also gets refined by this new more accurate perceived reality (see the path between the perceived reality and the sixth sense in Figure 2). The experience of perceiving the unseen goes to our sixth sense, as any other experience, and positively affects it. Therefore, this will make the mind accurately process the information coming from our five senses as this information is compared with cleaner and purer information from the sixth sense. Namely, increasing the openness of our seventh sense will have the wonderful effect of uncovering the fallacies of our belief systems, dogmas, conditionings, traumas and any other limitations that our past experiences instilled in us. In this case, our sixth sense will become more compatible to our noble goal of spiritual realization.

## The Sixth Sense and Mental Attributes

Our mind evolved as a sophisticated instrument to distinguish, sort and classify the inherent differences among the components of this physical world. Our mind very efficiently compares each current experience with an enormous database of previously acquired knowledge (sixth sense) and establishes the corresponding associations. From these associations, our mind distinguishes an object or situation from another object or situation. We learn how to group together based on common attributes and how to separate and discriminate one group from another based on their different attributes. Our mind does this all the time, very quickly and efficiently.

Mental attributes are indispensable to categorize our experiences. A mental attribute, as mentioned in Chapter 2, is a label with which we store experiences and objects allowing us to classify them as good, bad, dangerous, or as any other required category. This categorization or classification allows humans to anticipate possible outcomes based on the comparison between the current circumstances and previously acquired information. Based on this capability to anticipate, we survived as a species for millions of years as we foresaw dangerous and threatening situations and, therefore, took the necessary well-thought-out steps[2] to avoid them.

---

[2] The term "well-thought-out-steps" is another way to refer to the development of our intelligence. Intelligence entails elaborated mental associations and connections that lead to complex deductions and conclusions. The development of sophisticated tools constitutes a typical example of our intelligence.

Nevertheless, for those unavoidable and immediate "fight-or-flight" threats, which were very common in our far distant past, a fast, automatic and more primitive mind was necessary during our evolution: the subconscious (instinctive) mind. For millions of years, the subconscious mind—a subset of the whole mind as we will see in the next section—developed a sophisticated reaction mechanism originally intended to preserve our physical integrity. This mechanism has stayed with us to this day, and we use it for the non-life-threatening situations of our modern lives at a high cost to our well-being. For example, stress, this contemporary source of disease, is nothing but a typical subconscious instinctive response to unfavorable circumstances such as a bad situation at work or the sensation of being stuck in heavy traffic. We could lose our job or be late for an appointment but we could never die in either of these situations; however, our mind seems not to recognize this fact. This is not because the mind is malfunctioning, but because the two outcomes, losing a job and being late for an appointment, have been previously recorded with an attribute that indicates they are high threats to the individual's integrity.

Mental attributes constitute an important factor for our mind to interpret the stimuli from the outside world in our daily lives. A swimming pool, for instance, is more than the object "swimming pool." For those who had a traumatic drowning experience that kept them from learning how to swim, a swimming pool perhaps represents a source of fear and anxiety about falling into its waters; in this case, a swimming pool is recorded by the mind as a very dangerous object. For those who know how to swim, a swimming pool could mean a source of endless hours of fun and enjoyment. For competition swimmers, a swimming pool could signify the living memory of many hours of exhausting training that they would rather avoid altogether. Whatever "swimming pool" really entails for each individual constitutes a subjective perception of the object "swimming pool." We imbue this perception with a lot of extra components—the results of our previous experiences and learning—on top of the raw sensorial image.[3]

---

[3] There is no way to know if the raw sensorial image reflects faithfully the physical object or not; our senses just receive information. The five senses constitute our interface to the physical world; they are not the physical world.

The perceived reality that our mind composes considerably affects the individual; whatever our mind senses is real within us and immediately affects us irrespective of the objectivity of the situation that is being perceived. Using again the "swimming pool" example, we can think of somebody who could feel so threatened being close to a swimming pool that they could have a panic attack triggered by their subconscious instinctive mind. In this case, this person feels all the physical manifestations of a real death threat: fast heartbeat, high blood pressure, adrenaline rush, etc. The mind does not realize that the threatening situation does not really exist. The mind only acts according to the information that it has been presented with: "swimming pool equals threatening object."

We can go even further and illustrate this situation with an example of collective behavior. After 9/11 a large part of the U.S. population anticipated and feared the worst and their feelings and emotions corresponded to those of a constant conventional war attack that did not actually exist. The senseless 9/11 terrorist attack, though cruel and criminal, was an isolated attack not comparable, for example, to the continuous and persistent attack that London's civilian population suffered due to the German Luftwaffe bombardment known as the Blitz campaign; or the attack that the German civilian population endured during the air raids that the Allies routinely inflicted on Germany in the final years of the Second World War.[4] Nevertheless, the idea that a terrible war had just started was accepted by many people; fear and anxiety then grew among these people. No doubt the mass media fed this fear as did actors in the political arena to justify the reelection of a

---

[4] To have a vivid idea of what British and German civilian populations went through during the Second World War, we can refer to Wikipedia's 'The Blitz' and 'Strategic bombing during World War II' articles: "The Blitz ... began with the bombing of London for 76 consecutive nights. By the end of May 1941, over 43,000 civilians, half of them in London, had been killed by bombing and more than a million houses destroyed or damaged in London alone..." "By 1943, the United States had significantly reinforced these efforts [bombing efforts on Germany]. The controversial fire bombings of Hamburg (1943), Dresden (1945) and other German cities followed... The attack on Dresden killed at least 24,000 people, nearly half the number of those killed in the entire Blitz campaign."

"war president" who led the U.S. to the Iraq invasion–a long war that turned out to be as bloody and costly as it was unjustifiable.

## The Subconscious and the Conscious

Our magnificent mind represents the result of millions of years of evolution. Originally, the mind evolved to protect our physical integrity above all and for that purpose the mind split into two different minds: the subconscious mind and the conscious mind (or simply the subconscious and the conscious). Both of them are unique and wonderful tools for our spiritual growth if we know how to use them.

The subconscious functions without our will or awareness and operates following the three components described in Chapter 2 and depicted in Figure 1. Without our involvement, the subconscious receives an incredible amount of stimuli from the outside world every fraction of a second, compares it with stored past information and composes a perceived reality that makes us act correspondingly. That is, the subconscious is an automatic mechanism of the mind.

This explains why, for example, we can drive a car and maintain a conversation or listen to the radio at the same time. In this case, we can notice that most of our actions and reactions needed to drive a vehicle are quite automatic due to many years of driving practice. Similarly, after practice, keeping one's balance during biking turns into a subconscious task, thus the biker can focus on other aspects of the biking experience, or perhaps something else. If every time we drive a car or ride a bike we had to pay attention as much as we did when we were learning these activities, we would never enjoy them as they would overwhelm us.

This property of the subconscious applies to not only physical but also to mental activities such as solving a logic problem, a puzzle or any other analytical problem. The practice of solving many problems of this type conditions the mind to detect quickly and efficiently the right mental associations or links that helps to solve similar problems without the individual's intervention. The "eureka moments"–those moments when scientists find a solution to a problem when they are not thinking about it–constitute good examples of the subconscious working solely on the individual's behalf.

In every activity we learn, there is an initial stage when we pay most attention to and focus on what we are learning, but when the physical or mental activity is mastered through practice, the subconscious takes over and automatically runs a major part of the actions that the activity in question requires. This is an important feature of our mind because without it many quotidian activities would require enormous mental effort every time we undertake them, and life itself would be exhausting.

But perhaps the best known role of the subconscious lies in its deeper and more primitive layers: the innate and acquired instincts for self-protection. The innate instincts stem from the evolutionary past that shaped the survival and supremacy of the *homo sapiens* species on Earth. These are the instincts that explain, for instance, why people automatically turn their head trying to find the source of an unusual sound in the midst of any activity they might be focused on. The other type of instincts, the acquired instincts, develop constantly as the subconscious never stops working and accepting all kind of stimuli from the outside world. At this point in life, we surely have already established many acquired instincts that trigger automatic reactions based on our individual belief system, and right now we keep on establishing new ones as we proceed with our lives.

These instincts are meant to protect us from the recurrence of past suffering. They make us anticipate any possible "threat" and act accordingly. We then act, based on our goals or ends, for "self-preservation." Our jobs, our relationships, our ranks in the social context, all of them become the ends for our "self-preservation." In furtherance of this "self-preservation," we are susceptible to impatience and frustration as the ends of our undertakings do not materialize as fast as we wish. From frustration to anger at the people and circumstances that seem to impede our progress, or to depression because we doubt our capabilities, there is only one small step. In either case, when our acquired instincts make us take that small step, we feel compelled to do anything we deem necessary to achieve our "self-preservation" goals, meaning that our actions, as we can infer, will probably be unharmonious and disruptive; this is the case when the means justify the ends.

Examples of this behavior abound all around us inasmuch as most people worry about their "self-preservation," but I always remember Orson Well's classic film "Citizen Kane" as a good illustration of how the excesses of money and power bespeak fear rather than confidence, and in the end are always destructive. In the movie, all the money and all the power that the fictional character Mr. Kane amassed to avoid the sense of abandonment he deeply felt inside were not enough to get rid of his fear contrary to what he could have ever thought. His decrepit health took him to a solitary death in the shadows of what was once a luxurious mansion. Kane's death reflected his life. He was always lonely amid his power and wealth since that winter day of his childhood when his mother sent him away. Mr. Kane's fate could be anyone's fate if this precious life is wasted through excesses, and the essential loving connection with all is never made because of our subconscious fears. The lesson to learn, therefore, is that the resolution of a subconscious fear consists in eliminating the fear itself, not to build a fortress around it.

The other mind is the conscious. The conscious mind runs under the individual's control when the individual pays attention to, focuses or concentrates on an activity, thought, idea or problem. The conscious also operates following the mind's three components described in Chapter 2 and depicted in Figure 1 but more selectively. In other words, we can select at will the information we want to focus on. It is similar to tuning your radio to a particular station. Your radio in the background (as your subconscious) is always receiving all the signals from the radio stations in your city, but when you dial your radio to tune to your favorite station, you listen to only one station. Likewise, you can always tune your mind to consciously select your thoughts.

Unlike the subconscious mind, the conscious does not run all the time, only when required by the individual. Furthermore, the conscious is much slower than the subconscious and cannot perceive all the stimuli from the outside world; in fact, humans are not consciously aware of much of what they continually sense.

The subconscious has the vital task to sense and process the information from the five senses faster than the conscious can ever detect. For example, the subconscious can perceive hidden or fleeting images that the conscious can never notice. This fact constitutes the reason behind subliminal conditioning in public messages and advertisements. It explains as well why the preferred way to advertise a product on TV, video or film employs fast succession of images and words. These fast successions of images and words attempt to create a subliminal message by accentuating the subconscious over the conscious. In addition, since physical self preservation is paramount, these subconscious subliminal messages become much more effective if the fleeting images are negative or entail signs of danger. [5, 6]

Despite this picture that portrays the subconscious governing most aspects of our lives due to its fast perception, fast response, and around the clock schedule, the conscious can bring the unconscious under control by erasing detrimental subconscious patterns—the belief systems described in Chapter 3—that act as programs ready to run when the right stimuli are present. The conscious achieves this outcome by focusing on new information and learning new patterns. Nonetheless, for the conscious to successfully erase one detrimental program, we must acknowledge, as an initial step, that such a detrimental program resides in our subconscious. If we do not recognize that indeed we are conditioned and if we think that a particular response or reaction of ours represents the manifestation of what we really are, then the subconscious will always take precedence over the conscious, leaving us with the detrimental program intact and functional.

---

[5] "Researchers at Columbia University Medical Center have found that fleeting images of fearful faces—images that appear and disappear so quickly that they escape conscious awareness—produce unconscious anxiety that can be detected in the brain with the latest neuroimaging machines." *Fleeting images of fearful faces reveal neurocircuitry of unconscious anxiety*, by Karen Zipern, Medical News Today, December 18, 2004, http://www.medicalnewstoday.com/releases/18022.php.

[6] "Professor Lavie believes that the ability to subconsciously pick up fleeting signals could have developed as a way of picking up fleeting warnings. 'Clearly, there are evolutionary advantages to responding rapidly to emotional information,' she said. 'We can't wait for our consciousness to kick in if we see someone running towards us with a knife or if we drive under rainy or foggy weather conditions and see a sign warning 'danger' ". *Subliminal advertising really does work, claim scientists*, by Richard Alleyne, The Telegraph, September 28, 2009, http://www.telegraph.co.uk/science/science-news/6232801/Subliminal-advertising-really-does-work-claim-scientists.html.

The conscious plays the utmost important role in our spiritual journey. Thanks to our conscious we can concentrate and bring control to our thoughts whenever we wish. With concentration we start mastering our mind as we can discriminate more wisely the information from our five senses and the sixth sense. Concentration opens the doors to meditation[7] in which we open our seventh sense fully and reality manifests itself in its entire splendor. As reality becomes clearer, our sixth sense and subconscious align themselves with our spiritual path and life become more fulfilling and abundant.

Amazingly true, many walk on Earth without having control of their lives because subconscious programs, or instincts, command them while subjugating their consciousness; nevertheless, the good news is that they can always change their situation through their conscious. Through their consciousness, they can identify old harmful programs, modify them or create new ones to train the subconscious in the wonderful possibilities of ultimate realization.

## Energy and Intelligence

Mind and energy are intimately related. Our thoughts are energy. The activity of our brain can be registered through devices that detect its electromagnetic waves. The information from our five senses is transmitted to our brain via electrical currents that travel along the nerves of our body. Electrical currents and their associated electromagnetic waves are a form of energy. Our organs, endocrine glands and tissues are all connected through complex nerve pathways, and each cell itself is able to emit electromagnetic radiation (biophotons) that the entire body uses for its operation. Moreover, as we consider the wisdom of ancient traditions, we need to include aspects of subtle energy not recognized by Western science. Subtle energy is known as *prana* (Hindu tradition) or *chi* (Chinese tradition) and circulates in our body through *nadis* or *meridians* respectively.

From the energetic point of view, it is difficult to confine the mind to an organ or some other limited region in our body. Our full mind does not reside exclusively in our brain, though we

---

[7] Meditation is discussed in Chapter 7.

could consider our brain as a gigantic and complex "central station," in which a massive amount of information is received, transmitted, stored and processed. The full mind starts revealing itself as the (Great) Mind, with upper case 'M,' when we realize that the Mind controls and transforms energy. Since energy represents the essence of the physical realm, our Mind has the potential to transform our lives in this physical world by transforming energy. Our Mind encompasses our nervous system, including the brain, all our senses (sixth and seventh included), our entire body, the electromagnetic and subtle energy in and around our body, and much more. It goes beyond our physical limitations to connect us with the entire Creation. In fact, our Mind is a powerful antenna that receives, accumulates, transforms and transmits energy throughout the universe for the greatest good. The Great Mind is an *Intelligent User* of energy. In this section we deal with this idea of the Mind as we unveil the concept of energy and Intelligence (with upper case 'I').

*****

The physical realm that we appreciate in our daily lives is extremely diverse and complex. Its myriad forms overwhelm our senses and flood us with information every fraction of a second. Nevertheless, in an astonishing demonstration of profound commonality, we find that at its smallest elementary level all the elements present in the universe are made of the same stuff.

Atoms, for example, are composed of the same fundamental atomic particles in all the known elements; the way these atomic particles are arranged within the atom determines the element in question. But atoms and their particles—electrons, protons and neutrons—do not constitute the most fundamental level of our physical universe. Scientists know that the atomic particles are made of sub-atomic particles, and that sub-atomic particles can be modeled using "strings and membranes" of pure energy. In other words, the most promising model that attempts to explain our physical universe states that the utmost fundamental block that constructs our physical realm is pure energy arranged into inconceivably small strings or membranes. These strings and membranes vibrate according to basic patterns and frequencies, which in turn originate the different sub-atomic particles respectively.

How can we imagine pure energy confined in ultra-small things such as strings and membranes? The most common notion of energy has to do with its effects not with its pure representation. We can appreciate the effects of energy all over around us. Energy makes things move, flow, and vibrate, and energy can travel as light and other electromagnetic radiation, or as electricity; energy can be stored in batteries or dams; and energy can transform from one of its many forms into another making the dynamism of this universe possible. But what is energy actually? We can see its effects from the explosion of a nuclear bomb to the most trivial activity we engage in every day such as brushing our teeth, but we cannot conceive of it in its pure basic essence. Any typical physics textbook defines energy as "the capacity of doing work," but now scientists say that energy, the unconceivable, is the uttermost fundamental component of which everything, the conceivable, is made of in the universe. Energy creates everything, but nothing creates energy. Energy just is. If we take again the expression "nothing creates energy" to scrutinize it a little further, we arrive at this ancient maxim: God–the void, the nothingness–creates the universe (as noted in Chapter 2).

But it's one thing to pour energy into the creation of this universe, and another to organize it to make sense of it. This is God's superb intelligence in action. The evolution of the universe since the Big Bang and the evolution of life are products of this intelligence. The causality laws that rule the universe's physical phenomena constitute the first manifestation of God's intelligence. Science can backtrack energy and, through causality laws, explain how some phenomena derived from other phenomena, and probably can predict, too, some events in the future following the same causality laws. Nevertheless, all causation chains have proven to have a limit.

Once certain elements and circumstances are given, an always-approximated scientific model–out of potentially many others–can explain what is coming next; but, how did those first elements and circumstances appear to begin with? For example, the Big Bang theory can explain the major features of our universe from a certain point in time after the initial bang, but no answers exist to the questions: What caused the bang? Where did the energy come from? Why exactly that amount of energy, no more, no less? What happened between the initial bang and the point in time mentioned above? To acknowledge the lack of physical understanding of this phenomenon, scientists call the Big Bang a "singularity" or "discontinuity." Similarly, another "singularity" or unexplainable leap occurred with the rise of life on this planet. After the first initial primitive form of life emerged, the evolution theory can explain the diversity of life on Earth, but we are still wondering how the leap from no-life to life ever occurred in the first place.

"Singularities" constitute the second expression of God's intelligence. They indicate a set of initial conditions that at some time were given or appeared all of a sudden. These initial conditions are very subtle or unelaborated, but once they are present, the causality laws of the universe (the first expression of God's intelligence) begin to develop more complex manifestations of the physical world. This explains why nothing physical is created instantaneously in its full complexity, but rather in the most basic raw form so the universe and its laws can take over from the moment the singularity appears. And it also explains why our expanding universe is always evolving by means of God's intelligence. Singularities and causality laws constitute indications that the Creation, God's creation, is still unfolding.

In conclusion, we can state that our physical realm has two main components: energy and Intelligence. Energy is the raw material and Intelligence is the underlying organizational agent that sets laws and initial conditions (singularities); both of them are needed for the universe and life to continuously evolve. Science always acknowledges the energy in the universe, but science does not recognize the presence of an intelligence that pervades the entire cosmos even though it always hits a hard end in its explanations: The primeval cause of any causation chain can never be causal. Spirituality, conversely, acknowledges both and recognizes the importance of God's intelligence because, as we progress in our spiritual journey, we realize that God's intelligence is our own Intelligence.

We can use our Intelligence, the intelligence of our Mind, not to change nature's laws but to establish the initial conditions, or singularities, from which the natural laws of the universe—the seen—will follow towards happiness and fulfillment. Consequently, our Mind will always direct and transform energy to the noblest goals.[8] This harmonious energy manipulation will set the subtle singularities in a special realm better known as the quantum realm, where the unseen and the seen merge, as detailed in the next section.

## The Quantum Nature of the Physical World

(Note: This section attempts to describe our quantum nature in order to highlight its connections with spirituality. I have noticed that many people are fascinated by the relationship between quantum physics and spirituality; for them this section might be of interest. However, for others, this section could be heavy in content. I have tried to express my understanding of quantum physics in layman's terms as much as possible; nevertheless, I acknowledge that my effort may not have been enough. Please jump to the next section, page 105, if you discover this is true for you. The next section summarizes the main aspects of this section allowing continuity in your reading.)

### The discontinuous universe

The quantum realm is the world of the extremely small, the world of the infinitesimal, which quantum physics attempts to describe; however, the word quantum (plural quanta) is more related to discontinuity than to smallness.

The term quantum comes from the Latin word *quantus* which means "how much?" and was used by Max Planck to explain the electromagnetic radiation emitted by a heated element at different temperatures in 1900. Planck postulated that energy can be absorbed or emitted only in quanta or packets, in other words, the absorbed or emitted energy is quantized since it can take only discrete values. In this regard money is similar to energy. You can receive and give only discrete values of money. Money is not continuous because its value is always in increments of one cent. You can have $1,000 but you can't ever have any money between $1,000.00 and $1,000.01.

---

[8] If our goals are selfish and, consequently, our actions are not harmonious, we are not being guided by our Mind but by the limited mind that does not include the seventh sense.

In order to understand further how stunning Planck's postulate was, imagine that you live in a physical world where speed is quantized indicating that your car can go at only certain speeds, for instance 10, 20, 30, 40 miles/hour, and so on. From 20 miles/hour you can speed up to 30 miles/hour, and then to 40, and then to 50 miles/hour without transitions between one speed and the next. That is, the speed varies in discontinuous jumps. There is no way for the car to go at 25, 31, 47 miles/hour, or, for that matter, any other speed different from the given discrete values; these other speed values do not exist in this hypothetical physical world.

Assume also that space is quantized in your world and the quantum length is 10 meters and you want to walk 100 meters from A to B, as you head to B you appear 10 meters away from A; you cannot be, say, 5 meters away from A because this travelled distance is smaller than the quantum length. As you keep on moving towards B you then appear away from A by 20 meters, 30 meters and so on until you finally reach B. In this hypothetical world, space does not exist between steps. Time could also be quantized with a quantum of 1 second in some imaginary universe. In this case, existence vanishes every second to emerge again the next second; time would not exist between one second and the next in this universe.

Of course, all of these sound bizarre to us because our universe is different. The quanta of the universes of the previous examples are simply too big for our comprehension. Fortunately, the physical nature of our universe embodies a much, much, smaller quantum,[9] so small that we cannot ever perceive any discontinuity in the normal scale world as everything around us seems very smooth and continuous. It is like comparing a 1000-pixel digital picture, so coarse that we can see all the pixels, with another one with 10 million pixels, so smooth and perfect that it is impossible to determine whether the picture is digital or not.

But even the 10 million-pixel picture will become coarse and show its pixels when we zoom enough into it; likewise, if we

---

[9] I think our "smaller quantum" is just a subjective concept. Perhaps the inhabitants of other universes got accustomed to their quantum size as much as we did to ours, which tells us that time and space might be concepts more related to our perception than anything else.

could zoom enough into our physical world to the infinitesimal scales below the sub-atomic realm, we would see how this physical world breaks down and escapes our everyday perception.

The fact that energy can be transferred only by packets or quanta implies that all electromagnetic radiation, including visible light, are composed of many of these packets or quanta that behave as massless particles called photons. Due to the very small quantization of our universe, the energy of one photon of visible light is not enough for our eyes to discern, but it is big enough to affect an electron inside an atom. The changes that occurred in the atoms of an object when light illuminates it are discrete changes due to the quantization of light; every time photons hit the object, the object changes to a new discrete state, and every time the object releases the excess of light (reflected light) as photons, it changes also to another discrete state. There are neither transitions nor intermediate values between one state and another. What we see, through the reflected light from the object, are snapshots of a physical object, and what the object looks like between snapshots eludes our perception.

Besides sight, our other four senses are also affected by the quantization of our universe as they are based on friction or contact between objects: air and ear drums, food and tongue, objects and skin, and odor molecules and olfactory receptors. When two objects are in contact, the atoms or molecules of their respective surfaces interact through electromagnetic forces. This creates energy exchanges that these four senses detect. As expected, these energy exchanges are quantized implying that these senses, too, process only snapshots of a quantized physical realm.

In this universe, all the interactions that have occurred and still occur among atomic and subatomic components cause a discontinuous exchange of energy. The state of matter, thereby, changes abruptly from one snapshot characterized by a set of conditions to another one with a different set of conditions. What happens between consecutive snapshots cannot ever be known using physical means because there is no physical information, no space, no time, between consecutive snapshots. As an example, consider a film or video which consists of still pictures that when in motion give the illusion of continuity to our eyes and brain. In this case, we have no way to know what happened between one still picture and the next because that information does not exist in the video or film. Likewise, we do not exist physically between one quantum snapshot and the next one. We, ourselves, abruptly change from one instant to another as if something were remaking us every time. Between one instant and the next, we cease to exist and then we are born again completely different and yet apparently preserving our identity. Something makes all our constituents remain together in the quantum cycle of death and rebirth.

In order to better comprehend these discontinuous snapshots, we should know how quantized our universe is. Scientists mention that the *Planck length* (about $10^{-33}$ cm, a millionth of a billionth of a billionth of a billionth of a centimeter) for distances and the *Planck time* (about $10^{-43}$ s, a tenth of a millionth of a trillionth of a trillionth of a trillionth of a second) for time are the theoretical minimum values for distance and time intervals above which physical reality can make sense. As we can see, these values are unimaginably small, so small that in no way would we see any appreciable discontinuity in our daily lives. Even for atomic particles the Planck length is enormously small. A proton, one of the particles that form the atomic nucleus, is $10^{20}$ (100 times a billion times a billion times a billion) larger than the Planck length, but the size of the energy strings that compose the variety of sub-atomic particles is in the order of the Planck length. Therefore, we can state that at these infinitesimal scales of time (Planck time) and space (Planck space) the physical realm, as we know it, breaks down as time and space cease to exist and the universe's matter changes through imperceptible, minuscule and discontinuous energy changes.

### The empty space energy

But it's not only matter whose energy fluctuates by jumps. The empty space also has energy that fluctuates in a discontinuous fashion. The energy of the empty space is called zero-point energy or vacuum energy. This energy is a direct consequence of the quantum nature of the universe, and specifically of Heisenberg's uncertainty principle.

Heisenberg's principle states that it is impossible to know exactly both the position and the velocity of a particle at the same time. A typical way of interpreting this result is by saying that the more accurate the particle's position or velocity is, the less definite its velocity or position is, respectively. If we know perfectly the particle's position, then its velocity is completely unknown, and *vice versa*. We can take Heisenberg's principle as a statement about the information that, in theory, we can access from this universe. Presented using everyday language, this principle says that this universe, due to its quantization, establishes fundamental limits for our observations. In other words, this universe will never provide us with information that violates its quantized nature, since said information does not exist physically. Heisenberg's uncertainty principle is equivalent to stating that we cannot see what happens between two contiguous frames of a film.

The uncertainty principle is not detectable in the macro world. For instance, if you know accurately where your car is at a certain instant, there seems not to be a limitation in nature that prevents you from also obtaining an accurate measurement of the car's speed at that same instant. In fact, with the information we obtain from today's typical instruments, we are able to predict for all practical purposes where the car will be in the next 20 minutes, or how long it will take to arrive at some destination 10 miles away. At least in our macro world, knowing the initial position and velocity of an object is enough to predict with reasonable accuracy the final position of the object after a certain time or the time that the object takes to travel a known distance.

However, electrons are small enough for the effects of quantum mechanics to be observable on them. If you know the position of an electron with an extreme exactitude, which is to say that the actual position of the electron is confined to a very small initial region in space, then according to Heisenberg's principle the velocity of such electron is very uncertain. Its velocity can be anything between zero and a big value; therefore, one instant later that same electron could be anywhere within a much larger region of the universe. The smaller the initial region, the faster the electron moves away, and the harder to predict its final position. Conversely, if you know the speed of an electron with a very small uncertainty, then Heisenberg's principle implies that its current position lies anywhere in a large region of space. In this case too, the prediction of where this electron will be after certain time is very difficult since its current position is highly uncertain.

It is important to note that the same uncertainty principle applies to both the car and the electron in the examples above. The results are staggeringly different because of our appreciation of the scale. In the macro world, the uncertainties derived from Heisenberg's uncertainty law are so small that they completely escape our perception. Assume the car of the example above is parked and the uncertainty of its position in the parking lot is one meter. According to Heisenberg's principle, the speed of this car has also an uncertainty; the speed cannot be zero with absolute precision. If we know the uncertainty of the position, we can determine the uncertainty of the speed using Heisenberg's principle. The uncertainty principle tells us that the speed uncertainty for this car is around $10^{-40}$ Km/s, that is the parked car has any speed between 0 and $10^{-40}$ Km/s. This speed is so unimaginable small that at the max speed the car will take $10^{27}$ years, that is, 100,000 trillion times the current age of the universe, to move one centimeter. Obviously, the parked car is not moving for all practical purposes.

Now think of a region in empty space that has constantly no matter and no force fields.[10] Then that region apparently has and maintains a zero energy field, for which we know its energy value (zero) as well as its energy rate of change (also zero) with perfect exactitude, violating Heisenberg's uncertainty principle. To understand why zero energy along with zero energy rate violates Heisenberg's uncertainty principle, imagine a single particle that happens to be in an empty space region as such. The particle then will maintain the same position forever as the field forces are all zero and no energy can be exchanged with the particle in question; consequently, we can predict its position (some fixed point in space) and velocity (always zero) with zero uncertainty, again violating Heisenberg's principle and, therefore, the quantization of this universe.

---

[10] A region in space has a force field, or simply a field, when particles inside that region are affected by the field's characteristic forces. For instance, Earth has a magnetic field that affects the atoms in our bodies, as well as a gravitational field that prevents us from floating aloft in space; light and other electromagnetic radiation consist of both electric and magnetic travelling fields; the strong forces that keep protons and neutrons together in the atom's nucleus constitute another example of a force field.

As a consequence of Heisenberg's uncertainty principle, empty space cannot have zero energy. Energy has to materialize somehow in this empty space and jitter from one discrete value to another. Since energy cannot be created in the physical realm, this energy simply emerges from the void into the physical realm pervading all space, including the relatively vast amount of space present within atoms and molecules of all matter.

The quantum nature of our universe implies that empty space really does not exist. Because energy and matter are equivalent according to Einstein's $E=mc^2$, particles and anti-particles are constantly created and annihilated in space following the quantum fluctuations of the vacuum energy. Space is energy from the void. Within one cubic meter of "empty" space there is as much energy as the Sun produces in 1,000 years.[11]

## The wavefunction explanation for the entanglement of the universe

The quantum world is a tumultuous realm with abrupt changes fostered by quantized energy exchanges among all the constituents of the universe—space, matter, and fields in all their diverse forms—and quite remarkably, these exchanges propagate through the entire universe since an interconnected fabric seemingly entangles space, fields and matter throughout the physical realm. In this respect, Quantum Physics offers a probabilistic model that describes observable phenomena emerging from the quantum world and satisfying Heisenberg's uncertainty principle. This quantum model, known as the wavefunction model, (a) describes the quantum realm as an entangled fabric through which any quantum variation propagates as a wave, and (b) uses probabilities to predict the likelihood of the wave causing a specific quantum change (wave collapse) somewhere else in the universe.

Let us dissect this description with more details and examples, beginning with our basic notion of waves. Waves in the macro world propagate away from their source in all directions as long as there is a medium in which they can travel. The waves in a pond travel in the water and the sound waves we hear travel in the air;

---

[11] *The Quantum Universe* by Brian Cox and Jeff Forshaw, DaCapo Press, Boston, MA, 2011, p. 212.

in either case, the motion of the wave (wave momentum) is transmitted in all directions away from its source as one molecule pushes another molecule which in turn pushes another molecule and so forth in their respective medium. Anything in the path of the wave front will be affected by the wave and the wave itself will be affected too as it transmits part (not all) of its energy to the object in question.

Consider now a photon in the micro world. We accurately know the photon's speed because all electromagnetic radiation travels at the speed of light; therefore, according to Heisenberg's uncertainty principle, its position must not be definite, which agrees perfectly with the verifiable notion that electromagnetic radiation travels as waves. In this sense, when an atom produces a photon, which constitutes a quantum variation, the momentum of this photon can potentially reach anyplace in the universe as it travels as a wave at the speed of light in a very special medium, the quantum fabric itself. This means that the photon (which could be pictured as a particle as well) exists all over its wave front,[12] like being simultaneously in many places at the same time. Nevertheless, unlike the waves in the pond or the sound waves that can transmit part of their momentum to more than one object at the same time, the photon can transmit only the totality of its energy at once and at only one point in the universe, causing a quantum leap. This is when the wave "collapses" into one point as the photon exchanges its energy. In order to know where the photon wave will collapse, the wavefunction model uses probabilities. The use of "probabilities" indicates a lack of source knowledge (that cannot be physically obtained).

Once you understand how the wave-like approach of quantum physics explains the entanglement of our universe, think for an

---

[12] The photon (which has no mass) travels as a wave and, due to the quantized energy exchanges of the universe, interacts as a particle at once in only one point. This wave-particle dual behavior is also characteristic of particles with mass such as electrons. An electron travels on a wave front, which tells us that potentially it can be in many places at the same time (even though it can be observed only at one place at a time). When you drive, your car also travels on a wave front, but the probability that Quantum Physics predicts for you to be found somewhere away from your actual path is infinitesimally small, zero for all practical purposes.

instant what a quantum change represents in the world of the infinitesimal. We cannot think here as we think in our macro world. A quantum change constitutes a huge change in the world of the ultra-small. As a huge change, it affects the universe's constituents that surround it. For instance, when an atom changes its quantum state because a photon hits it, its electromagnetic interactions with other atoms will change too, forcing new quantum changes in the atoms nearby. Generalizing this phenomenon, we can state that every quantum change generates other quantum changes that trigger even more quantum changes in a chain reaction that travels as a wave in the quantum fabric, thus affecting the evolution of the universe.

## The Quantum Spirituality

The last paragraph of the previous section states a fact that has a very important spiritual interpretation: our real greatness, our true happiness, can be found only when we become small and humble, for this constitutes the way everything connects within the Creation. Everything that lies in the big scale world seems disconnected with everything else, yet as we zoom into the infinitesimal world we can appreciate how the quantum fabric interconnects the entire universe; any pull or push of any of its threads will reverberate throughout all of existence.

If you throw a pebble into the ocean, it seems that your action cannot make any difference in the macro world. When the pebble hits the water, it produces ripples so tiny that the ocean waves are unperturbed; however, think of the changes that the little pebble caused at the quantum level of the infinitesimal. That little pebble has created an entirely different quantum state whose effects propagate throughout the entire ocean, throughout the entire planet, throughout the entire universe because when you threw that pebble into the water you pulled an invisible thread of the universal quantum fabric; you changed the universe.

Think now about that energy that jitters in empty space, including the space present in atoms, molecules and any matter in general, including our bodies, organs, cells and DNA. This is the energy created by force fields that appear and disappear in any space as a reminder that the Creation is still unfolding. Describing this vacuum energy escapes science's causality laws since energy pouring out of nothing is not causal at all, and describing how this energy, due to the quantum entanglement, affects the universe cannot ever be dreamt of in scientific terms. Nonetheless, from the spiritual point of view, the energy that emerges from the void is a mere consequence of the Creation still unfolding at the quantum realm. As God's creation continues forever, the empty space energy expands the universe at an increasing rate.

The quantum realm constitutes the threshold where the unseen merges with the seen and where events and circumstances start forming. Hence, envision yourself accessing your Intelligence, that is to say, the same God's intelligence. Then you would be a creator as you alter the quantum realm to manipulate empty space energy and establish singularities in the infinitesimal world. As a creator, you maintain and contribute to the harmony of the Creation; you do not disrupt the universal flow, but you follow it; you are not a subject of fate, but the object of your own creation; you are not engulfed by hubris in the awareness of your capabilities, but you are uncovered by the most beautiful humility in the appreciation of being with God. However, in order to access your Intelligence and become a creator, you must start with your conscious mind to learn new patterns and *see* more of reality. As your consciousness grows by means of a spiritual practice,[13] it will eventually transcend the little mind[14] until you reach the (Great) Mind. This occurs because your conscious reprograms your subconscious with new absolute and real patterns of faith (trust), love and compassion. These new patterns dissolve all destructive fears caused by your belief system and set you free.

Through concentration (as detailed in the following chapter), our conscious brings our sixth sense under control, which makes more room for the seventh sense's information to come into our awareness. Therefore, we will *see* more of reality, and our thoughts will start turning pure and pristine. Our pure thoughts' electromagnetic waves alter the quantum world inside and around

---

[13] This spiritual practice is described in Chapter 8 and the principles of this practice are discussed in Chapter 7.
[14] The little mind is a subset of the Mind. If we don't see reality the way it is, we are not using the Great Mind fully.

us to enhance the energy field, or aura, that every human has. In Chapter 2, we tacitly mentioned this aura when we described the seventh sense of intuition. In fact, our quantum realm, or aura, and the seventh sense are the same thing. Consequently, our seventh sense function is two-fold: (a) to *see* the unseen and (b) to propagate the quantum changes that will set the singularities for creation. Putting it differently, as we perceive the unseen through the seventh sense, we become the unseen itself; we become creators with the power to alter the quantum realm (see Figure 2).

What starts with a willful effort to apply our conscious reverberates as a positive feedback cycle of infinite and splendorous possibilities. As our will to be conscious opens the doors to our seventh sense, the increase of information from the seventh sense augments our awareness, which opens even further our seventh sense. When the seventh sense is fully expanded, the conscious effort naturally becomes meditation (as explained in Chapter 7) intensifying our creator role. In this state, the seventh sense, the quantum realm, represents the furthermost expression of our Great Mind in the ultimate bliss: union with God and, thereby, with everyone and with everything. It's in this state that reality turns as clear as crystal.

When you are able to produce the quantum changes—or singularities—in the infinitesimal world according to your harmonious creator role, you are changing your life to serve your desires for love, peace and happiness for you and all. Notwithstanding the initial imperceptibility of these changes, they represent the fundamental dynamism through which the universe manifests the perceptible events of the macro scale, that is to say, the scale of everyday life. Whatever will happen tomorrow is already happening now as the energy exchanges of future events are forming and arranging in this precise moment in subtle and undetectable ways at the quantum level. Everything starts in the quantum world of the infinitesimal, and the magnificence of the gigantic cosmos is nothing but a consequence of the infinitesimal world.

# 7
# THE SEVEN PILLARS OF SPIRITUALITY

In the previous chapters we have discussed the nature of spirituality and the hindrances to it. We have also stated that achieving spirituality, the exact awareness of reality, relates to a journey of self-discovery or, perhaps, self-reencounter as we start perceiving reality as it is, in all its magnificence. Many obstacles and detours may appear on our spiritual path and hinder our journey, but we have learned also from previous chapters that none of those hindrances is real. We create our own limitations and, therefore, we can demolish them at anytime.

In this chapter, we describe the Seven Pillars of Spirituality that support our journey and prevent us from straying from it. The Seven Pillars of Spirituality, when interpreted properly, present similarities with the Eight Limbs of Yoga and the Noble Eightfold Path of Buddhism (see Appendix A). As the Eight Limbs of Yoga and the eight precepts of the Buddhist path, the Seven Pillars are meant to work together synergistically; trying to develop any of them in isolation will not produce the desired result. The Seven Spiritual Pillars of Spirituality, on which the spiritual practice described in Chapter 8 is based, are:

1.  Emotional recapitulation
2.  Devotion and Prayer (Faith)
3.  Body Purity
4.  Mind Purity (Intention and Concentration)
5.  Meditation
6.  Deep connections with others
7.  Union with God

I owe the Seven Pillars of Spirituality to an inspiration I received as a response to my desire to put spirituality in practical terms. The Seven Pillars state the fact that spirituality is an individual undertaking in which we need to acknowledge and understand how our mind directs us (pillar #1 emotional recapitulation) not necessarily for our best interest. They establish that in the midst of a dire situation, there is a perfection that can be approached, a perfection we can tap into (pillar #2, faith). Even if the idea of God is extraneous to us, we all know that there exists always a way, "the way," to make any situation evolve to an optimal and harmonious resolution regardless of our ability to see it or not. Trusting our ability to see "the way" constitutes the *sine qua non* of the human spirit. When we have faith in this human spirit, we express our devotion to humankind and its potential to find the optimal way to resolve any situation. Between this optimal way, "the way," and God I don't see any difference. The pillars also indicate that spirituality is all-encompassing. It covers our physicality: body and mind. Body and mind must work in unison to bring us the best experience of our physical realm (pillars #3 and #4, purity of body and mind). But as reality extends beyond the physical, meditation (pillar # 5) will expand our perception towards the immaterial, the unseen. As we increase our awareness of reality, deep connections with others (pillar #6) strengthen and spread out without limitations. We feel our universality and appreciate the union with all. Pillar #6 is the barometer that measures the intensity of our spirituality. Observe how deeply you connect with others regardless of their social condition, physical attributes or beliefs, and your observation will tell how spiritual and happy you are. Finally, Union with God, the ultimate realization, is not more than the expected consequence of being dedicated to your spiritual path.

## Spiritual Pillar # 1: Emotional Recapitulation

Very likely we all know the type of emotional recollections that harm us. As indicated in Chapter 5, these are the recollections that make us incessantly dwell in the past as we reenact some stories of our lives as if the past were still alive. Technically, reenacting the past in this way is not a recapitulation but a capitulation. In this case, we capitulate and acquiesce to our subconscious fears as we relinquish the precious control of our present moment, that is, our life itself. However, if we find ourselves "capitulating" at some moments of our daily life, we might take note of the events that make us capitulate and bring them for a session of recapitulation as explained below.

Emotional recapitulation is rather a conscious act wherein the individual revisits with full attention the events of their past. This pillar makes the individual sensitive to their actions and reactions. The individual through conscious recollection will be able to identify those moments when anger, anxiety, frustration, depression, suffering, or excesses of any sort arise taking over their behavior. In this stage, the person interested in obtaining more awareness of reality must watch one of those moments in their mind, perhaps the most recent one. Then he or she should be able to scrutinize this moment by answering these three basic questions:

*What were the circumstances and the events of the moment in question?*

Answering this question, the individual must be able to reproduce in their mind the chain of events that caused their reaction. For instance, if I had a bad day at work and I lost my temper, I should try to remember what happened when I lost my temper. Perhaps I got offended because somebody said something about me that I didn't like. Then I focus on remembering what was said to me and how I reacted. I try to reproduce as faithfully as possible the things that I said and the things that I did, and what others did. As I remember the circumstances and events of the moment in question, I should pay attention to the emotions and feelings that are triggered by my memories in order to answer the next question.

*How will I respond next time when similar circumstances arise again?*

Before answering this question, try to remember the basic feeling you felt. Was it about anger? Was it about depression? Were you suffering? Was it about greed or ostentation? Was it about judging and discriminating others? Was it about feeling emotional pain due to a loss? As you replay your memories in your mind, you should acknowledge the emotions and feelings you feel now and compare them with the ones you felt when the actual events occurred. Is the feeling or emotion you experienced during your reaction still alive? Or do you feel guilt, shame, or embarrassment about what you did?

If the memories of your uneasy past behavior bring you the same feeling or emotion you experienced during your unharmonious reaction, you will indeed repeat such reaction again because very likely your reaction makes perfect sense to you. For example, anger is a natural human emotion and gives you the energy to defend yourself, depression helps you to clearly determine your limitations for you not to bother "surmounting the insurmountable" and accept your victimhood condition, ostentation makes the statement of who you are since people need to know how relevant you are, and discrimination sets you apart from "low quality people," including "evil doers." In other words, you are justifying and validating your excessive behavior and, therefore, you will maintain it.

Conversely, if your memories make you feel guilty, embarrassed or ashamed, you could be restricting yourself too much, becoming repressed and inauthentic and, consequently, susceptible to reacting in the opposite way you initially did. As an example, you could have fallen into depression due to a relationship breakup in the past. During this depression you felt worthless as a sense of rejection overtook you. Your partner abandoned you for somebody else who you thought was better than you. Then, after a while of feeling depressed you start feeling ashamed of how low you came, of how much you suffered because someone decided to hurt you. You wonder how somebody had so much power over you, being able to harm you that way. It was a complete embarrassment and you proudly promise yourself never to let anyone humiliate you like that again. Your self is now much more important than anything else. You develop, thereby, a sense of cautiousness and vigilance in your subsequent relationships; you become suspicious and ready to take action if any new partner does not behave according to your expectations. Now, you know your worth and you will protect it at all costs; as a result, you easily become angry to defend your point and, if necessary, you will not hesitate to break up the relationship if you want to save your integrity. This way, any of us can transform one emotion into its exact opposite (depression to anger, in this particular example) indicating that we are still restricted, unable to manifest our pure self.

Nevertheless, as we replay our past maladroit behavior in our mind, we could experience another kind of feeling, a more authentic and harmonious feeling completely different from those exemplified above. The best way to describe this feeling is through an analogy in which the actor–the observed–of a movie stops being an actor and becomes the spectator–the observer–sitting in the movie theater, as explained next.

When we watch a movie, most of the time we are moved by the events and circumstances depicted in the movie. We cry because of the pain and sorrow we see in it, we hate its bad and despicable characters and feel anger at them, we laugh at its funny situations, we feel the stress and the fear caused by its violent actions and orchestrated suspense, but also we feel inspired due to its rendering of heart-moving events. When we see a movie, we just sit there and experience a variety of emotions with some sense of detachment, very likely, because we know that, after all, it's nothing but a movie. In many aspects our past resembles a movie; for example, we cannot change it as we cannot change a movie, and the people involved in it (including ourselves) followed their own scripts written long ago in their subconscious through programmed belief systems. Unfortunately, these belief systems constitute the only guidance that most people have; therefore, we certainly must assert that those implicated in our past truly acted at the best of their knowledge and abilities. And despite the fact that some movie actors are cast in roles that fit their personalities, the people involved in our past stories do not necessarily have to behave as they did when they followed their past roles, for those roles were never meant to be permanent.

There exists a fundamental difference, however, between the way we approach our past and the way we approach a movie. Unlike a movie, we frequently look at our past with a strong attachment. When we recall our past, we have the propensity to attach ourselves to the events, circumstances and people of our memories. We forget that we are the spectator now and end up acting in the movie again. In this case, we relive the past emotions so intensely that they have a long-lasting effect on us. As expounded before, they still affect us in two drastic ways: (a) we rationalize our unharmonious actions and justify them, getting ready to react with the same unharmonious behavior next time or (b) we feel guilt, shame and embarrassment because of our unskillful actions and thus become prone to react with feelings and emotions opposite to those that originated the sense of guilt and shame. Attachment to our stories (as explained in Chapter 5) creates a disharmonious attitude that harms us and others as it renders us emotionally imbalanced.

Only when you can watch the movie of your past with detachment, or equivalently, when you are just the observer–spectator– and not the observed–actor–will you know that your old ways of reacting are becoming obsolete. This holds true even if similar circumstances to those that triggered your past reactions reappear again.

In the detachment mode, you observe the characters of your past story movie but pay special attention to the main character who used to be you but is no longer. The main character is your old, antiquated self but is still the special one, nevertheless; it's the one you follow the most because it's the only one who appears in all your stories. During detachment you will experience the emotions and feelings of your main character as well as the emotions and feelings of the other characters of your stories, just as you do while watching a movie, that is to say, detached from the movie and in the comfort and safety of your own seat. Being detached, then, does not signify that you turned into a cold-emotionless machine but that you transformed yourself into a sensitive human being capable of feeling deeply in the comfort and safety of your own awareness, which gives you the conscious control to act harmoniously. Irrespective of what the movie of your past shows, when you are detached from your stories you know that you can always restore the harmony in your behavior. More specifically, you know that you can now direct your actions towards easing the pain of those hurt by the main character of your past story movie. In an allegoric sense, you ease their pain in the same way you clean the floor of pieces of glass and wipe away the spilled water after you dropped a glass of water. You cannot recover the broken glass and the spilled water as you cannot undo the pain you inflicted with your past recklessness, but you can always clean up your mess for them and for you by just starting with a sincere heart-centered apology—that is, an apology that does not excuse or justify your actions.

Regarding those who made your old self suffer or have a hard time, while you observe them in the movie of your past with no attachment, you will understand that they were playing their role to the best of their abilities with the knowledge they had. To hate them or to keep any resentment against them makes no more sense than to despise the actor that plays the evil guy in any movie, especially if you consider the fact that they cannot give the glass they broke and the water they spilled back to you.

Remember also that because of your old past choices, you have contributed to your own suffering, or more precisely, the suffering of the main character of your movie. These were the moments wherein you did not manage your pain well and transformed it into suffering. Unlike suffering, pain is unavoidable. Pain exists to let us know that we need to correct the course of our actions. Without physical and emotional pain as feedback[1] to live our lives, we will have a short and chaotic existence. Usually we withdraw from a source of physical pain but incredibly, in many circumstances, we seem to be stuck to sources of emotional pain. In the latter case, the feedback mechanism is broken and pain becomes suffering. Suffering is avoidable because it is the exacerbation of pain. Suffering happens when you add to your pain; you add to your pain when your mind is not attuned with reality. Suffering puts more

---

[1] Feedback is fundamental for vehicle navigation. NASA spacecraft use it and you use it, too, every time you drive. You know the trajectory you should follow and your eyes tell you where you are. Any discrepancy between where you should be and where you are automatically induces a correction in your driving to go back to the desired trajectory. This process happens in your mind and you don't even notice it. The small deviations that actually happen are seemingly imperceptible. Close your eyes and start driving to see if you can reach your destination without feedback. In this case, your driving is erratic and dangerous as you lose your sense of orientation and location. Similarly, if you don't feel pain—life's feedback—your life is erratic; you are disoriented and you don't know where your spiritual path is. This doesn't mean life has to be painful *per se*; it means that, as we progress in our spiritual endeavors, we learn how to transform pain into awareness until some time when, as for those grand spiritual masters, pain is seemingly imperceptible.

pain on top of the existing pain with drastic emotional and physical consequences for the well-being of the individual. Suffering grows as it feeds itself to enormous proportions; pain, when used as feedback to correct the course of a human life, transforms itself into awareness as the individual starts *seeing* reality as it is. Suffering makes you react, pain makes you consciously act with serenity and equanimity. You can still experience peace and contentment while in pain; in suffering, you break down into pieces as your subconscious mind exacerbates your pain in a futile attempt to guard you against it.

Because you have contributed to your own suffering, you must forgive yourself, as well as those who hurt you, from deep inside your heart. Only then will you be assuring your happiness, for forgiveness is the key to emotional freedom and authenticity—the emotional freedom that stems from knowing that you will never repeat the unskillful actions of those who acted in the movie of your past. Forgive and then forget that you have forgiven, for everything starts all over again with radiance and harmony.

### *Why am I so sensitive to the events and circumstances that originated the incident?*

If by answering the previous question you still find yourself attached to your stories justifying your anger, frustration and excesses or feeling guilty and ashamed due to your past actions, and especially incapable of forgiving, then you need to do a deeper introspection. The recent event that triggers all these uneasy feelings is just the manifestation of some unconscious program whose existence perhaps you wouldn't admit, but at least you have gained awareness of your feelings and emotions as you went through it. Once you have recognized your feelings, acknowledge them as they are, for they all are valid. At this point it is better not to rush and to let the natural forces take their course. Your next step is then to try to remember a different incident farther in your past in which you reacted similarly, and then try to remember another one even farther in your past; keep on doing this as far as your memory goes. Can you see a pattern in your behavior? Can you identify a common cause for the same reaction in these old events of your life? You need to admit that the only common character in all these past stories is you; therefore, within you, and not others, lies the original cause for the behavior you expose.

As your introspection intensifies inevitably you will reach your adulthood early years, adolescence and eventually childhood. In this introspection do not try to look for traumas and rationalizations because the most important thing you must do is to remember what you were told, what others did to you, what you did as a response and how you felt. While you go through your memories, seek not to judge your own situation and that of others. Just recount, recapitulate your early years and remember it is perfectly fine to re-experience all the emotions of those days. While you develop your consciousness through the other six spiritual pillars described in the following sections, you naturally assist yourself in finding the harmful connections that your subconscious has established between your previous life experiences and your current circumstances. Once those connections are found, you can answer this third and final question of the first spiritual pillar and place yourself closer to your total freedom.

## Spiritual Pillar #2: Devotion and Prayer (Faith)

In order to survive, human cubs rely on their parents. Their survival is directly related to the attachment they have to their parents. It is natural for children, then, to look at their parents as almighty beings that provide them with protection, care and love. This evolutionary instinct extends to human religion expression as we can see with the development of religions over the course of history. Mother Earth, Mother Nature, Heavenly Father, are all expressions for the divinity that is out there to care for, protect and love us.

Thus most people are easily inclined to the idea of God as external to us. Through devotion we develop a profound personal relationship with God. The devotion practitioner chooses the kind of relationship she or he wants to establish with God. God could be a father, a mother, a benevolent master, or any other related figure depending on the devotee. In any case, God is always all caring and loving, and God's love extends to all without distinction.

During devotion, devotees worship God through rituals and ceremonies that express their affection and awe. Usually, devotees hold these rituals and ceremonies in shrines, temples and churches, all of which are endowed with elevated energy as these places are set apart for people to bring in their best intentions and thoughts.

Devotion includes talking to God through prayers to ask God for help in moments of need and to express joy and gratitude for the gift of precious human birth and existence. Prayers cultivate the devotees' faith in the belief that the uncertain will become certain and fears will vanish. This faith is not the dogmatic faith, the one that makes devotees blindly accept dogmas, belief systems and prejudices without reasoning about them. This is the faith that makes devotees see that we all are equal and that God has no preference for any sector of the population in particular. This is the faith that as a powerful force opens the devotee to the extraordinary splendor that unchains the faithful from fears and limitations. As such, faith encompasses an intrinsic gratitude that devotees feel and openly express because they have the certainty that what is asked will be bestowed by God since God always wants for each of us the highest good in perfect harmony with all.

Devotees can call God by any name of their preference and can also call upon the virgins, saints, angels, gods and goddesses, and other pure spiritual beings characterized by love and compassion. Devotion represents the opportunity for us to unconditionally love whom we consider our personal purest expression of good. Devotion is also the surrender of our imperfections to God, for God always shows us the perfect way. For these reasons, devotion with its observances is fundamental to open the individual to God's pure love and constitutes an important initial step to set the intentions for each day of our life, thus the same pure love can also be found within later on (especially through the next spiritual pillars).

## Spiritual Pillar # 3: Body Purity

Mind and body constitute inseparable aspects of our Great Mind (see Chapter 6); nevertheless, people talk about them as separate entities. What affects the mind affects the body; what affects the body affects the mind. Both of them must work in tandem to achieve physical purity and, consequently, spiritual realization.

The extended misconception that the body is of no concern for spiritual realization, because allegedly spiritual focus must be only on the "soul or spirit," causes too much confusion for the individual. Definitely, we must find our pure essence, the one beyond the physical realm, to appreciate our sameness with God and, therefore, with everybody else. As explained in previous chapters, not appreciating the sameness among us has led humankind to the excesses that we all are familiar with throughout the course of history (including these present days). On the other hand, by realizing our sameness we treat one another with compassion, we try to help each other, and we try to mitigate other people's pain. This human pain is caused by physical necessities that are not satisfied because of conditions such as poverty, diseases, wars, exploitation, discrimination, etc. Patently, when we try to help others following our spiritual true nature we assist them in their physical needs. Therefore, wouldn't it be laudable and spiritual to assist ourselves in our own physical needs too?

Spirituality is the awareness of reality—the seen and the unseen—and our individual physical attributes, body and mind, definitely form part of reality. Spirituality, therefore, should lead us to attend our own physical needs as part of our spiritual realization. The greatest physical need we have is that of creating and maintaining a healthy body-mind combination through physical purity. What does purity mean in the spiritual context? An object's purity denotes the absence of "impurities," that is, of anything foreign, inappropriate or extraneous that does not contribute to and quite often diminishes the function and the beauty of the object in question. A pure body is a body free of dirt, pollutants, and toxins, and without energy blockages as all its organs, senses, tissues and glands function in perfect harmony with life and the flow of the Creation; therefore, a pure body is healthy and full of vitality and vibrant energy. A pure mind is a mind free of destructive, unharmonious and selfish thoughts; a pure mind creates powerful intentions that alter the quantum realm to create and sustain the individual and the collective well-being (see pillar # 4).

## Outside body purity

The purity of your body on the outside relates to your personal hygiene. Keeping your skin free of dirt and foreign substances represents an important step towards physical purity. Here, however, you have to be careful about the products you use to clean your body since they could be even worse than the dirt you try to remove. Your skin is the largest organ of your body and absorbs anything that you put on it directly into your bloodstream. Unfortunately, commercial skin products are even less monitored than are products for human consumption.[2] Since most skin product manufacturers are motivated only by profits, many questionable ingredients end up in these products.[3] By reading the many unpronounceable names of these chemical ingredients on the product label, you should get the intuitive guidance to avoid those products.

A natural cleansing requires only a good scrub and water. Without putting chemicals on your skin, the scrub will provide you with an excellent massage that activates your blood circulation and stimulates the segregation of the skin natural oils that moisturize your skin and protect you against germs. Water is the purest element for cleansing and has a special spiritual significance as it is used in many religious rituals including baptism, Ganges ritual bathing and others. In this sense, I consider water very sacred to me. As I take a shower, I visualize the water coming out of the shower as pure universal energy pouring onto me, flushing away my fears and all other mind impurities. This way I make a body cleansing a mind cleansing too (more about mind cleansing in the next spiritual pillar), and for that reason I express gratitude towards the water for purifying my body and mind. In order to complete your external body cleansing and in order to nourish and soothe your skin, you can use natural oils and botanical products that you can find in your garden or natural food/products store. I particularly use aloe vera, coconut oil, and argan oil on my skin.

---

[2] Cosmetic and skin care products do not require approval from the U.S. FDA before they are found in the stores.
[3] Among these questionable ingredients we have: diazolidinyl urea, imidazolidinyl urea, sodium laureth sulfate, polyethylene glycol, oxybenzone, octylmethoxycinnamate, phthalates, parabens, triclosan, aluminum and many others with bad reputations, including that of being carcinogens, hormone mimics, mutagens, Alzheimer's disease promoters, etc.

## Inside body purity (food quantity)

The purity of your body in the inside relates to both diet and physical activity or exercises. The two dietary aspects that you must consider are quantity and quality of the food you ingest. Quantity is a concern for people from affluent societies because they tend to eat much more than they should according to evolution's human body design. Affluent societies have made food widely available, relatively cheap and abundant like never before in history. A vast population in these countries has access to plenty of food and they ingest it when their bodies do not need it. People eat three copious meals a day and in between meals they have snacks usually made with sugar and refined flour. Their refrigerators are always available with easy food 24 hours a day, 7 days a week; everywhere they go they find food and they eat it; they eat when they are not hungry and when their bodies have not finished digesting and assimilating their last meal or snack; their entire digestive systems have been working at full capacity without a rest for many years. Amid all of these, they perhaps have not fully realized that digestion itself requires energy, energy that is taken away from their bodies during the digestive process, the reason that they feel tired all the time. Paradoxically, while they feel tired lacking energy, their bodies have accumulated excesses of energy deposited as fat—which, besides storing the energy excess, also has the purpose of storing away the toxins and pollutants[4] that find their way to the human body especially through tainted food as described below.

People eat out of habit to distract themselves from whatever they want to get away from. When we are focused and enjoying an activity we can skip eating very easily, but when we are not interested in what we are doing we find any excuse to fetch some food or drink. Eating, including drinking beverages, has become excessive as people need more distraction and do not recognize the real needs of their bodies. We definitely must enjoy what we eat and drink, but we also must make our minds attuned to the real

---

[4] If toxins and pollutants were not stored in fat tissues, they would be more available in the bloodstream causing even more damage to the body organs. It is interesting to notice the resourcefulness of the human body as it tries to protect humans from their bad choices.

physical needs of our bodies. We must eat only when we are really hungry, when our stomachs are completely empty and the gastric juices give us the burning sensation typical of hunger. We never should eat until we feel full but until we feel approximately ¾ full. And most of all, we must give our digestive system a break by moderately fasting according to the evolutionary design of our human bodies.[5]

## Inside body purity (food quality)

As if the excessive quantity of food were not already a big impediment to our body purification, we have, too, the poor quality of modern day food. The food industry, including the large-scale farm industry, has adulterated the natural food needed for human consumption in order to make it profitable rather than wholesome. Therefore, we need to increase our awareness of what is out there posing as food. The processed food includes preservatives, artificial colors and flavors, and other chemicals to increase their shelf-life and appeal to the human taste; vegetables and fruits are contaminated with pesticides, herbicides,[6] fungicides, nemacides (to

---

[5] The human body reached its evolutionary zenith with the Paleolithic people who lived before the Agricultural Revolution more than 10,000 years ago. For millions of years the human body adapted to fast due to the not-too-available food. Periods of food scarcity were common and hunting was a tough and dangerous activity. If we hadn't had the capability to fast, the *homo sapiens* species would have become extinct tens of thousands of years ago. And now, the current human body is practically the same Paleolithic body with the same needs and requirements because, after all, 10,000 years is nothing in terms of the millions of years that evolution took to perfect the human body.

[6] The use of pesticides and herbicides is completely unnatural. Nowadays, the modern agriculture industry requires such chemicals because of its extended practice of monoculture. This illustrates the typical case when something gone wrong is patched with something even worse. Monoculture constitutes the dedication of acres and acres of land to cultivating only one type of crop, as nature never intended. The lack of genetic diversity makes all the plants equally susceptible to any particular disease or pest to which they do not have resistance. If that pest or disease attacks a plant, the entire crop will be lost. To avoid this, instead of diversifying the crops, pesticides and herbicides are heavily used.

protect roots), plastic-like coatings, artificial growth accelerators,[7] petroleum-based fertilizers and other chemicals, all of which improve their appearance and shelf-life while rendering them unsuitable for human consumption.

Genetically modified (GM) crops are extremely poor quality food. They have damaging effects in animals and humans when consumed. "Studies link GMOs [genetically modified organisms] with toxins, allergies, infertility, infant mortality, immune dysfunction, stunted growth, accelerated aging, and death."[8] They also destroy the natural diversity and promote the excessive use of pesticides and herbicides which creates the right conditions for the alarming rise of herbicide-resistant super weeds and pesticide-resistant superbugs.

Many human consumption animals are placed for a long time in confined environments (feedlots locations) with highly stressful, crowded and unsanitary conditions that weaken their immune systems. To avoid the diseases caused by their confinement, these animals are given huge amounts of antibiotics that remain in their meat, which contributes to the generation of antibiotic-resistant bacteria. The same animals are then fed[9] with food extraneous to their natural diet to quickly fatten them beyond their constitution.[10] In the U.S., they are also injected with growth hormones to increase their milk production. In these extreme circumstances,

---

[7] The news about exploding watermelons in China that circulated in May 2011 brought to the public knowledge the chemical forchlorfenuron used to accelerate the growth of fruits. The drug is legal in China and the U.S. What is the reason to expose people to this chemical? Answer: profits for those who taint the food supply.

[8] Jeffrey Smith. See the webpage http://www.responsibletechnology.org of the Institute of Responsible Technology founded by Jeffrey Smith for more information about the pernicious effects of GMOs.

[9] Animals for human consumption are fed in what are called "concentrated animal feeding operations" or CAFOs. With this sophisticated technical name for what should otherwise be a natural feeding process, we shouldn't expect anything good out of it.

[10] For example, among these extraneous foods we have chicken litter (which includes manure, feathers and anything found on the floor of a chicken feedlot) and GM grain to feed cows (which are ruminants, i.e. grass eaters), arsenic (a known human carcinogen) and cow parts to feed chickens, and cow parts and chicken litter to feed farmed fish.

their health worsens even more, pushing for more antibiotics in their already weakened bodies. Eating any product of these animals constitutes an attempt to intoxicate and harm the human body.

The evolutionarily-recent acquired staples of sugar and grains (especially wheat)[11] have become too prevalent in the modern human diet and constitute the prevailing cause of obesity, diabetes, insulin resistance, digestive and elimination problems, high blood pressure, cancer, and other cardiovascular complications, the well known "civilization diseases."

Therefore, eating these kinds of profit-based food products affects our wholeness as spiritual beings since by doing so we, knowingly or not, damage our physical bodies and support the destruction of the environment; in other words, we disrupt the harmony of the Creation, we become unharmonious beings. Purifying the inside of your body requires taking important measures concerning your diet. If you care about yourself as you should care about any constituent of God's creation, you should eat and drink what Mother Nature has designed for you. You cannot fall into the trap of an economic system eager to obtain short-term gains for the few at the expense of the health of the many, and more

---

[11] Eating grains is a recent event in evolutionary terms. Man evolved for millions of years eating animal fat, animal meat, fruits and other plant parts, all of which constituted the Paleolithic diet. We started eating grains only 10,000 years ago or so mainly because grains could be stored for a long time and provided the food in times of scarcity. Our digestive systems might not be well adapted to eat grains as indicated by 10% of the population with gluten intolerance and by the fact that grain carbohydrates break down into sugar that later on is accumulated as excess fat in the human body. For evolutionary reasons, grains cannot be the main staple of the human diet regardless of what the infamous food pyramid says, and their consumption must be reduced considerably; more specifically, eliminating grains with gluten, such as wheat, becomes paramount for good health even if we don't have perceivable symptoms of gluten intolerance. Added sugar is even much more recent. Sugar consumption has increased tremendously in the last 100 years or so, and many studies link the high sugar consumption to obesity, cardiovascular diseases and diabetes (see the presentation "Sugar: The Bitter Truth" by Robert H. Lustig, M.D., Professor at UCSF, http://www.youtube.com/watch?v=dBnniua6-oM). Added sugar without the nutrients that usually accompany fruits and other sweet products of nature is toxic and foreign to human diet.

principally, you shouldn't fall into the trap of your own limiting belief system.

Spiritual realization always starts with yourself; you ought to love yourself, you ought to marvel about that wonderful body of yours with its internal organs, tissues, senses and glands, and align your thoughts and actions to its God-given perfection. In this sense, I recommend that you consider the act of eating and drinking a sacred one. Consider the food and the beverages you ingest an offering to yourself, a measure of love and thankfulness towards the purity and perfection of your body; hence, pick the food that nourishes you and keeps toxins and other strange elements out of your body. Organic food in general, such as vegetables, fruits, fermented food,[12] grass-fed beef and other animal products free of hormones, antibiotics and other chemicals, is your best choice.[13] Do not eat industrially processed food including pasteurized (high temperature cooked) products and minimize, or completely eliminate, the grains (especially wheat) from your diet, and definitely stop consuming sugar and its artificial substitutes. Make raw food—including raw milk from naturally raised cows and goats—an important part of your meals because its nutritional value and enzymatic content are superior to those of cooked food, and drink also plenty of water, for water is cleansing and has a powerful spiritual significance. Bless your food and water as you put the best of your intentions to enhance their properties and energetic content by favorably adjusting their quantum realm.[14]

---

[12] Fermented food, such as fermented vegetables and yogurt, provide you with probiotics (beneficial bacteria) which constitute the first line of defense against harmful bacteria and other germs. Probiotics also enhance digestion and nutrient absorption.

[13] Unfortunately, organic wholesome food is more expensive than conventional food; but if you consider that you also should eat less, then you could compensate the organic food cost by eating the right amount of it.

[14] Blessing food and water is very healing. Particularly, blessing water is practiced in many cultures. Water has interesting properties since water molecules form perfectly symmetrical water crystals (see *The Hidden Messages in Water* by Masaru Emoto) when they are blessed.

## Physical exercise

Besides diet, we also mentioned exercise as another way to purify our internal physicality. Humans beings evolved to be active, to move, to spend calories and to apply their physical strength to earn their food. Our Paleolithic forebears knew that they had to exercise hard when they got hungry, that is, they knew they had to go out and literally chase and then fight their food. In contrast, modern human beings barely move and if they are hungry, they just open the refrigerator and sit on the couch to watch TV. The same physical capability that the prehistoric hunters and gatherers had more than 10,000 years ago remains in the modern human,[15] but dormant. In order to awaken this capability we don't have to do strenuous exercises, spend money to join a fitness center or become a professional athlete; we just need to exercise to gradually build back our strength and mobility according to our own physical limits. We need always to remember that the less we move the closer we are to a stiff dead body.

The long walk, the run, the charge, the wrestling, all these demanding physical activities freed our hungry ancestors from their fears and worries, set their conscious mind with only one purpose and made them live the moment in its all intensity, for survival was at risk. With the subsequent fall of the big animal, there was the euphoria, the satisfaction, the joy caused by the release of endorphins and by the fact that life had been granted one more time. This picture reflects what exercising should mean to us. Exercising tells our bodies that we are alive and that we want to remain alive; exercising strengthens our muscles and bones making us disease-proof; exercising increases blood circulation and oxygenation, thus more nourishment is brought to all the cells in our bodies. Exercising increases our metabolism and makes us sweat, thereby, toxins and waste material do not stay inside our bodies and are easily disposed; exercising releases endorphins and other neurotransmitters that alleviate pain (both physical and emotional), it provides a sense of accomplishment and elevates mood. For all of these reasons exercising has a purifying effect; it unblocks the body channels so energy can flow freely throughout the body

[15] As proven by modern athletes.

and sets our mind in the right state to continue its own purification.

## Mind and body working in unison

We already know that mind and body are inseparable parts of the Mind. Spiritually speaking, we cannot separate them; they must work in unison as they affect each other.

When you purify yourself through a wholesome diet, you will notice not only that your health and energy increases, but also that your mood and attitude begin to change for good. You will become more serene, in control, and especially more joyful because, after all, "we are what we eat" as the old adage states. There exists a gut-brain connection that has been acknowledged by medical science termed *neuro-gastroenterology*. Problems with the digestion system as it deals with toxins and other extraneous substances have been associated with psychological and psychiatric disorders and developmental malfunction (e.g. autism, attention deficiency disorder, etc.). These mental disorders and problems constitute clear signs of the gut-brain connection. Therefore, by eliminating the food that unnecessarily loads and stresses the digestive system, we will start purifying not only the body but also the mind.[16]

Most diseases have a psychosomatic (emotional) component that needs to be treated by dealing with its root cause. Treating a disease by dealing only with its symptoms or its physical manifestation in the body is a mistake. When a sickness strikes, the pharmaceutical industry encourages the use of drugs with harmful side effects. These side effects are frequently so damaging that other drugs are required to treat them. The prescription of drugs to treat the side effects of other drugs is shocking, to say the least, and has become quite common. As mentioned in Chapter 5 (see its footnote 7), the motivation of the pharmaceutical industry is led by profit, not healing, and therefore we should not blindly trust drugs that debilitate our bodies with extra burdens. The spiritual solution is to support the mind and the body to effectively help in the healing process. When the mind works on its purity the body comes along with it and *vice versa*, when the body works on its purity with a wholesome diet and exercise the mind then joins the body

---

[16] Probiotics play an important positive role in this brain-gut connection.

to a higher state of purity. Once in this stage, in which both mind and body are synchronized, a unique symbiotic process between the mind and the body starts and healing becomes certain and permanent. The mind should achieve its purity through spiritual pillar # 4 considered in the next section.

## Spiritual Pillar # 4: Mind Purity

The purity of mind consists of clear and constructive thoughts. Fears, worries, uncontrollable desire for power, money or sex, envy, jealousy, hatred, depression, all of these represent detrimental states of the mind brought up by the subconscious with the pretext of defending us. Only when the conscious eliminates every single detrimental program from our subconscious and updates it with new programs in accordance with the only reality that exists, shall our mind be pure and become the Great Mind.

### Intention

To achieve mind purity, a consistent intentional effort must be applied to put our conscious in charge of the situation and, thereby, start living life more fully in the present moment. As an initial step, this process can be initiated by simply repeating a positive affirmation, denying a bad thought and replacing it with a positive one, praying a comforting prayer, or chanting a mantra to set up the mind in the right initial condition to start a more intense process towards its purity.

Intention is the ability to consciously take our thoughts away from recurrent and disturbing trends of worries and fears. Essentially, with intention the individual is able to stop the current thoughts in order to create a new more positive thinking trend. A prayer, a mantra or an affirmation embodies the essence of spiritual intention. Through spiritual intention, one expresses a good desire for one's self or for others; expressing a good desire can be done through thoughts, words, actions, gestures and the use of symbols. For instance, the traditional Christian sign of the cross or the symbols of Reiki bring forward the intention of protection and healing. The hand positioning in Reiki and the hand motion in

Qigong[17] have the objective of conducting the life force energy (known as *qi* or *chi* in Chinese tradition and *prana* in Indian tradition) for healing purposes. The simple words "I have faith, I have no fears, there is nothing in God's creation to be afraid of" have the objective of dissipating fear by creating trust in God. In all these cases, spiritual intentions positively alter the quantum realm that surrounds and permeates our bodies; it creates the right conditions to deepen our spiritual awareness through concentration and meditation.

## Concentration

Concentration is the ability to consciously stay focused in one particular area of interest; the longer we stay focused the stronger our concentration. Concentration requires the participation of our senses, including our mind through its conscious. During concentration we synthesize, analyze, study, observe or feel the object of our attention. The activities that we undertake in our daily lives require some degree of concentration that directly correlates with the affinity we have for the activity in question. If we love to do something, we don't mind spending a long time and putting all our senses and mind on the activity we enjoy. Conversely, if we don't like what we are doing, our concentration is poor and very likely we would be absent minded.

Concentration is a conscious function. When you concentrate on something, the conscious does most of the work while the subconscious is relegated to a very minimal operation. This explains why concentration constitutes an essential spiritual tool to deal with the subconscious. Through concentration, the conscious can regulate the subconscious by directing it from the unneeded "fight-or-flight" mode to the trusting, loving and caring mode implied by spirituality. Through concentration, we select the memories we want to use by regulating our sixth sense. Through concentration we live the present moment because no concentration resides in

---

[17] Typically, The Reiki healer keeps his hands steady to transmit the *chi* to a particular area of the patient's body. In the ancient self-healing Chinese practice of Qigong, the *chi* is conducted by the hands of the practitioner through gentle wavy motion.

the past or the future. During concentration, the mind becomes an object of our will indicating that we still control our lives.

Concentrating on our actions constitutes an important spiritual exercise. For the sake of spirituality, our actions and the results or ends of our actions must be harmonious. Namely, what we do and what we expect from what we do must not be at the expense of anybody belonging to this or future generations. As the ends do not justify the means, we need to be very careful to not become obsessed about the ends or goals of our endeavors, even if they are noble and just. If we only care about the ends, we will do unharmonious actions in our zeal to attain our goals (see Chapter 8). What we do now, not what we will obtain later, is what really matters. Our actions in this present moment will tell the world how spiritually deep we are.

To exercise spiritual concentration you could start by focusing on any of the activities you engage in daily and not on the results of the activity in question. As you willingly concentrate on what you are doing in the present moment, you keep your subconscious thoughts away from you. These subconscious thoughts encompass worries, events from the past, possible future events, daydreams, and other kinds of distracting mental images/thoughts that keep you away from the actions of the present moment, your actual life. By keeping the subconscious away as you concentrate on the actions of your current activity, you gain control of your life through consciousness and awareness–a control that you can increase to unimaginable limits if you also do specific concentration exercises that focus on your body, as explained in the following.

## Yoga concentration exercises: pranayama and *asanas*

We have categorized Reiki and Qigong above as tools to create intention rather than concentration. Nevertheless, they also help to develop concentration. The reason for our categorization is that both techniques do not resist the natural tendencies of the body. They flow with the body, which is good and complements the other two techniques from the ancient Indian tradition of Yoga described below.

Dedicated yoga concentration exercises comprise breathing exercises (*pranayama*) and postures (*asanas*). *Pranayama* and *asanas* are part of the Eight Limbs of Yoga according to the tradition of the Sutras of Patanjali.[18] In these exercises, the practitioner has to concentrate to resist the natural tendencies of the body. These yoga exercises create willpower that can be used to eradicate the pernicious patterns and programs of the subconscious.

During the breathing exercises you consciously control your breath and pay detailed attention to your breathing and its effects on the body. *Pranayama*'s purpose is two-fold. First, *pranayama* strengthens your consciousness as you deliberately control a process that operates automatically as an indication that you can control, too, the automatic responses of your subconscious. Secondly, *pranayama* augments the primal energy, or *prana*, that generates vitality and establishes harmony among all the vital systems of your body (in fact, purifying your body). In this concentration exercise, the *pranayama* practitioner transforms the breathing air into pure energy that he or she directs at will. Consequently, the practitioner, with full attention, follows the inhaled or exhaled air by feeling all the sensations that this wonderful energy produces in the body and by increasing the consciousness and awareness of the body. In *pranayama*, the mind controls the breath so the natural tendency of the body to breathe automatically is resisted and then controlled accordingly.

In general, an *asana* is an unusual body posture with specific actions to hold the body steady and safe. Notwithstanding these actions might require physical strength and endurance, concentration and body awareness constitute the key to practicing yoga *asanas*. In other words, the *asana* is mastered by the power of the mind, not by the power of the body and, as for any concentration exercise, holding an *asana* long enough is crucial for *asana* practice.

*Asanas* are closely linked to *pranayama* in that *pranayama* requires certain postures or poses and *asanas* require a controlled breath. For example, in his aphorisms, Patanjali stresses the steadiness and the control of a seated pose while an equally controlled breath is achieved. In any *asana*, you can develop your concentration and open more doors to your spiritual realization.

---

[18] See the Appendix A for more details about the Sutras of Patanjali.

Strength, vitality and innumerable health benefits represent some of the wonderful side effects of *asana* practice; they constitute the effect, not the cause, of the expansion of consciousness due to *asana* practice. Yoga postures energize the body; in an *asana*, the body behaves as an open antenna that receives and transforms energy. These new energetic possibilities of the mind/body combination positively alter the quantum realm towards the individual's fulfillment.

Over the course of thousands of years the yoga *asana* science has developed numerous poses which embody physical challenges for many people. The idea of putting the body into twisted and difficult contortions prevails in the minds of many and actually intimidates most people. The good news, however, is that nobody needs to be extremely flexible or super strong to practice most yoga *asanas*. In fact, many *asanas* are physically within the reach of many people through a gradual learning process that stresses safety and the use of simple props. The intensity level of each pose must be suitable to the physical limitations of each person, and at each level of this process, from the early stages of learning to the latter stages of mastering a particular *asana*, concentration always plays the most fundamental role.

Each *asana* must have a physical challenge that the practitioner must overcome through concentration in order to experience the ease in the unusual pose. As an example, the cross-legged sitting position on the floor, which has become one of the most preferred icons for yoga poses, has its own challenges. As in any *asana*, the cross-legged position entails absolute stillness, and particularly requires the back completely straight and erect, upper chest lifted up while lower ribs are drawn in and down, and head straight up as neck and shoulders are fully relaxed. If a person cannot do the cross-legged position at all, they may instead find an adequate level of physical challenge while sitting straight up on the edge of a chair. In any case, the straight back is paramount for the pose since according to yogic science the spine is the main energetic channel. Through concentration the practitioner can then overcome the natural tendencies of the body to wrestle the initial discomfort and eventually find the ease in the pose. When this ease is achieved, the practitioner deepens even more the concentration and gets ready for applying the newly acquired concentration skills in daily life, living life moment by moment with a less reactive subconscious and a stronger conscious. The previously impossible will become possible.

## Spiritual Pillar # 5: Meditation

Concentration requires us to narrow down the use of our five senses and the sixth sense. Meditation requires only one sense working: the intuition sense, the one we have termed the seventh sense in Chapter 2 and later on we called the quantum realm in Chapter 6. With concentration we master our mind and sensory perceptions by directing them to the object of our attention. As we progress during this mastery, we start focusing on the object of our concentration in such detail that the six senses are no longer needed as the essence of the object is complete in our mind. Continuing this process, we get ready for the greatest concentration test ever: to reduce the object of our attention to "nothing," as if we were concentrating on the void.

How can we concentrate on nothing? Does concentration intrinsically imply an object? Yes, it does if you are the observer of the object for which reason you need all your five senses and your mind; however, when your concentration on the object reaches its full potential you will come to the most profound awareness whereby you realize that the intrinsic nature of the object is your own, the eternal and immutable sameness. At this highest level of concentration, all differentiation between you and the object vanishes and you become one with the object; thereby, you, the observer, become the observed. The object has disappeared from "out there," there is nothing "out there," everything exists within; the void "out there" turns into everything within, everything within turns into the void "out there." When everything exists within, the five senses, the recording (sixth sense), the analytic and the composing components of the mind are no longer needed because there is nothing physical to observe (see Figure 2).

The ideal concentration ends with true meditation as the Great Mind manifests itself in its full splendor. You have achieved the paradoxical situation when you have used your mind to transcend its own functioning: "The mind has been the instrument, and the world [has been] the object of the experience whereby the experiencer [observer] has come to know the *Atman* [true object's nature], his real nature. The mind has been used to transcend the mind, just as we use a ladder to 'transcend' a ladder. Once we have reached the sill of the window against which it rested, the ladder can be kicked away; we do not need it anymore."[19] You will not even need the ladder to come down because once up there, you will have myriad different ways to do so.

Meditation, then, is achieved at the highest point of concentration when the seventh is the only active sense. This situation is very similar to enhancing your auditory capability by covering your eyes. As you don't get distracted by the images of your vision, your auditory sense sharpens up and suddenly you can appreciate the richness of the sound world around you. Likewise, when the subconscious and conscious are quiet and sensory perceptions mean nothing to you, you will start appreciating the vast richness of your eternal essence, the same God essence that now you can perceive fully during meditation because your seventh sense is no longer overwhelmed by the other senses.

As mentioned in Chapter 6, the seventh sense surrounds and permeates the human body as a magnificent field or aura. This aura is the quantum realm that serves as the passage between the void and existence. By crossing this passage during deep meditation, the dedicated practitioner has access to all the knowledge of the Universe with which the path to creation turns clear. This is the path for anyone to become a creator, a creator who creates from the unseen, as God does, always harmoniously with the solid foundations of love and compassion.

## Spiritual Pillar #6: Deep Connections with Others

By observing the previous five spiritual pillars we have done the right actions for us. We have gained awareness of the obstacles that impede our fulfillment (pillar #1). We have prayed with faith and certainty, not with fear and hesitation (pillar #2). We have purified our body (pillar #3) and mind (pillar #4 and #5) clearing our

---

[19] *How to know God. The Yoga Aphorisms of Patanjali*, translated by Swami Prabhavananda and Christopher Isherwood. A Mentor Book New American Library, 1969, p. 96.

path to health, abundance, comfort, joy and happiness. We surely will live a better life after implementing the previous five pillars.

As our well-being increases by observing the first five pillars of spirituality, we should find that our sense of connection with everyone intensifies; in other words, the way we relate to others becomes more harmonious and constructive. Notwithstanding its individual approach, the spiritual life has the important effect of increasing our sense of connection with others as we realize our immutable eternal sameness. If this sense of connection is rather limited, the spiritual-motivated individual should focus on the re-capitulation of pillar #1 to scrutinize those personal beliefs that impede the spiritual progress.

We all have the "response-ability" to contribute to the harmony of the world through our right actions and according to our means. This ability strengthens with spiritual practice (as the one detailed in Chapter 8) until it becomes a very natural facet of our lives. At this point, reaching to others turns into reaching to ourselves; no difference exists between the way we treat ourselves and the way we treat others. More importantly, by helping others, by healing others, by bringing a little joy to others in their moments of need, and also, by feeling the enthusiasm and joy of those blessed with happiness and grace, we experience an enormous sense of gratitude towards God, for God has bestowed us with such beauti-ful "response-ability."

This gratefulness feeling grows along with a powerful feeling of humility inasmuch as the true "reaching-to-others" has no hid-den agenda. The idea of being grandiose when helping others does not exist; reaching to others, helping to restore the harmony of this world with the means we have at our avail is natural, basic and simple. If we subconsciously or consciously seek recognition, ad-miration, importance, or we just want to display the control we have on people's lives when we help others, then we are complete-ly missing the point. If the need for importance and control is true for you, revisit pillar #1.

Humility constitutes perhaps the most revealing emotion of connection, of merging with another human being; it constitutes also a true joy impossible to describe: it is the joy of union, it is the joy of grace and freedom, it is the photon that can go to any-where in the universe but that finally is accepted by one single atom. As discussed in Chapter 6, to see the connection of all the constituents of the universe, we need to look into the scale of the ultra-small; similarly, to really connect with someone, we need to be small, we need to be sincerely humble.

I consider myself fortunate as I have often felt this moving feeling of humbleness. In particular, I remember when I felt completely humble and blissful for being able to heal a much loved one. It was on the occasion of performing a remote Reiki healing[20] for my mother when she came to California for a long visit. During the session I certainly knew that I had the capability to heal my mother; I had no doubt that I was doing so. I also saw her life from childhood to being a young mother; I understood her as her life's vicissitudes were being projected in my mind, and then I knew the causes of her ailment. I felt as if I were her, and maybe I was; I felt the union between us and tears filled my eyes. They were tears of joy in a silent and yet powerful cry. I felt this immense power of being so close to my mother and able to heal her and to provide the comfort she needed. I felt grateful for such a blessing. My tears were a manifestation of the joy of being humbled by such a gift. My mother recovered well and had a good time during her stay.

How do we know that our actions are the right actions to connect with others? One way to answer this question is by verifying if you have followed Don Miguel Ruiz's Four Agreements,[21] or equivalently by answering these questions: Have I been impeccable with my word? Have I taken anything personally? Have I made any assumption? Have I always done my best? If you answer yes to any of the first three questions or no to the last question you should go back to the "drawing board" (i.e., Pillar #1). It is clear that if your word is not impeccable when you address or talk about somebody, you demonstrate no connection with that person. Perhaps it is the other way around, that is, when you are the object of harsh words, wherein you might not show connection. If you take it personally and react by feeling attacked, or if

---

[20] A remote Reiki healing occurs when the person you are trying to heal is not there with you.

[21] *The Four Agreements* by Don Miguel Ruiz, Amber-Allen Publishing, Inc., San Rafael, California, 1997.

you make assumptions that prompt you to judge the other person in question, then you have failed to see beyond the other person's harsh words and, thereby, you are unable to feel connected to that person. Finally, doing your best does not mean to be efficient in reaching the goals you have set but to be harmonious and respectful with the natural flow of the Creation. In other words, doing your best means not to harm or take advantage of anyone ever in all your undertakings.

Not exercising our "response-ability" renders us completely limited. Why does anyone want to be limited when reality is boundless? Perhaps they don't know. Only ignorance can explain the zeal of many to amass money, power and lusty desires beyond all logic. Only a lack of awareness of reality can explain the excesses that pit humans against one another. Only the total lack of experiencing true happiness through the hearts of others can justify the belief systems that stress the need for an exaggerated materialistic and disconnected life. No delusion can come close to true happiness, the one that is achievable only through union with everyone and everything.

## Spiritual Pillar # 7: Union with God

Pillar #7, Union with God, is the unutterable transcendental state of equanimity in which the void is experienced in all its magnificence. The seventh spiritual pillar is the natural consequence of the previous six pillars. After dedicating our efforts to the first six pillars, Union with God comes naturally at its due time. Union with God is attained during the deepest part of meditation, but also can come in dreams, near death experiences or spontaneously during special moments. As we intensify our spiritual practice and master the art of the deepest meditation, we will have more moments of Union with God and a real transformation will start occurring in us, in which full awareness becomes a norm in our daily life.

The full knowledge of God makes the enlightened one transcend the physical realm; all past, present and future knowledge unravels to the enlightened; pain, suffering, attachments, wants, even joy and contentment, all of them cease to exist within the equanimity of the God-knowing person. Love and stillness, love and sameness, are equivalent to the one who has attained Union with God. That one will be each of us, for enlightenment, fully knowing God, constitutes the ultimate reality in which we all will dwell eternally.

## The Final Words of this Chapter

To understand the reigning despair and contention within us we need to practice spirituality. If we try to fix ourselves without realizing our spiritual nature, we are doomed to repeat the same mistakes that brought us to our present erratic emotional state. Previous chapters explained how our belief systems dominate us with a tangle of dysfunctional emotions. We cannot untangle our emotional situation using our belief systems because they are the ones that create and maintain our current emotional havoc. We need to step out of our box of beliefs in order to align our lives with our longing for happiness. The Seven Pillars of Spirituality of this chapter describe the way to experience reality for our transcendental happiness. In the next chapter, we put the Seven Pillars of Spirituality into a succinct practice.

# 8
## A PRACTICAL SPIRITUAL PRACTICE
## (TO PERFORM ON LIFE'S STAGE)

A practice is a set of activities and actions that we do repeatedly in order to acquire, maintain or improve a skill needed to attain a specific goal. The individual first needs to establish a goal to start a practice. You may ask yourself: What do I want to achieve? For instance, many athletes train to become an Olympic gold medal winner or a well-paid professional, and some pianists rehearse rigorously to perform as an acclaimed soloist. Second, the individual must follow a discipline or routine intended to increase the proficiency needed to attain the desired goal.

Under these precepts, life itself may be seen as a practice continuum as we find ourselves repeating many of our daily activities day after day as we try to achieve some goal. In many instances of our lives, we want to get better at what we do in order to achieve some specific goals. When these goals are so strong that they grow fixated in our minds, we justify our actions despite their consequences as long as they serve the purpose of attaining our goals. For example, since work constitutes an important practice in our lives, we could damage our health and neglect our families working extra long hours for that promotion at work. Or, to illustrate even more, as GMO corporation executive-owners desiring bigger bonuses and profit sharing, we could have become too good at putting the corporation's interest over everybody else's, and rush untested genetically engineered food to the market potentially harming the environment and consumers. Namely, when the ends, whether they are laudable or not, indiscriminately justify everything we do, the joyful life seems to come to a halt as we obliterate our present moment and think about only that future day when we attain the so-desired goal. Our obsession for the ends practically takes us over and makes us act in detriment to ourselves and to the world around us as we try to maximize our future gain. We sacrifice the present moment, the only source of happiness, for a "promise of future happiness" without realizing that true happiness belongs only to the right now right here.

## The Ultimate Spiritual Practice

Indeed, life constitutes *the ultimate spiritual practice*. This practice must occur in the present moment, for spiritual realization is not confined to specific times or places. As with any practice, *the ultimate spiritual practice* entails a goal and a discipline with the right actions to achieve such goal. But unlike any other practice, the goal is never an obsession and consequently the discipline never becomes a burden. The goal is guaranteed to every single human being since permanently becoming one with God will happen to each of us regardless. Indeed, enlightenment dwells within us already whether or not we've decided to realize it yet. *The ultimate spiritual practice* is like participating in a race that you know you will win irrespective of your speed. The first prize is already yours; the only thing you need to do is to show up at the place and time of the race and simply keep on moving to the finish line. That place is right here, and that time is right now, and whatever you do must be along the direction towards the finish line.

If you ever feel bothered, anxious, contentious or depressed as you are still obsessed by the ends you want to achieve, then you must know that either you are not showing up yet for the race or you are getting off track. In both cases it's an indication that you are still ignoring your truth within. Nevertheless, you must know, too, that you are not irremediably lost but delaying your destiny until the Universe reminds you of the path to your spiritual realization and you decide to step on it. Be assured that if you don't do it this time, the Universe will never leave you alone until you do it.

When we know the final outcome of our endeavors, when we know its solid certainty, and especially when we know that it encompasses the greatest fulfillment ever, we detach ourselves from it not because we do not care about it, but because we do not worry about it. In this situation, we focus on our actions entirely, we make sure we align our actions to the greatest purpose of being one with God while never desiring or contending for a particular outcome. Why do we need to fret about the final outcome when our actions, as little as they can be, harmoniously go with the Creation's flow? If we do fret, if we do become anxious and obsessed about attaining a goal, then we must take these feelings as an indication that we are indeed opposing the Creation's flow and consequently damaging our well-being.

Acting for the sake of our actions per se requires living the present moment as we engage in them. Future and past have no relevance; only the present moment matters to our sense of well-being. Observe what you feel in the present moment to determine whether what you do flows with the Creation or opposes it. Contention, anger, frustration, anxiety, depression, even sickness and physical unfitness (both of which have emotional origin) represent signs of reality denial, present moment neglect and unfulfilling actions. In this context, this chapter offers a practice that will help most people to recognize reality as it is, thus they can live their present moment fully focusing on obtaining the best out of their actions—the only way to find peace and happiness. In other words, this chapter offers *a practice* to fully experience *the ultimate spiritual practice*, life itself.

## The Philosophy of this Practice

Specifically, a spiritual practice involves a set of actions targeted to enhance the awareness of reality thus the practitioner may live life in joy and peace. A helpful spiritual practice must be aligned with the Seven Pillars of Spirituality expounded in Chapter 7 in order to holistically cover all the meaningful aspects of life.

Every single individual on the face of the earth is able to connect to their eternal immutable essence and become one with God regardless of their beliefs or situation. Everyone possesses this beautiful potential to find one's self reflected in other people's souls as a manifestation of human sameness. Each human being can become a creator of their own fate in which everything flows effortlessly along the perfection of God's universe. Therefore, a true spiritual practice must be universal and applicable to all faiths and religions. It must be self-contained without requiring special places, devices or apparel, it must rely only on the practitioner's willingness and intentions, and finally it must release the practitioner from any anxiety about the end results as these unveil positively and surely.

Contrary to some popular beliefs, a spiritual practice should never be thought of as austerity or some sort of self-torture. Certainly, a true spiritual practice never drains energy away from us. Quite to the contrary, it brings us energy and vitality along with enthusiasm as we enjoy the practice. With an authentic spiritual practice, there is a lot of gain without suffering.

We can now concisely state the fundamental outcomes of the spiritual practice recommended in this book (referred to as the practice henceforth):

- ✓ The practice will enhance your awareness and consciousness in order to fully live the process of your life moment by moment, which will naturally accelerate your spiritual realization.
- ✓ The practice will bring you energy and vitality along with enthusiasm as you enjoy the practice.
- ✓ During the practice, your fears and the sources of your discontent will be pinpointed.
- ✓ During the practice, you will associate your fears and the sources of your discontent with subconscious programs that make you react with anger, depression, frustration, anxiety, stress, cravings, excesses and other defensive mechanisms that separate you from your real essence, i.e. God, and, therefore, from all the people that surround you.
- ✓ During the practice you will never blame yourself or others. Your subconscious has done what our past evolution trained it to do. Your subconscious is always unaware; its major duty is to protect you. With this practice, you will appreciate and thank your subconscious and realize how useful and important it is. You will know that your subconscious contains wonderful tools available to you. The only reason for which it makes you react inappropriately in most circumstances stems from its bad programming.

✓ During the practice, you will increase your awareness and develop your consciousness; thus, you can reset your subconscious by cleaning up your sixth sense, clarifying your memory and past stories. Consequently, you will replace the old subconscious programming–source of your unhappiness–with faith, love and compassion as you feel the certainty that your present and future needs are already taken care of by the abundance of the Universe.

✓ During the practice, you will continuously increase your consciousness and awareness as they are not physically bounded. As your conscious mind starts transcending towards the Great Mind, and your subconscious aligns with your highest purposes, you will experience a shift that betokens the ascent of your creator role.

✓ At this stage, you have control of the quantum realm inside and around your body. You know how to employ your Mind for the greatest good. Your intuition develops enormously and you start understanding the importance of feeling small and humble to connect with everybody and everything in the entire universe. Your aura grows tremendously and people around you feel your presence as peaceful, healing and uplifting.

✓ Your reality then starts forming, and no matter what you create for yourself, your reality will always be harmonious with God's creation as you holistically care for yourself and everyone, and express your love without bounds. You will never advocate for excesses and always will help others to find their own path of fulfillment.

✓ In this spiritual practice, you will profoundly comprehend that you are a creator and that as such you ought to create and maintain harmony, not a self-centered world that fosters competition and destruction.

The practice is based on a set of activities repeated every day for 40 days. The number 40 is chosen for its special spiritual significance as denoted by religions such as Judaism, Islam, Christianity and Hinduism, and among other things it is mentioned in the Bible and Quran many times. In this respect, I have found this excerpt on the Internet that succinctly describes the spiritual relevance of the number 40:

> The number 40 is a very familiar one in the Bible. In the story of Noah and the flood, it rains 40 days and 40 nights (Gn 7:4, 12, 17; 8:6). After the sealing of the covenant at Mt. Sinai, Moses is with God on the mountain for 40 days and 40 nights (Ex 24:18). When the prophet Elijah is being pursued by Queen Jezebel, he flees for his life and travels 40 days and nights until he comes to the mountain of God at Horeb (Sinai) (1 Kgs 19:8). The number appears also in the New Testament. Jesus is tempted in the desert for 40 days and nights; his ascension to heaven occurs 40 days after the Resurrection (Acts 1:3)...
>
> Forty denotes a period of preparation for some special action of the Lord; it is a time of grace...
>
> After the flood in Genesis, a new creation begins. After Moses converses with God, the covenant is renewed. After Israel's wandering in the wilderness, they will enter into the Promised Land. After Elijah's journey, God strengthens him to resume his prophetic ministry. After Jesus' temptation, he begins his public ministry; after the Ascension, we enter the age of the Church. At the end of the season of Lent, we celebrate Holy Week and the great feast of Easter. [1]

Therefore, the forty days of the practice constitute the "period of preparation" for you to realize God within you and open the doors to the myriad wonderful possibilities that await you.

## How to Approach this Practice

The following spiritual practice was given to me through inspiration, direct intuitive knowledge and indirect knowledge from a

---

[1] *In the Dessert with Jesus: Biblical Themes of Lent*, by Michael D. Guinan. Catholic Update, February 2005, http://www.americancatholic.org/ Newsletters/CU/ac0205.asp.

number of worldly sources. As you engage in this practice, please follow these guidelines:

- As in any physical activity you want to practice, you should consult with a physician to evaluate your physical conditions and limitations before engaging in the practice.
- Get familiar with the exercises before you start the 40-day practice. This way your mind will be more focused and you will not be distracted by the learning process. Go through all the exercises and practice each of them independently until you feel comfortable with executing them.
- All human bodies are different. They have different physical conditions and physical constitutions. An exercise may be easy for some but hard for others. This is completely normal. Yet, even though this spiritual practice is suitable for most people, you will find alternatives for some exercises that you can employ in case the original exercises turn out to be hard for you. The list of alternatives offered here is by no means exhaustive. To exactly adjust this practice according to your physical condition and constitution requires the dedicated effort of a spiritually-guided professional.
- Similarly, the pace of the practice is up to you. Each exercise has a suggested duration time. But since they are just that, suggestions, you need to pay attention to your body and adjust the duration of each exercise according to your physical condition and constitution. As you progress in your practice, you will notice that your intuition will lead you to intensify and spend more time on those exercises you need the most. The practice typically takes an hour and a half.
- Pay attention to and focus on your exercises to obtain awareness of your body and mind. Notice where your body is stiff, loose or painful, and never intensify the exercises beyond your body's capabilities. Get to know your body and mind and remember that mind (through

intention and concentration) and body must always work together.

▪ Ideally, during the forty days, the practice should be done around the same time each day to establish a cycle that imprints a new program on the subconscious and all the cells of the body. Early in the morning after waking up is a recommendable time for the spiritual practice, but any other time is good too.

▪ For the practice, the stomach must be completely empty so the practitioner may feel hungry. Make sure you haven't eaten anything for at least four hours before the practice. Doing the activities while one is hungry has beneficial effects for the human body, especially in reducing aging and increasing the body's growth hormone production. Remember that hunger brought our forebears into physical activity as they had to move to hunt and gather food. Evolution has adapted our bodies to be quite energetic after not eating for some time. Therefore, being hungry is not a limitation but a plus for the spiritual practice.

This practice has wonderful side effects. As you progress in this practice you will notice an overall improvement in your health. Remember that in this practice you deal with the emotional issues or psychosomatic factors that cause many diseases. Moreover, the physical exercises described below tone and strengthen the body enhancing the immune system, internal organs and endocrine glands.

The practice consists of activities and exercises grouped into seven parts, all of them described next. The practice is also illustrated in Appendix B with a series of pictures and detailed instructions.

## Part 1: Emotional recapitulation and intention

Recapitulation is the process to acquire awareness of your own emotions and actions as indicated in spiritual pillar #1 (Chapter 7). Essentially these are the emotions that trigger your unskillful actions, your suffering and your excesses. You want to bring them to the practice so you can release yourself from them:

1. In this step the practitioner recapitulates while sitting in a comfortable position. Remember not to judge, not to search for traumas or solutions, just be aware of the emotions and the feelings that the recapitulation causes in you as you watch the movie of your past (try to respond to the questions in the emotional recapitulation pillar of Chapter 7).

2. Still sitting in a comfortable position, express your intention to release yourself from the subconscious programs that triggered the emotional crisis that you revisited in the previous step. Express also your devotion through prayer and affirmations or mantras. These are powerful intentions that set your mind on the right path. As you pray, express your gratitude for this point in your life that you have achieved and express also your faith, your conviction that God, or your highest being self, will always provide you with what you need as the prayer "Faith" in Chapter 4 asserts. Next, in your prayer, ask for anything you need, such as health, money, job, a fulfilling relationship, and envision it as a reality because, indeed, it is a reality. Do not forget to ask God that whatever you are asking be granted to you in perfect harmony with everybody and everything through the perfect way that only God can create. Then finish your prayer expressing again your thankfulness, for God has already altered your quantum realm for you to receive what you have just asked for.

(See Appendix B for recommended sitting poses during recapitulation).

## Part 2: Knowing our potential

In order to be in control of your life situations you need awareness and the knowledge that comes with it. The awareness of your potential prepares you to resolve your issues in life, including the issue you brought up in your recapitulation in the first part above. Similarly, the human body needs to get acquainted with its possibilities. The first step prepares the body for what it is next. By warming-up and strengthening the muscles of your legs, hips and belly you start to appreciate and acknowledge the parts of your body that allow you to stand up and walk on Earth. Your body warms up and becomes prepared for the more challenging exercises next, as if you were saying to yourself: become aware of your real potential to resolve the difficulties you are facing in your life.

(See Appendix B for detailed instructions of the exercises covered in this part 2.)

## Part 3: Living the ruling circumstances (this moment is unavoidable)

Many times in our lives we think that we are tossed and carried away by the winds of our circumstances. These are the times when we feel the need to either defend ourselves with anger or give up with depression; these are the times when we believe that we are forced to do this or that, when we rush from here to there or keep ourselves busy with stuff that seems not to make us happy. This part of the practice resembles those moments in our life, but this time we apply the intention to be in control.

The third part of the practice is designed to strengthen your heart muscles and increase blood and lymph circulation, oxygenation, and waste removal by doing a brief but high intensity cardiovascular exercise. Running in place is a good alternative when running outdoors is not possible. As you run as fast as you can (according to your own physical condition), you accept the current circumstances of the world. These are the circumstances you cannot ever change because they belong to the present moment, and this present moment, with all of its connotations, is unavoidable.

In this activity you also experience the rush and the physical struggle that our ancestors, the Paleolithic humans, experienced while hunting big dangerous animals. They had to accept their circumstances and knew what to do about them, and so can you. As your endorphin production increases and your blood irrigates all your body, purifying it (pillar #3, body purification through exercises), you are in full control because now you certainly know of the benefits you will receive. You follow your intention and make the statement that you are not tossed and carried away by anything (pillar #4, mind purification through intention).

(See Appendix B for more details about part 3.)

## Part 4: Dissolving and removing the delusions

Part 4 of the practice is about recognizing the delusions that we usually cling to when trying to satisfy our emotional needs. To reject our obsolete subconscious patterns we need to be firm and strong. After all, these subconscious patterns exist to assist a primitive and powerful instinct: the instinct of survival. In this sense, part 4 develops the strength of our chest and arms to be able to remove the objects that block our way, which translates into dissolving and removing the harmful mental structures that our subconscious has created.

(See Appendix B for detailed instructions of the exercises covered in this part 4.)

## Part 5: Bringing up clarity and receptivity

Part 4 of the practice dissolves and weakens the subconscious harmful structures that limit us. But now, after loosening up the dirt we need to flush away the residues. Through an ancient Chinese practice called Qigong in this part of the practice, we will be able to make energy flow through our body cleaning our energy channels. As an empty vessel, we will feel more receptive to new and more harmonious content after the Qigong practice.

Energy flows following the path of least resistance like water running down hill. It is natural to think that the life force energy, called *chi* in the ancient Chinese tradition, flows endlessly and gently in the Universe. Qigong brings us such energy by imitating the natural flow of *chi* with soft, continuous and undulated slow motion with our hands. In Qigong, the hands represent the main vehicle to cultivate *chi* and direct it towards our mind and body. As we do Qigong we visualize the energy being managed and collected by our hands in order to reinstate the harmony of the Creation in us, that is to say, in order to heal ourselves.

Note that Qigong exercises complement the exercises of the previous part. The strength and vigor of part 4 is balanced by the gentleness and softness of part 5. Qigong actually guarantees that the energy of part 4 will not dissipate quickly as usually results after a regular workout. As Qigong unblocks the meridian channels, *chi* can flow freely without the resistance that causes energy dissipation. Furthermore, Qigong increases the electrical currents that flow along the meridian pathways of the body (bioelectrical conductivity), producing powerful healing effects (similar to those produced by acupuncture). We know also that these electrical currents generate electromagnetic fields, which in turn will alter our quantum realm and prepare it for the next activity (the *asana* practice).

(See Appendix B for detailed instructions of the exercises covered in this part 5.)

## Part 6: Rooting down in Earth to fill the empty vessel

Part 6 seals the pact between you and Earth. This part will ground you on this planet for you to know exactly the harmonious role you need to play on life's stage. You will earn this knowledge by imitating the tall and noble tree whose stillness and quietness represent the serene power of our spirituality. As the tree fills itself with the nutrients of Earth, you will be able to fill your mind and body with the awareness that brings consciousness.

Through the concentration and focus facilitated by the yoga exercises of this part, you will live a long and healthy life, you will increase your control and will power, and you will be able to control your cravings and addictions. Your subconscious will be more attuned with reality and your body will become a powerful antenna capable of interacting with the universe through the quantum realm.

In the exercises of this part, hold each pose as steady and still as possible and close your eyes if this contributes to your concentration and the body's balance is not at risk. Maintain a serene expression that relaxes your face and breathe using the victorious breath (*ujjayi* breath) unless indicated otherwise. The Sanskrit word *ujjayi* can also be translated as "towards-victory" symbolizing that the practitioner is already on the path to their certain liberation–liberation from obsolete subconscious programs, limiting beliefs and disease. Since liberation is certain, the practitioner does not think or worry about future events because it is in the present moment when everything that will happen is currently being created. The *ujjayi* breath is carried out only through the nostrils. It is an audible, long and deep breath in which inhalations and exhalations have about the same duration. The sound of this breath in inhalation and exhalation derives from constricting the air passage in the back of the throat as we usually do when we whisper. This sound is used as feedback to bring the mind within, to the source of the sound. In this breath the intake is directed to fill the lower part of the lungs first as the belly expands freely, and then it naturally rises to the upper parts of the lungs.

The mountain pose (*tadasana*) described in Appendix B is also fundamental as its key points are maintained in many other poses. (See Appendix B for detailed instructions of the exercises covered in this part 6.).

## Part 7: Reaching beyond the realm of forms

Just like the tree that grows its roots deep down as well as it reaches up for the sunlight, you have already grounded yourself and now you reach up to perceive what there is beyond the realm of forms. Your conscious now understands much better and has started creating more harmonious patterns in your subconscious. You know already about your role and the creative potential you possess through the Great Mind. Thus you create the singularities that later on will become the events and circumstances that advance your peace and happiness. As this happens, you will regain your rightful place on Earth as the creator you are. It is time, then, to go further ahead.

In this part of the practice, you intentionally start a gradual process of shutting down your six senses and releasing your mind of all the *asana* concentration you have done in the previous parts. In fact, you want your mind to be free from any attachment to the physical world and *see* the unseen using your seventh sense. Notice though that you need to consciously use your mind through concentration in order to free it from any activity. In other words, you need to use your mind in order to go beyond it; this is when concentration becomes meditation as explained in Chapter 7 (Pillar #5, meditation).

This part of the practice is for you to transcend your own physicality and encounter the other part of your reality. Thus, you will fully experience your absolute essence, the immutable sameness we discussed in Chapter 2, and realize that God has always dwelled within you. In this gradual process, and since you know that the attainment of your highest goal is completely certain, you will not be concerned about the final outcome and will dedicate your effort to the present moment only.

(See Appendix B for detailed instructions of this part 7.)

## The Other Aspects of this Practice

The practice above takes approximately an hour and a half of your daily routine. But how can you align the rest of your life to your new spiritual endeavors? No doubt that as you progress in your daily practice, you will be making better choices for your well-being on a daily basis. Keeping in mind the precepts of the Seven Pillars of Spirituality is always a good help at any time in our daily lives. During the forty days of the practice, do your best to:

❖ Eat only organic vegetables, fruits and other botanical products.[2] If you are not a vegan, make sure the animal products you eat are from animals that eat an organic diet according to what Mother Nature has designed for them. Do drink plenty of water free of chlorine, fluoride,[3] and other contaminants as they are all dangerous toxic chemicals.

❖ Eat plenty of raw food.[4]

❖ Reduce your caloric intake by eating only when you are really hungry and eat until you feel three-quarters full. Only two things have been scientifically proven to significantly increase your lifespan and the quality of your health: lower

---

[2] Visit http://www.ardentlight.com/body/wholesome-recipes.php#Organic to learn more about the importance of eating organic food.

[3] The interested reader should watch the video "The fluoride deception (interview with Christopher Bryson)" at http://video.google.com /videoplay?docid= 7319752042352089988&hl=en# (posted in 2006). This video is based on the findings that Christopher Bryson exposed in his book *The Fluoride Deception*. The rationale for water fluoridation follows the same pattern that corporations have used previously to defend DDT, tobacco, asbestos, etc. In my opinion, the idea that this toxic chemical helps to fight tooth cavities is ludicrous. Why would Mother Nature ever design us to rely on a toxic chemical to maintain healthy teeth?

[4] Visit http://www.ardentlight.com/body/wholesome-recipes.php#Raw to learn more about the importance of eating raw food.

caloric intake and lower basal metabolism.[5] Meditation will help lower your basal metabolism.

❖ Bless your food and water before consuming them to enhance their healing and nutritional properties.

❖ Eliminate processed food[6] including pasteurized dairy (organic raw dairy from grass-fed cows works better for you as it has more nutrients and enzymes to help its digestion). Considerably reduce the consumption of grains, especially those with high levels of gluten, and added sugar (or any other artificial sweetener) where most bad calories come from. Remember that obesity, diabetes, insulin resistance, heart diseases and cancer are mainly caused by sugar and grains. The idea that saturated fat, including animal fat, is the cause of these civilization diseases has been debunked by many scientific studies. We have been eating animal fat for millions of years, and most fats are required[7] for the human body to operate properly. The problem stems from the excesses of sugar and grains that have unnaturally become the staple of the human diet.

---

[5] Basal metabolism is the minimum amount of energy required to maintain vital functions at rest.

[6] Visit http://www.ardentlight.com/body/foreign-substances.php to learn more about the chemicals present in processed food.

[7] The only really bad fat out there is trans-fat. Trans-fat is produced through the process of hydrogenation. During this process, hydrogen is added to vegetable oil to solidify it and make it last longer increasing its shelf-life (again corporate tactics to increase profits at the expense of human health and life). Trans-fats are unnatural to human diet and they have been associated with heart diseases, cancer, diabetes, and other illnesses. Vegetable oils also become bad fat when they are used to cook or bake. The high temperatures turn the unsaturated vegetable oils into bad fat. Saturated oils, such as coconut oil and palm oil, despite the propaganda against them, are actually loaded with wonderful healthy properties, and are ideal to cook or bake with because they can withstand high temperatures without breaking down. Saturated fats are necessary for cell metabolism (our brain cells need a lot of saturated fat), hormone balance, fat-soluble vitamin assimilation, vitamin D production, etc. See http://www.ardentlight.com/help/coconut-oil.php for more revealing information about the dangers of cooking with vegetable oils and the critical role of saturated fat in our diet.

❖ Make your breakfast and lunch your main meals with no dinner at all or a very light one (small and easy to digest) early in the evening at least three hours before bedtime.

❖ Do not consume any drug, alcohol, or smoke. If you do have a drug or smoking problem, reduce their consumption gradually day-by-day to mitigate the withdrawal effects, and target not taking them at all by the thirty-first day of the practice. Likewise, reduce your caffeine intake to nothing, especially if you depend on the caffeine to wake up, have a boost of energy or do your job. Nevertheless, consider any reduction in the consumption of addictive substances an important improvement.

❖ Eliminate hygiene products that contain chemicals and toxic ingredients. Replace them with natural products or ways to clean yourself.

❖ Take one or two of your normal activities at work or home to be present using your conscious. Focus on every single detail of the activity you choose and give your subconscious a break.

❖ Try to observe yourself daily and take note of any maladroit behavior of yours that you would like to explore in your daily spiritual practice. Observe especially how deeply you connect with people. These observations give you the feedback you need in order to assess your spiritual progress.

❖ Consider the possibility of fasting for one or two days at a time during the 40 days of the practice. Fasting is not unnatural to humans; eating three times a day or more every day is. If human beings had not evolved with the capacity of fasting, our species would be extinct by now. You can moderate your fasting with fresh homemade juices until you are able to fast for one or two days with only water. Fasting will help your body to detoxify and your mind to become more peaceful.

❖ Create a shrine in your home to practice the daily sessions of the spiritual practice. Prepare this shrine according to your personal devotion beliefs and make it special for you, perhaps with incense, flowers, holy water, candles, singing bowls, images, pictures, etc. As you practice in this shrine every day, this area of your home will accumulate special energy that will assist you in your spiritual transformation. Nonetheless, if you happen to be away for any reason, you can make any place special with your intentions.

## Conclusions

The spiritual practice of this chapter might seem difficult to start, but once started it creates the conditions through which energy is cultivated and harvested with ease and joy by the practitioner. With this practice, our well-being increases further and further on a scale undreamed-of as we commit fully, in body, mind and spirit, to the execution of the seven parts of the practice.

By simply not having eaten anything for at least four hours before the practice, we increase the control to direct our lives and augment the vital energy that sustains our bodies. In most cases, after each session the practitioner feels less hungry or not hungry at all due to an increase of energy and an elevation of consciousness. It is common for people to lose weight, become healthier and have a better relationship with their food after this 40-day practice.

As people become healthier with this practice, which is itself a spiritual accomplishment, they also become more connected to everyone, to the world around them and to nature. They feel at ease, content and open. Since they no longer have obstacles, the abundance of the Universe harmoniously manifests itself to them and through them for others to find their own realizations. They will realize that this spiritual practice is worth continuing.

# 9
# THE UNIVERSAL BELIEF OF SPIRITUALITY

The first time I saw my oldest son he was around 11 years old, just the age he is now as I write the final chapter of this book. I was changing the oil of the car and he was just standing there with a calm and peaceful expression. He looked so beautiful, like an angel watching over me. He made sure he stayed long enough for me to detail his physiognomy very well: his Asian dark eyes, his nose and mouth, his long shiny black hair with the bangs on his forehead and his face color with the nice tan he gets now when he goes to the beach. At that time my wife and I were living in an apartment, but I saw him in the garage of the house where he would be born ten months later. When I woke up I knew he was coming.

A few months later my wife told me she wanted to have our first baby at home; specifically she wanted to have a home water birth. I looked at her. There was the girl I met one November morning of 1992 during her college years while I was pursuing my Ph.D. degree. This was the girl whose circumstances led her to spirituality and meditation whereas my circumstances led me to sensuality and self-centered adoration. I tried to do good to people but I did not know how to really connect with them. How could two dissimilar people, so opposite in many aspects in life, start a life together? I have always loved my wife and have watched for her physical safety, but have I always been aware that I loved her? Have I always taken care of her emotional needs? Being so un-skillful at that time, how could I comprehend her desire to have our first baby at home and in the water? Her safety and the baby's safety should be above all. Why to reject the technology and the experience of the medical community to safely deliver a baby?

Was she insane? All these thoughts came to me, and before I opened my mouth to say something I saw again the face of my son yet to be born; it was the same face I saw in the dream I had before he was conceived. I saw his calmness and serenity; he was speaking without words. He had decided the way he wanted to be born, and my wife simply received the message very well. Her intuition and self-awareness were above any fear I could develop. Thus, I joined them happily and enthusiastically and looked forward to the day of his birth in the water, at home.

Then I realized how misguided I could have been. How could I ever believe that the excessive medical intervention during the process of human birth constitutes the "natural" choice? Human birth is a natural process that does not require much medical technology and medical intervention. Humans were designed to have babies and they have done it for millions of years very naturally without any specialized equipment or drugs. For example, epidural anesthesia is a drug commonly used in hospitals to reduce the pain of women in labor. This drug renders the mother unable to participate in the birth of her baby as it numbs her. The application of the drug starts a chain reaction of additional interventions. As the mother's pushing is hampered by the epidural drug, another drug, Pitocin, is used to induce labor, and if this new drug does not work, a pair of forceps, a vacuum extractor or a cesarean section (cut) becomes necessary. As if all this were little, the epidural anesthesia can cause the mother's blood pressure to drop suddenly which would require more medications, intravenous therapy and oxygen. What is natural in these fabricated interventions for human birth? What is natural in the fact that in the U.S. one out of three women delivers her baby through a cesarean cut? Why are cesarean cuts continuously increasing in the U.S.?[1] None of these medical interventions to assist a woman to give birth in the cold environment of a hospital sounded natural to me after my son to be born and my wife spoke to me.

Maximilian (Max) started signaling his arrival on a Monday morning at 4:00 by breaking the waters before any labor

---

[1] *Why has the USA's cesarean section rate climbed so high?* by Rita Rubin, USA Today, published on August 30, 2010, http://www.usatoday.com/ yourlife/parenting-family/babies/2010-08-31-csection31_ST_N.htm

contraction began; I proceeded then to call our midwife. My wife Ngoc and I were alone that morning. Ngoc was very calm in a meditative state to receive her son. She never screamed, she never complained of any pain. I was very calm and very certain that Max was already with us. I never felt any fear or had any hesitation (I knew the future already, why worry about it?). More than three and a half hours went by and our midwife hadn't shown up yet, but Ngoc and I were still confident, serene and happy. Ngoc was already in the bathtub submerged in water and Max was already emerging. I was ready to assist her all by myself when finally our midwife rang the doorbell. Maximilian was born at 8:00 a.m. I took him and exposed his face to the air for him to start breathing. Max inhaled his first breath and did not cry. Then, I put him on his mother's breast so she could feel him, our gift from God, and he could feel her in a different way, skin to skin. The scene was beautiful, the peace was incredible. The birth of a human being is a spiritual experience in which we instantly feel an unconditional connection with the newborn baby. The baby's soul is our soul, sameness is all what it is, no differences exist, no barriers and fears to separate but love to unite. My wife and I experienced again the same joy and peace with the births of our other two children in our home. Renzi, our second son, was born on a Wednesday night after two hours of labor at 11:00, and Allegra, our little girl, was also born on a Wednesday after four hours of labor at 12:00 p.m. Both of them were born in the same bathtub as their brother, but with relatives in the house and our midwife arriving on time.

Our children's births were unique and elevated spiritual experiences that my wife and I tried to facilitate to the full extent of our awareness. Were we deceived by a belief system? Were we rationalizing an unharmonious behavior? I'll let the reader answer these questions. The only thing I can say is that few times in my life have I felt the certainty and the peace that I experienced with the birth of each of my children. I was not concerned at all with the outcome as I already knew the outcome; I never panicked or rushed to go anywhere because I didn't have to; and, I didn't have to witness unnecessary interventions for the natural birth process which is meant to get us closer to God. When we feel this tranquility and calm certainty about an outcome, we are manifesting a spiritual realization, we are living the moment and enjoying the process knowing that its outcome is positive because our actions are harmonious: This is happiness. If I can manifest these spiritual realizations in most facets of my life, I would be transcending my limited existence and getting closer and closer to the infinite realm of God. If my entire life becomes one ecstatic spiritual experience, I will have reached enlightenment.

A spiritual realization is direct knowledge that comes to us from the unseen by means of our seventh sense (see Figure 2). The universality of spirituality was already stated in Chapter 2: "Notice that since the information from the past and the information from the five senses do not play a role to perceive the unseen, the perception of the unseen is (a) universally the same and (b) free of contention because the information received through the seventh sense does not need to be scrutinized and weighed against old beliefs and conditioning."

As we perceive the unseen we realize that spirituality is universal. It does not depend on cultural or religious values. Spirituality recognizes and embraces the differences that characterize us as human beings along with the diversity of our belief systems; spirituality accepts all of them as natural and unavoidable. At the same time, spirituality goes beyond our differences and belief systems to find the substratum from which everything emerges. This subtle and invisible substratum is the non-physical sameness that threads us from heart to heart in a wonderful fabric that extends to all and everything without exception. Some people call this fabric God, the Creation, the Universe, Great Spirit, but regardless of its name and the social context in which we unfold our lives, we intuitively know there is "something" beyond any possible physical description that connects us in the same universal way.

The greatest fact about spirituality is that it drives people to live their lives based on this principle of universal sameness. The spiritually motivated people can see the reflection of their souls in anyone without distinction and in everything that has been created in this universe. Conversely, people motivated by dogmas and belief systems fail many times in seeing their essence within and therefore they are unable to recognize it when it shows in somebody out of their immediate group; they cannot even see themselves in nature, in its brightness and beauty. If you ever feel above or below others, if you abide one hundred percent by your dogmas without questioning them, if you are unable to see when your mental fixations fail to apply the universal principles of God to ALL, and if you ever feel disconnected to yourself as your actions degrade your well-being, or connected only to those who belong to your religion, country or social group, then you should know that your fears are ripping the divine fabric in the section that corresponds to your life. In this case, you must amend your life by reconnecting to the universal harmony, the same harmony that God always grants to everyone in order to fulfill their lives with joy and contentment.

When in doubt of your beliefs, look for inconsistencies between your ideals and actions. It is common to act contradicting ourselves when spirituality is not really settled in us. For example, knowing that something you consume is harmful and yet you consume it; frequently experiencing anger and depression to try to protect yourself when in reality you are harming your health and well-being; supporting the security of your country by justifying the "collateral damage" of war that kills the innocents of another country; judging and labeling others when you are incapable of examining yourself; loving your children and feeling hatred or contempt for someone, and many other inconsistencies so easy to find in our individual lives. Moreover, always remember to apply the wisdom of the following quote attributed to the Buddha:

*Believe nothing,*
*no matter where you read it or who has said it,*
*not even if I have said it,*
*unless it agrees with your own reason and*
*your own common sense.*

If your common sense—which can be defined as the however small section of your intuition that your belief system cannot close—says that what you do and experience goes against the universal harmony of our sameness including your own well-being, then stop and do something about it. Begin with yourself. Heal yourself to start experiencing your spiritual realizations and then let your presence and actions help the world to heal.

*What you hear, you forget; what you see, you remember; what you do, you understand...*
(From an ancient Chinese maxim attributed to Confucius)

# APPENDIX A
# YOGA, BUDDHISM AND
# THE SEVEN PILLARS

Yoga and Buddhism originated in India thousands of years ago within a society that embraced Hinduism as its major spiritual trend. I have chosen both of them in this appendix because they include a number (eight to be exact) of precepts or principles that embody the core of their philosophies. Among those precepts is meditation, which represents their very distinctive signature. I particularly consider meditation crucial for spiritual attainment.

## The Seven Pillars and Yoga

Most people think that Yoga consists of a particular kind of exercises that require bending like a pretzel, stretching like a piece of play dough or having gymnastic skills. Our Western society is so used to competition for recognition that it has embraced Yoga mainly from the physical point of view.

But Yoga entails much more than exercises for the body. Doubtlessly, physical exercises are excellent for the body and when the body feels good, the mind indirectly will benefit too. But when our mind and spirit are left out of the picture the benefits of just exercising are not deep enough, or long-lasting enough, to realize our shortcomings. When one uses a tool halfway, one obtains only half of the expected results derived from using such a tool.

The physical yoga that the West embraces derives from *Hatha* Yoga. *Hatha* Yoga is one of the different kinds of "yogas" documented in the literature. These different "yogas" are described next.

## *Raja* Yoga

The word *raja* is a Sanskrit word that means royal. The mind is considered the king of the body. *Raja* Yoga deals with the mind, hence its name. *The Yoga Sutras of Patanjali,*[1] written during the third and second centuries BCE, sets the fundamentals of *Raja* Yoga. Patanjali in his second sutra established that the goal of Yoga is to control or restrain the thought-waves of the mind. As the mind, if left alone, can create a sense of identification and attachment to the physical world, the *raja* yogi seeks to calm his mind to perceive what is beyond the physical forms.

*Raja* Yoga establishes that each individual has a separate but identical *purusha* (*Atman*, our immutable and eternal sameness that dwells within us) and that the purpose of a *Raja* Yoga practitioner is to unite or merge with their *purusha*, thus God can be experienced. This path of union is described by Patanjali as a process that comprises eight limbs (the Eight Limbs of Yoga) of which we speak later.

## *Jnana* Yoga

The Sanskrit word *jnana* means "knowledge." From the *Jnana* Yoga's point of view, "knowledge" must be cultivated to differentiate the immutable and eternal from the temporary ever-changing forms of the physical world. "Knowledge" is acquired by using the reasoning capabilities of our intelligent mind: association, discernment and abstraction.

Perhaps starting from 800 BCE ancient scholars and philosophers wrote the *Upanishads* to establish the principles of their monistic philosophy, in which *Atman* (the eternal essence from within) and *Brahman* (the ALL infinite essence, God, of the manifest and the unmanifest) are one and only one. Through *Jnana* Yoga the ancient sages tried to convey the message of this monistic philosophy to the people.

At this point, it's good to emphasize the words of the Buddha as we engage in practicing *Jnana* Yoga: "Believe nothing, no matter where you read it or who has said it, not even if I have said it,

---

[1] *How to know God, The Yoga Aphorisms of Patanjali,* translated by Swami Prabhavananda and Christopher Isherwood. A Mentor Book New American Library, 1969

unless it agrees with your own reason and your own common sense." In other words, we should not confuse reasoning with rationalization (of belief systems).

## Karma Yoga

The Sanskrit word *karma* means action. In Chapter 3 of *The Bhagavad Gita*, written around 300 BCE, Krishna explains the mystic meaning of Karma Yoga in verses 3.6 and 3.7:

> He who controls his actions
> but lets his mind dwell on sense objects
> is deluding himself and spoiling
> his search for the deepest truth...
> The superior man is he
> whose mind can control his senses;
> with no attachment to results,
> he engages in the yoga of action.[2]

A spiritual practice embodies what Karma Yoga is all about. Put in simple words, Karma Yoga actions follow the harmonious path of least resistance, wherein action matches inaction similar to the Taoist principle of *wu-wei*,[3] and contribute to the well-being of the whole world. Karma Yoga actions bring happiness; other actions bring disarray and contention. By engaging Karma Yoga, we make the law of Karma, the law of cause and effect, work towards our fulfillment.

## *Bhakti* Yoga

The Sanskrit word of *bhakti* denotes devotion. *Bhakti* Yoga is the yoga of devotion, the yoga of love towards God, the Beloved. *Bhakti* Yoga is the yoga of feelings and emotions where the intellect is secondary.

---

[2] *The Bhagavad Gita* translated by Stephen Mitchell, Three Rivers Press, New York 2000, pp. 62-63.
[3] "The concept [of *wu-wei*] refers to a kind of intuitive cooperation with the natural order, which is perfect and harmonious when left to work without the interference of ignorant human action" by Yi-Ping Ong. Lao Tzu, *Tao Te Ching*, translated by Charles Muller. Introduction by Yi-Ping Ong. Barnes and Noble Classics, New York, 2005, p. xviii.

*Bhakti* Yoga is the practice of faith, prayer and mantras; it is the practice when we openly worship the Beloved using altars, images, incenses and any other rituals that we consider necessary. During *Bhakti* Yoga we thank the Beloved, we ask the Beloved for what we need and we look up to Him longing for the eternal connection. *Bhakti* Yoga needs *Jnana* Yoga and vice versa, for feelings and emotions need knowledge and knowledge needs feelings and emotions.

## *Hatha* Yoga

The Sanskrit word *hatha* has one meaning derived from the Sanskrit words *ha* (sun) and *tha* (moon) denoting the dualism of opposites (feminine-masculine, *yin-yang*) that characterizes every human being. But it has also the connotation of willful or forceful. In either case, the term *Hatha* Yoga refers to the physical aspect of Yoga, the cultivation of the body to reach higher realms.

The original source of *Hatha* Yoga is attributed to Swami Swatmarama who compiled the *Hatha Yoga Pradipika* about the 15th century CE. *Hatha* Yoga consists of a series of *asanas* or body postures that are meant to achieve physical steadiness to intensify concentration and contemplation. A steady body induces a steady mind; a steady mind eases meditation and transcendence.

*Hatha* Yoga *asanas* have also the purpose of cultivating the subtle and the coarse energies in the body. *Hatha* Yoga practice produces innumerable health benefits by cultivating both types of energy. In other words, *Hatha* Yoga practice affects our quantum realm to favorably condition our physical and mental health and sense of connection to that which is all.

## There is only one Yoga

Why are there many "yogas"? Which one should we practice? These questions are really not well posed. By reading the first paragraph of the book *Light On Yoga* by B. K. S. Iyengar, we can comprehend the real nature of Yoga:

> The word Yoga is derived from the Sanskrit root *yuj* meaning to bind, join, attach and yoke, to direct and concentrate one's attention on, to use and apply. It also means union or communion. It is the true union of our will with

the will of God. "It thus means," says Mahadev Desai in his introduction to the *Gita According to Gandhi*, "the yoking of all the powers of body, mind and soul to God; it means the discipline of the intellect [*Jnana* Yoga], the mind [*Raja* Yoga], the emotions [*Bhakti* Yoga], the will [*Hatha* Yoga], which that Yoga presupposes; it means a poise of the soul which enables one to look at life in all its aspects evenly."[4]

Yoga, therefore, is all the "yogas" above. Yoga is life itself. It is a very comprehensive spiritual practice for daily life inasmuch as it holistically addresses the key facets of our human condition. There are not different yogas; there is one and only one Yoga that harmoniously yokes our body, mind and spirit to one another.

We have mentioned before that devotion (*Bhakti* Yoga) and reasoning (*Jnana* Yoga) must operate together to counteract each other. Excess of devotion denies reasoning and brings fanaticism; excess of reasoning dulls the heart and brings hubris. *Asana* practice (*Hatha* Yoga) for the sake of the body brings attachment to the body as we seek the temporary euphoria caused by endorphins; conversely, *asana* practice in the spiritual context brings concentration as we develop will power to tame the mind for meditation (*Raja* Yoga). Meditation leads us to transcendence, to the realm of the unseen, that is, God, and transcendence naturally increases our devotion towards God as our intellect becomes brighter and brighter and our actions become impeccable (Karma Yoga).

## The Eight Limbs of Yoga

The sutra 2-29 of Patanjali states the Eight Limbs (or Eight Petals) of Yoga. They are (with their Sanskrit names):

1. *Yama* (abstention from actions that negatively affect others).
2. *Nyama* (observances that benefit one's self directly).
3. *Asana* (body poses).
4. *Pranayama* (controlled breath).
5. *Pratyahara* (withdrawal of the senses).

---

[4] *The Light on Yoga* by B. K. S. Iyengar, Schocken Books Inc., New York, 1979, p. 19.

6. *Dharana* (concentration).
7. *Dhyana* (meditation).
8. *Samadhi* (Union with God).

As limbs or branches that sprout from a common trunk, each limb of Yoga stems from the same core and, therefore, has the same essence as that of the core. The Eight Limbs of Yoga overlap each other and each of them is as important as the others.

*Yama* and *Nyama* are interrelated as everything in our lives. Harming others will eventually bring distress in our lives, and not taking care of ourselves will, sooner or later, harm others.

*Yama* is abstention from harming others directly, or, equivalently, from disrupting the harmony of the Creation, and comprises non-violence, truthfulness, non-stealing, celibacy, non-greed and non-coveting. Non-violence includes not inflicting pain of any kind (physical or emotional) to anyone, not abusing or taking advantage of anybody for personal gain, and not damaging the natural flow of God's creation in general (e.g. not polluting, not killing animals unnecessarily, etc.). Truthfulness is always needed because whoever deceives and conceals consequently harms others. Celibacy in this context does not mean abstention from sex but enjoying sex derived only from the deepest sense of union with another human being; otherwise, sex would be just a tool to exploit others for personal pleasure. Coveting must be avoided because it represents a source of contention.

*Nyama* consists of purity, contentment, mortification, study of spiritual books and devotion to God. By not practicing the *Nyama*, we will hurt ourselves directly, which will eventually impair our surrounding, including its people. Purity involves purity of the mind and the body. The mind must be free of disturbing thoughts and the body must be free of toxins on the outside and the inside. *Asana* practice and *pranayama* exercises contribute to both a pure mind used to concentrate and focus, and a healthy body full of energy and vitality. Contentment is indispensable because if you are not content with your situation then you are uneasy, restless, anxious for something to happen, and therefore in disharmony. Contentment goes beyond feeling content because you have a good material life; instead, in contentment you naturally and selflessly exercise your creator capabilities to spread your contentment all around, especially to those who need it the most. Mortification is not self-torture, deprivation or extreme austerity, nor is it seeking suffering. Mortification in the context of the sutras is the certainty that any sorrow or pain we could have in the present is an opportunity for spiritual growth and for positioning ourselves better off in our spiritual journey.

The word *asana* derives from the Sanskrit root *as* which means to stay. It also means to sit or seat. Patanjali's sutra 2-46 specifies that *asana* must be steady and comfortable. In other words, an *asana* is a body posture or pose that must be maintained firm and steady for a period of time and with a sense of easiness and comfort. If the *asana* practitioner can breathe deeply and smoothly through the nostrils, the easiness and comfort has been achieved. Only then can the practitioner focus and concentrate the mind on the subtle energetic sensations that the posture produces and not on the process of getting the posture right. This concentration opens the door to higher levels of consciousness. In order to facilitate this process, each *asana* of a spiritual *asana* practice must be mastered before engaging in the practice. Furthermore, as a spiritual practice is an individual endeavor, best results are obtained when the practitioner is alone or counts with the guidance of a spiritual master.

*Pranayama* stems from the Sanskrit word *prana* which means the life force or energy that creates motion and changes in the entire universe. The breath is a source of *prana*. *Pranayama* is the intentional control of the breath through its inhalations and exhalations. *Pranayama* and *asana* are interconnected. To practice *pranayama* we need a steady pose, usually some version of the cross-legged sitting position, and to practice *asana* we need a smooth controlled breath. *Pranayama* increases concentration and focus liberating the mind from the subconscious chains. It also has beneficial side effects on our health and well-being.

Concentration (*Dharana*) constitutes a voluntary activity of the human mind. Concentration liberates us from our subconscious and can program and reprogram our subconscious. *Asana* and *pranayama* are excellent for concentration, but concentration, the ability that every human has to apply the senses and the mind to one specific purpose, can be practiced in any activity of daily life. Concentration represents a pure expression of living the "now."

*Pratyahara* (the withdrawal of the senses) indicates the relevance of not being perturbed by the sensations brought up by the five senses. During concentration we narrow the use of our senses to cover only the object of our concentration, but meditation (*Dhyana*) goes one very big step beyond. The goal of meditation is rather to shut down the five senses (and the mind) to open the doors to the non-physical, thus we can experience God. No meditation is possible without sense withdrawal. Meditation is not easy because shutting down our senses and mind is difficult; nonetheless, the preliminary stages in our quest for pure meditation are highly rewarding. Meditation can be mastered only after a daily and consistent practice.

*Samadhi* denotes the experience of the unseen, the unmanifest, God. There are no physical terms that can explain *Samadhi*, for *Samadhi* is non-physical. *Samadhi* is the unutterable transcendental state of being one with the Creation.

## The Seven Pillars and the Eight Limbs of Yoga

In the Seven Pillars we can identify the main Yoga principles but arranged in a different way as explained in the following.

Pillar #1 (emotional recapitulation)

Pillar #1 is not directly related to a yoga limb but it encompasses essential aspects of Yoga. In pillar #1 there is an implicit recognition of the fact that our most harmful actions result from automatic programs in our subconscious and since most of us are not aware of them, we should start our spiritual practice by identifying these subconscious programs. We cannot heal an emotional trauma if we do not acknowledge the trauma and its root cause.

The purpose of our subconscious programs is to trigger the defense mechanisms that are intended to protect us from a threat. In its zeal to protect us, our subconscious can make us dedicate all our mental energy to try to foresee possible future events in order to anticipate any course of action that best serves us. This mental activity that the subconscious triggers keeps the mind away from the present moment and represents what Patanjali calls *vritti* in his second aphorism. The word *vritti* is a Sanskrit word that has been usually translated into modifications of the mind or thought-waves. Patanjali's second aphorism reads: Yoga is the control and restraint of the thought-waves of the mind. Hence, identifying the origin of these thought-waves (pillar #1), that is to say, pinpointing the source of our traumas, insecurities and fears, becomes crucial if we want to reprogram our subconscious with harmonious and constructive programs—the only way to effectively control and restrain the thoughts-wave of the mind.

For example, the first and second limbs of Yoga tell us, among other things, that we should restrain ourselves from greed or from causing pain to others (*Yama*) and we should feed our body with the right quantity of pure and natural food (purity, *Nyama*), but many people fail doing this because they don't know they have destructive programs in their mind. Can a greedy person stop being greedy without understanding where the need to hoard money comes from? Can a man whose ravages of anger have disastrous consequences on others (and himself), get rid of his anger attacks without knowing the root cause of them? Can a woman who has been conditioned to consume processed food rich in sugar and grains, stop craving this unhealthy food without realizing that she has been programmed with this craving?

The emotional recapitulation involves the recognition of our behavioral patterns that adversely affect our state of well-being. As these patterns are unnatural and do not correspond to God's harmony, it is clear that they have been programmed, conditioned or implanted in us. The emotional recapitulation requires we dig our past to try to uncover these patterns from their roots.

## Pillar #2 (devotion and prayer)

Pillar #2 is one of the *nyamas* of the second yoga limb; it also corresponds directly to *Bhakti* Yoga. This pillar responds to everyone's need to start their spiritual journey from wherever they are. Most people cannot go directly to meditate to achieve Union with God because they are deluded in this physical realm and its delusions; for them it is hard to see God within. Nevertheless, the same people can be attracted to the idea of worshiping a benevolent and external God who is always pure, loving and caring, and has many names. It is just a question of time for these people to realize the external God within.

Pillar #2 has also the important role of solidifying faith in the individual. Faith is the real and powerful "placebo effect" that heals and sets the quantum realm for miracles to start to happen. Faith is the certainty that the Universe will provide us with what we need when our actions are harmonious and constructive.

Pillar #3 (body purity)

Pillar #3 is part of *Nyama* (yoga limb #2) and includes cleanliness, right food and exercises to maintain or restore a healthy body. Pillar #3 is important because our physical body is the vehicle of our spiritual practice in this physical universe, and as such we should honor it.

We honor our body by eating wholesome food such as organic raw vegetables and fruits, herbs, fermented food, and, for those who eat animal products, meat and dairy products from healthy animals. This includes animals that have been treated humanely, fed with the appropriate food for them (e.g. grass-fed cows as opposed to grain-fed cows) and free of synthetic hormones to fatten them. (Sugar and grains are not a natural food for us and they must be reduced considerably.)

Keeping a body active is necessary to keep our body close to its pure nature. Our muscles and bones were designed to move and lift things. Our legs are perfect to run; our bodies can swim; our muscles must both contract and extend. We need to make our bodies come back to their basic nature—the nature that this modern life has completely neglected.

Pillar # 4 (mind purity)

Mind purity (pillar #4) is achieved mainly through intention and concentration (yoga limb # 6) to tame our subconscious. Intention is placed before concentration to stop distracting thoughts. Concentration, as explained before, is practiced through *asana* (yoga limb # 3) and *pranayama* (yoga limb #4) to keep the mind away from distracting thoughts in order to restrain our subconscious.

Our subconscious operates all the time independently of our will. Concentration, instead, operates only when we consciously focus on something; concentration requires our will. Because of our will during concentration, we can reprogram our old harmful patterns that we have recognized in pillar #1.

## Pillar # 5 (meditation)

Pillar #5 corresponds directly to yoga limbs # 7 and #5 since meditation requires the withdrawal of the senses (yoga limb #5).

As discussed in Chapter 7, in pure meditation, there is nothing "out there," everything exists within. The void "out there" turns into everything within, everything within turns into the void "out there." When everything exists within, the senses are no longer needed because there is nothing to observe. You have achieved the paradoxical situation when you have used your mind to transcend its own functioning.

## Pillar #6 (deep connections with others)

Pillar #6 relates to *Yama* (yoga limb #1) since deep connections with others maintain the harmony of the Universe and follow God's flow. Not negatively affecting others with our actions comes naturally when a sense of connection with everybody (and everything) exists.

In Chapter 7 we stated that we all have the "response-ability" to contribute to the harmony of the world through our right actions and according to our means. This ability strengthens with our spiritual practice until it becomes a very natural facet of our lives. At this point, reaching to others becomes reaching to ourselves; no difference exists between the way we treat ourselves and the way we treat others. More importantly, by helping others, by healing others, by bringing a little joy to others in their moments of need, and also by feeling the enthusiasm and joy of those blessed with happiness and grace, we experience an enormous sense of gratitude towards God, for God has bestowed on us such beautiful "response-ability."

## Pillar #7: Union with God

The seventh spiritual pillar is the natural consequence of the previous six pillars. After dedicating our efforts to the first six pillars, Union with God, *Samadhi*, comes naturally at its due time. Union with God is attained during the deepest part of meditation, but also can come in dreams, near death experiences or spontaneously during special moments. As we intensify our spiritual practice and master the art of the deepest meditation, we will have more moments of Union with God and a real transformation will start occurring in us in which a permanent state of full awareness takes roots in more moments of our daily life.

# The Seven Pillars and Buddhism

Buddhism was founded by the Buddha, whose personal name was Siddhartha Gautama, around the 6th or 5th century BCE. The Buddha did not claim to be a god or any divine incarnation; he stated he was just a human being; he attributed all his spiritual attainments to normal human capabilities. In his book *What the Buddha Taught*, Walpola Rahula wrote: "Man's position according to Buddhism, is supreme. Man is his own master, and there is no higher being or power that sits in judgment of his destiny...He [the Buddha] taught, encouraged and stimulated each person to develop himself and to work out his own emancipation, for man has the power to liberate himself from all bondage through his own personal effort and intelligence."[5]

Since the Seven Pillars of Spirituality constitute an individual endeavor, we can see how Buddhism relates with the Seven Pillars. It is only through the individual effort that humans liberate themselves from their suffering and discontent. Our individual responsibility, Buddha taught, consists in knowing the nature of reality and exercising our capabilities to liberate ourselves from all bondage.

## Reality and the Four Noble Truths

According to Buddhism the Four Noble Truths with their Pali names are:

- *Dukkha*
- *Samudaya*, the origin of *dukkha*.
- *Nirodha*, the cessation of *dukkha*.
- *Magga*, the path to end *dukkha*.

---

[5] *What the Buddha Taught* by Walpola Rahula, The Corporate Body of the Buddha Educational Foundation, Taipei, Taiwan, 1978, p. 1.

## The First Noble Truth (*Dukkha*)

The word *dukkha* usually is translated as pain or suffering. However, the First Noble Truth *Dukkha* connotes a wider spectrum of meanings. *Dukkha* means pain and suffering and also means 'impermanence', 'essence-less', 'bondage', 'narrowness of perception'. The First Noble Truth tells us that pain and suffering are intrinsic elements of our physical world in which nothing lasts forever and everything decomposes and breaks down. Everything changes in an unstoppable series of quantum leaps (see Chapter 6 for the spiritual explanation of the quantum universe), and from one instant to another 'this' is not 'this' anymore. Nothing 'essential' remains in the physical world and our five senses and physical abilities are rather limited to actually perceiving the deepest meaning of our impermanence. More succinctly, the First Noble Truth states that irremediably, following the cause-and-effect law, our universe has its ways and that we fail many times in having full appreciation of them.

Because pain and suffering are the common translation of *dukkha*, Buddhism sometimes is portrayed as pessimistic and nihilistic. On the contrary, nothing is further from the truth as evidenced by the innumerable Buddha images that show him with a gentle smile and a serene and calm countenance. Buddhism in actuality emphasizes that no calamities and difficulties can ever upset us if we *see* how things really are. "It is extremely important to understand this First Noble Truth clearly because, as the Buddha says, 'he who [*sees Dukkha*] sees also the arising of *dukkha*, sees also the cessation of *dukkha*, and sees also the path leading to the cessation of *dukkha*'."[6]

## The Second Noble Truth (*Samudaya*, the arising of *dukkha*)

The main reason for the arising of *dukkha* is attachment, 'thirst' or 'craving'. 'Thirst' denotes desire for, and attachment to, belief systems of any sort: sensual pleasures, wealth and power, existence, becoming somebody and even becoming nobody (during depression). Egoistic wants and desires cause all the suffering in the world. Having egoistic desires can only stem from ignorance

---

[6] *Ibid.*, p. 27.

about the impermanence of our world and its law of cause-and-effect.

Naturally humans have the will to exist, to continue, to become somebody with some specific status. This has been our nature for eons and allowed us to survive as a species on this planet. The problem arises when the need to go forward for existence and continuity becomes so disruptive that, paradoxically, it obliterates the human condition. In Chapter 7, in the occasion of elaborating on Pillar #1, we differentiated pain from suffering. Pain is the natural consequence of us being in this world of *Dukkha* and suffering is the exacerbation of pain. Pain has a physical or emotional origin; for example, hunger creates physical pain and the image of a starving child creates an emotional pain. Suffering instead has a mental origin; for instance, the mental fixation of greed creates suffering for the restless and contentious man who hoards money for no real reason as if he were clinging for his mere life, oblivious to the toll he is paying anyway. From Chapter 7 we have the following excerpt: "Suffering puts more pain on top of the existing pain with drastic emotional and physical consequences for the well-being of the individual. Suffering grows as it feeds itself to enormous proportions; pain, when used as feedback to correct the course of a human life, transforms itself into awareness as the individual starts seeing reality as it is. Suffering makes you react, pain makes you consciously act with serenity and equanimity. You can still experience peace and contentment while in pain; in suffering, you break down into pieces as your subconscious mind exacerbates your pain in a futile attempt to guard you against it."

The Third Noble Truth (*Nirodha*, the cessation of *dukkha*)

The Third Noble Truth establishes that there is liberation from suffering. In order to stop suffering we must stop the arising of *dukkha*, which is 'thirst'.

As any desire to become, have, and enjoy ceases, suffering vanishes and the individual reaches the state of *Nibbana* (Pali) or *Nirvana* (Sanskrit) as it is more popularly known. According to Walpola Rahula, *Nirvana* is the Absolute Truth or Ultimate Reality. "A supra-mundane experience like that of the Absolute Truth" cannot be explained with words "just as the fish had no words in his vocabulary to express the nature of the solid land."[7]

*Nirvana* is related to pillar #7 (Union with God), *Samadhi* (yoga limb #8) or the unseen. The Third Noble Truth ensures that the unutterable state of *Nirvana* exists and is achievable through the Path. "[*Nirvana*] is 'to be realized by the wise within themselves'... If we follow the Path patiently and with diligence, train and purify ourselves earnestly, and attain the necessary spiritual development, we may one day realize it within ourselves—without taxing ourselves with puzzling and high-sounding words."[8]

The Fourth Noble Truth (*Magga*, the Path)
See the following section.


**The Seven Pillars and The Fourth Noble Truth (the Path)**

The Fourth Noble Truth describes the Path to the cessation of *dukkha*. The Buddhist path is known as the "middle path." Middle because it rejects the extremes of over-indulging in the pleasure of the senses, on one hand, and the extreme of self-denial through severe ascetic practices, on the other hand. The Buddhist path is also called the Noble Eightfold Path because it is composed of eight precepts all meant to work together as the eight spokes that maintain the structural integrity of a wheel (*Dharma* Wheel).

The Path is divided in three sections. The first section is about ethical conduct: How does the individual's life impact other people? This section relates to pillar #6 (deep connection with others). When we are deeply connected with others, love and compassion conduct our speech, actions and livelihood. Specifically, in this section the Path indicates:

1. Right speech (*Samma ditthi*): Right speech means always speaking with impeccable, benevolent, caring and gentle words. It excludes lies, words that bring hatred, disharmony and separation, any abusive language, gossips and meaningless conversations. "One should not speak carelessly: speech

---

[7] *Ibid.*, p. 35.
[8] *Ibid.*, p. 44.

should be at the right time and place. If one cannot say something useful, one should keep 'noble silence'."[9]

2. <u>Right action (*Samma sankappa*)</u>: Right action entails no harming, destroying, stealing, deceiving, concealing, and engaging in sexual dissipation. It includes reaching to others in acts of peace, love and assistance in order to lead others to live a fulfilling life.

3. <u>Right livelihood (*Samma vaca*)</u>: This precept indicates that our way to make a living must be aligned with the values originated by the feelings of deep connection with other human beings. Our jobs should not cause any harm to anyone now or in the future; they should be honorable, respectable and harmonious for the whole of society. It is clear that when we are deeply connected with others, our livelihood reflects the way we care about those who share the planet with us. In Buddhism, working for any company or army that benefits from war is immoral, as is working for companies that destroy the environment and take unfair advantage of the members of society. "[The] Buddhist ethical and moral conduct aims at promoting a happy and harmonious life both for the individual and for society...No spiritual development is possible without this moral basis."[10]

The next section of the Path is about mental discipline. This section connects with pillar #1 (emotional recapitulation), pillar #4 (mental purity) and pillar #5 (meditation). This section is comprised of three precepts, namely:

4. <u>Right effort (*Samma vayama*)</u>: Effort requires will and *vice versa*. According to Buddha's teachings, there are four main efforts: (a) the effort to prevent the arising of evil and unwholesome states of mind, (b) the effort to overcome and eliminate evil and unwholesome states of mind once they have arisen, (c) the effort to create good and wholesome states of mind that haven't arisen yet and (d) the effort to maintain and foment the good and wholesome states of mind

[9] *Ibid.*, p. 47.
[10] *Ibid.*

already in existence so that they would not disappear but grow stronger. These efforts are in connection with pillar #1 (emotional recapitulation) since emotional recapitulation is an activity of our own volition to understand the maladies of our subconscious programs, the ones that cause the unwholesome states of mind.

5. Right mindfulness (*Samma sati*): Right mindfulness requires being attentive to and aware of (a) the body, (b) feelings (good, bad or neutral), (c) the mind and (d) objects and their mental qualities. This spoke of the *Dharma* Wheel has to do with emotional recapitulation (pillar #1) because of the awareness of feelings, and with concentration (pillar #4, mind purity) because of the attentiveness dedicated to the body (as in yoga *asanas*) and other objects. In fact, concentration on the breathing (*pranayama*) helps to establish the right mindfulness by means of concentration.

6. Right Concentration (*Samma Samadhi*): According to Buddhist teachings, right concentration is a process of four stages very similar to the one explained in Chapter 7 wherein concentration (pillar # 4) becomes meditation (pillar #5) and then Union with God (pillar #7). In Buddhist terms, the first stage is characterized by applied and sustained thoughts. In the second stage, there are no more thoughts but a state of joy and bliss. Next, during the third stage, this state of joy and bliss starts disappearing for a sense of equanimity in which no sensation, joyful or not, is felt. Finally in the fourth and last stage of the process of right concentration, all thoughts, feelings and sensations are gone, and a pure state of equanimity of sameness and steadiness reigns in the individual.

The final section of the Path is traditionally called wisdom. We can interpret wisdom as the natural result of practicing the previous aspects of the Path, or their equivalent pillars. But also, this wisdom enhances and revitalizes one's ethical conduct and mental discipline. The eight aspects of the Path are linked together and mean to work simultaneously. As one sets the *Dharma* Wheel in motion, each one of the spokes helps the entire wheel to spin forward. The wisdom of the Path comprises:

7. Right thought or intention (*Samma sankappa*): Real, pure and genuine wisdom generate right thoughts and intentions. "[All] thoughts of selfish desire, ill-will, hatred and violence are the result of lack of wisdom—in all spheres of life whether individual, social or political."[11] This spoke means thoughts of love, compassion and selfless detachment.

8. Right understanding or view (*Samma ditthi*): In Buddhist philosophy, the right understanding corresponds to the internalization and comprehension of The Four Noble Truths. This understanding allows the individual to *see* reality as it is and, therefore, to break free from suffering.

---

[11] *Ibid.*, p. 49.

# APPENDIX B
# PRACTICE INSTRUCTIONS

## Instructions for Part 1 (Emotional Recapitulation and Intention)

1. Sit in a comfortable position maintaining your back straight, head aligned with your spine and the entire torso lifted up. Pictures 1a and 1b are suggestions of sitting poses for recapitulation.

 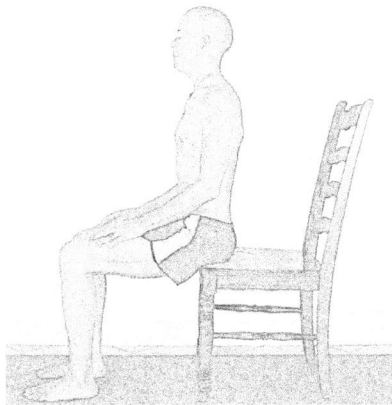

Picture 1a                    Picture 1b

# Instructions for Part 2 (Knowing Our Potential)

1. Stand on your feet and extend your arms overhead with your fingertips reaching for the ceiling. Stretch from the waist up through the four sides of your torso, armpits, shoulders and finally arms and fingers. Then lean towards your right side (Picture 2), come back to center and then lean towards your left side. Repeat a couple of times.

2. Stand with your arms alongside your torso and engage

Picture 2

your abdominal muscles slightly. Twist your upper torso to the right and then to the left (Picture 3). Repeat the twist from side to side several times. Intensify the twist with your abdominal muscles.

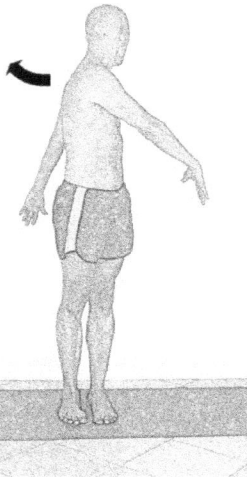

Picture 3

3. Stand with your arms alongside your torso, rotate your shoulders several times in one direction first and then repeat in the other direction (Picture 4). Now extend your arms out at your sides until they are perpendicular to your torso.

Rotate your shoulders moving the entire extended arms with small circles (Picture 5). When your shoulders start feeling the resistance of the motion, rotate your shoulders and arms the other direction.

Picture 4

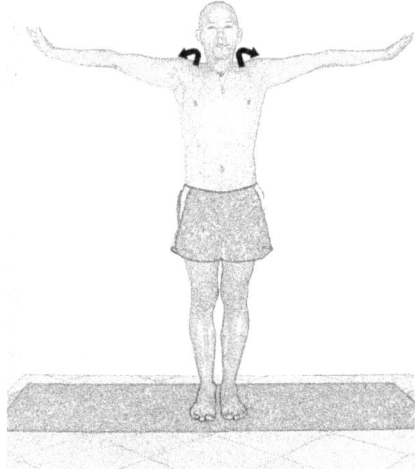

Picture 5

4. Stand on your feet and upon inhalation bring your upper back
   backwards into a small upper back bend (Picture 6a), look up,
   open your heart area and extend your arms out at your sides to
   receive energy from the universe; then during exhalation, bring
   your arms to the front and suspend them in the air as you round
   your back and look down (Picture 6b) at your body to let the
   energy just received settle in your body. Repeat a couple of
   times.

Picture 6a

Picture 6b

5. (This and the following four exercises are to strengthen the major muscles of your legs, your main connection with Earth, and prepare you for the next activities.). Stand on your tip-toes to engage your calf muscles (Picture 7). Slightly lower and lift your heels (do not let your heels touch the floor) such that your calves are active all the time. Breathe smoothly and with intention. Use a wall if you need it for balance. Stop when the strain in your calves is intense.

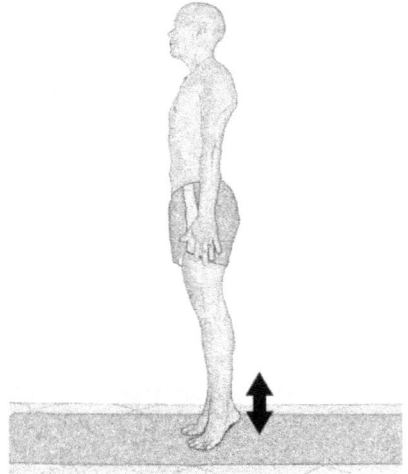

Picture 7

6. Stand with your feet two-shoulder-distance apart. Bend your knees to bring your sitting-bones down but not lower than your knees (horse stance) (Picture 8). Torso must be long and resting on top of the pelvis (not leaning forward). Hold the pose, relax the facial expression and breathe smoothly and with intention until you cannot bear the strain in the muscles of the front of your thighs (quadriceps).

Picture 8

7. Lie on your back (in a supine position), extend your legs on the floor and flex both feet (toes pointing to the ceiling). Lift your right leg straight up and bring it as close as possible to your chest while you engage your left leg and firmly press both heels away from the body. (If necessary, use a strap or belt around the right foot and use your hands to pull the strap and bring the lifted leg as close as possible to your torso) (Picture 9). Keep

the right knee straight as the right heel is firmly pressing away from the body. Relax your face, breathe smoothly, keep your intention alive and hold the stretch for as long as you can

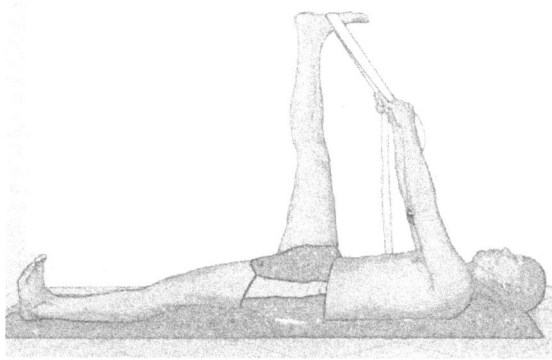

Picture 9

bear the stretch of the muscles of the back of the right thigh (hamstrings). Switch legs when you are ready and repeat for the other leg.

8. Still lying on your back, bring your knees to your chest and then open and straighten out your legs to opposite sides. Press out your heels in opposite directions keeping your knees straight to activate the inner thighs (Picture 10).

Picture 10

Relax your face, breathe smoothly, keep your intention alive and hold the stretch for as long as you can bear the stretch of your legs.

9. Lie on your left side with the right leg on top of the other and feet flexed. Hold your head with your left hand (right hand on the floor in front of you for balance) and lift your right leg as high as possible and press through the edge and heel of your right foot to firm the outer muscles of the lifted leg (Picture 11). Relax your face, breathe smoothly, keep your intention

alive and hold the stretch for as long as you can bear it. Switch sides when you are ready.

Picture 11

10. Lie on your back for the thread-the-needle exercise. Bend your knees keeping the soles of your feet on the floor. Place the right ankle on top of your left knee and flex the right foot. Thread the right arm through the hole made by and between the two legs while reaching your left hand around the the left leg and clasp your hands together holding the left thigh from the underside of the knee (or the left shin if your knee is not sensitive). Then pull the left leg in towards the left shoulder (Picture 12) while keeping the tail bone as close to the floor as possible. This opens your right hip muscles. Keep on pulling your left leg towards your chest as much as you can stand. When you are ready, switch to the other side to open the left hip muscles.

Picture 12

11. This exercise and the next two are to strengthen the abdominal muscles. Lie on your back, extend your legs on the floor and flex your feet. Inhale as you lift both straight legs (Picture 13a) as high as possible (try not to bend your knees) and exhale as

you lower them to hover just above the floor (Picture 13b). Keep on doing this until you feel the strain of your abdominal muscles. Rest for one breath.

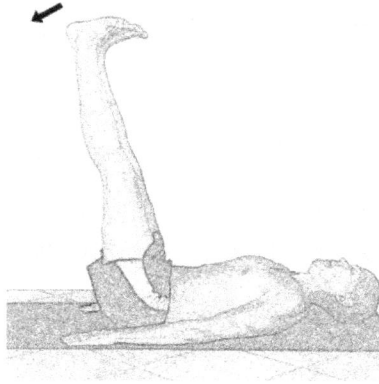

Picture 13a

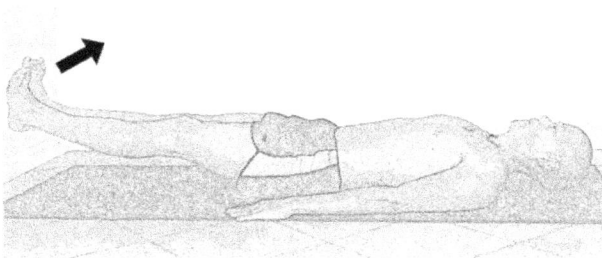

Picture 13b

12. Still lying on your back, bend your knees and bring both knees to your chest, inhale and extend your legs to hover above the floor (Picture 14a), exhale and bend your knees to be above your pelvis (Picture 14b). Repeat until you feel the strain of your abdominal muscles. Rest for one breath.

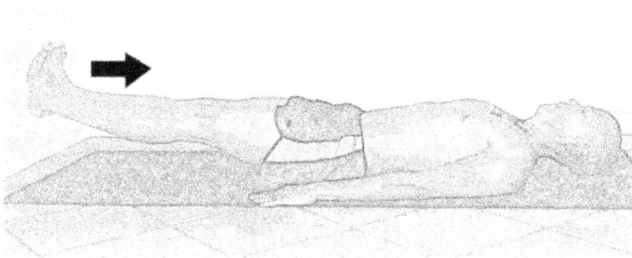

Picture 14a

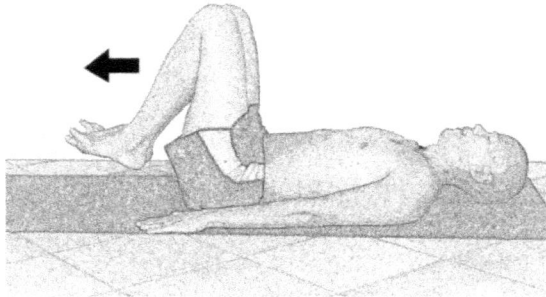

Picture 14b

13. Same as the exercise above but using one leg at a time (similar to bicycling) (Picture 15).

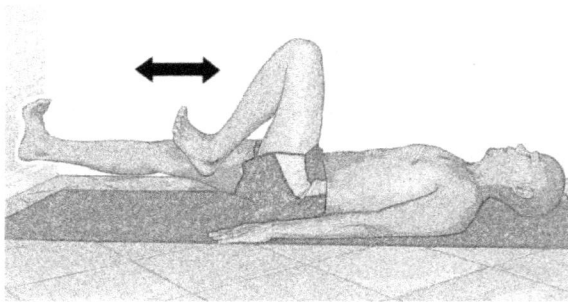

Picture 15

## Instructions for Part 3 (Living the Ruling Circumstances)

1. Run in place (or outdoors, if possible) at a moderate pace and then increase the pace to run as fast as you can (Picture 16). Run for at least four minutes leaving the last minute or so to run with full intensity. Feel free to do any kind of movement that brings more intensity to your workout. Depending on your physical condition, you may walk instead at a pace you can manage. The idea is to liberate the body to ease the mind. As the body works out, relax your face and breathe smoothly through your nose if possible. Remember you are in control of

your life (you could also inhale through the nose and exhale through the mouth if you feel short of breath). Do not make the common mistake of separating body and mind during this exercise,[1] make them work out together.

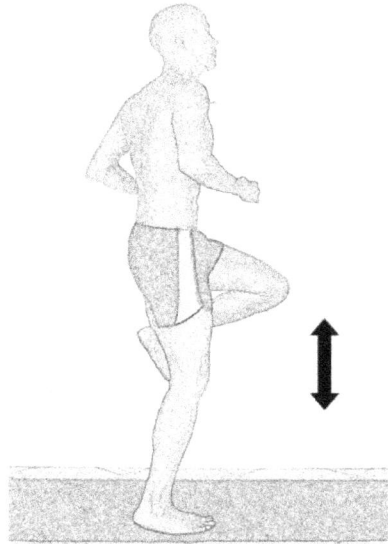

Picture 16

## Instructions for Part 4 (Dissolving and Removing the Delusions)

1. Lie on your belly (in a prone position) and do as many push-ups (Picture 17a) as you can (if this is too intense for you, use a wall instead of the floor (Picture 17b) or place your knees on the floor). Be very focused and intentionally strong. Inhale when you rise, exhale when you come down.

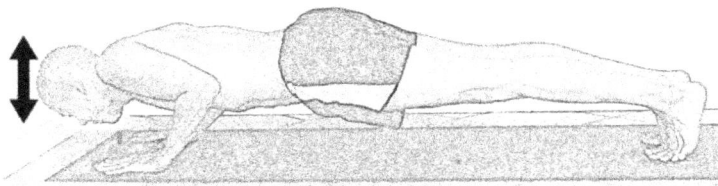

Picture 17a

[1] We can see this in gyms where people watch TV or read a magazine or are distracted by the loud music while they exercise.

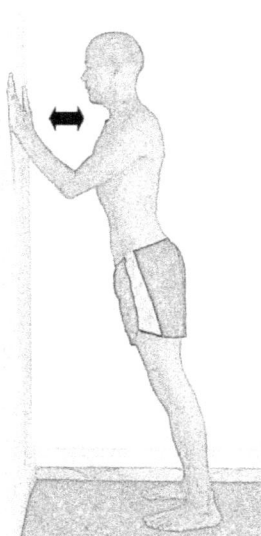

Picture 17b

2. Stand in a horse stance. Place your two fists around (or below) your waist. Tighten your fists and arms, contract the pelvic floor (the muscles between the genital and the anus), press your abdominal muscles in, expand your back and engage your upper chest while keeping a soft face and smooth breathing. Your expression must be peaceful as your body

Picture 18a

is as firm as it can be. Slowly cross your arms bringing the right fist to the left ear and left fist to the outside of the right armpit as you inhale (Picture 18a). Then, during exhalation, with full intention and strength move your right arm down so that the right fist is above the right thigh as you move the left fist to its original position (Picture 18b). Do the other side and repeat both sides several times. Do this exercise very strongly not releasing any part of your body but your face. Breathe with intention and ease. (You can think of this exercise as one intended to block the damaging old patterns of your subconscious).

Picture 18b

3.  Still in a horse stance, place your open hands around or below your waist with the palms facing forward, fingers down and curled in (Picture 19a). During inhalation, strongly and slowly press

Picture 19a

Picture 19b

and move the right hand forward by first rotating the entire hand so the knuckles are pointing up, the palm is facing forward and the arm is fully extended (Picture 19b). Exhale while pressing very strongly your right hand forward. Inhale, repeat with the left arm while you rotate and bring your right hand back to the initial position. Repeat both arms several times. Do this exercise very strongly engaging your abdominal and pelvic muscles, and the muscles of your torso and arms but keep your face soft similar to the previous exercise. Breathe with intention and ease. (You can think of this exercise as one intended to keep the damaging old patterns of your subconscious at a safe distance).

## Instructions for Part 5 (Bringing up Clarity and Receptivity)

1.  The Qigong practice requires that you maintain these six indications at all time in the exercises described below: (1) Stand with your feet a bit wider than shoulder-distance apart. (2) Bend your knees slightly to allow the natural flow of *chi*. (3) Slightly contract your anal sphincter and place the tip of your tongue on the upper palate of the mouth to close the microcosmic orbit. The microcosmic orbit is a circuit formed by the two main acupuncture vessels, the conception vessel for *yin* energy, which runs down from the mouth to the pelvic floor along the midline of the chest, and the governing vessel for *yang* energy, which runs up along the spine from the pelvic floor to the crown of the head and then down along the midline of the face to the mouth.[2] (4) Open your hands with fingers spread apart but relaxed to maximize *chi* manipulation. (5) Do not touch your body with your hands and (6) bear a gentle smile on your face.

2.  Make the palms of your hands face each other just around or below your navel while the upper arms are alongside your torso but not in contact with it. In this exercise do not let your hands touch one another and relax your shoulders and elbows

---

[2] According to *Taoist* medicine, the government and the conception vessels are the most important vessels to be trained with Qigong. From these vessels twelve main channels or meridians feed and they make possible for *yin* and *yang* to combine establishing the necessary balance for health and well-being.

while your back is upright. During inhalation, move your hands to each other until they are close enough (Picture 20a) that you can feel a sort of magnetic force between them; then exhale and move your hands away from each other (Picture 20b). Repeat several times and, at the end, stop the motion when your hands are separated about seven inches.

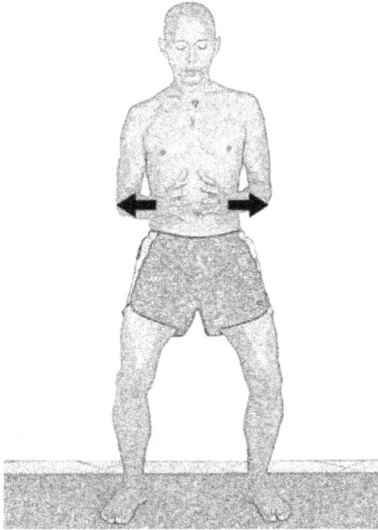

Picture 20a

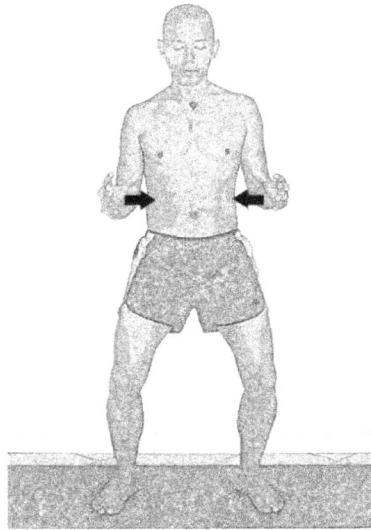

Picture 20b

3. With your hands separated as indicated in the previous exercise, visualize you are holding an invisible sphere of *chi* that you are shaping as round as possible (Picture 21a). Move your hands around this sphere but always keeping your palms facing each other on opposite sides of the sphere. When you feel that your sphere of *chi* has acquired enough *chi*, with your palms facing each other across the horizontal line and the

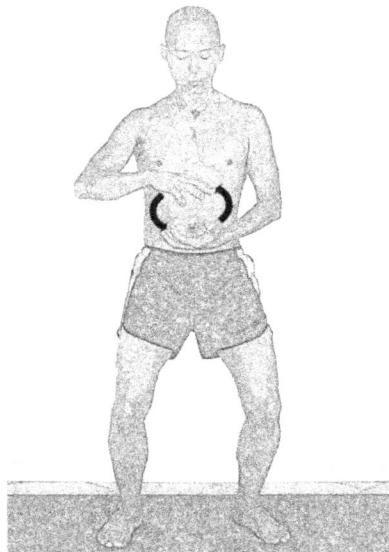

Picture 21a

sphere close to your lower belly, inhale while you lift the
sphere along the midline of the torso up to the forehead following an imaginary circle (Picture 21b), then, upon exhalation, lower the sphere along the other side of this imaginary
circle farther from the chest (Picture 21c). As you raise the
sphere, extend your legs (not all the way), and as you lower
the sphere, bend your knees (without straining them); thus
your body goes up and down with the sphere. Be very mindful
of this exercise, do it slowly with much intention and dedication. The circle represents the unity of everything that exists,
the *yin* and *yang*, the government and the conception vessels
connected as vital energy flows through your microcosmic orbit. Repeat the circle several times, and stop with your hands
in front of your lower belly.

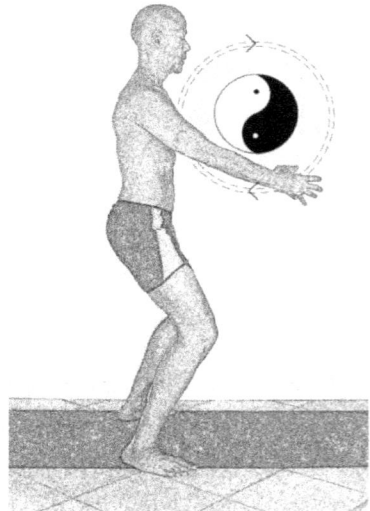

Picture 21b                    Picture 21c

4.  With your inhalation, raise the invisible sphere to the top of
    your head (Picture 22a, as always, do not touch your head or
    any part of your body with your hands). Upon exhalation bring
    the sphere down to your head and move your hands down
    along your body: ears (Picture 22b), shoulders, sides of your
    torso and hips to finally come to a rest facing the lower belly

for the next exercise (Picture 22c). The sphere's energy will spread from the top of the head all the way down through the back and front of your body.

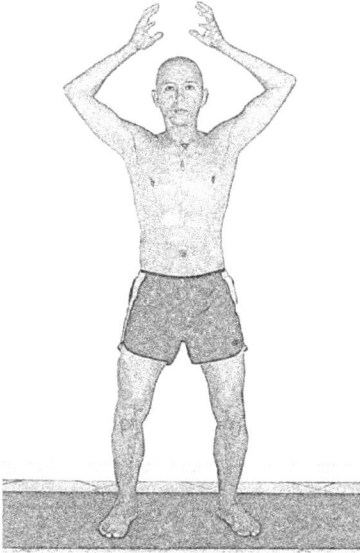

Picture 22a

Picture 22b

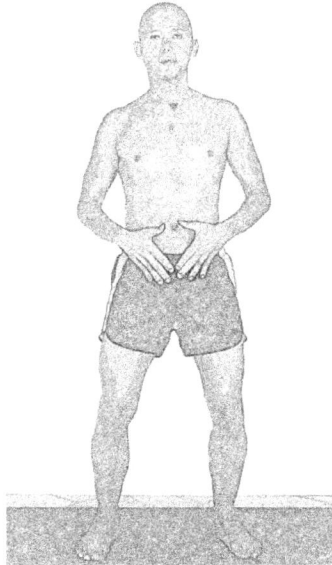

Picture 22c

5.  With the hands as indicated in Picture 23a and upon inhalation, move your hands upwards along both sides of the midline of your torso (Picture 23b) and take them apart as they reach the forehead to extend your arms wide open in a V shape (Picture

Picture 23a

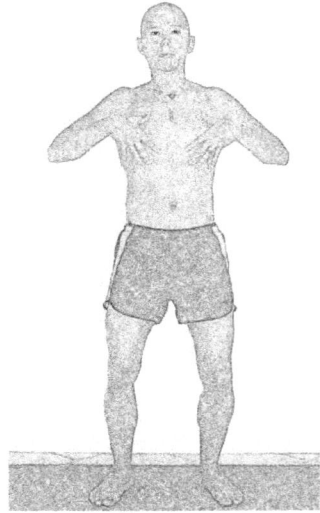
Picture 23b

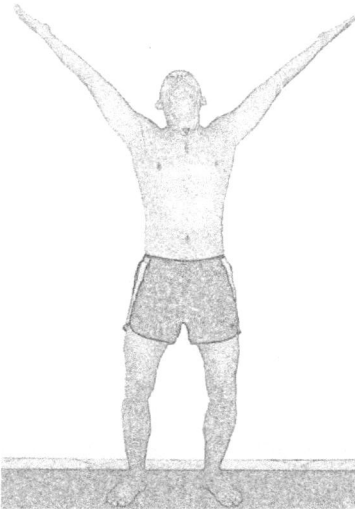
Picture 23c

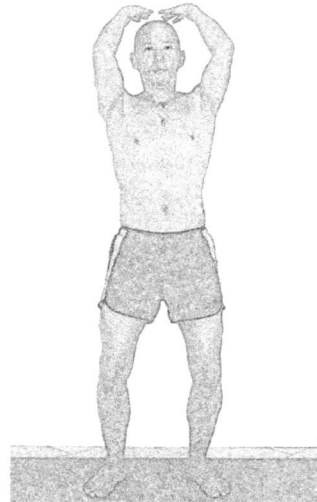
Picture 23d

23c). Look up to the sky, hold your breath, and bring your hands to the top of your head (Picture 23d), then start exhaling

Picture 23e                    Picture 23f

as your hands move along the face, the right side of the torso
(Picture 23e), the right pelvis, and the right leg all the way to
your right foot (Picture 23f) and the ground around it (bend
your knees as needed). Hold your breath for a few seconds,
and then extracting energy from Earth, initiate your inhalation
and move your hands upward. Let your hands travel your right
leg, right pelvis to the midsection of your torso until your
hands rest in front of your lower belly (initial position). Exhale
in this position. Now do this exercise for the left side to complete a cycle. Repeat several cycles. Remember to keep your
hands as close to your body as possible without touching it.
Move your hands slowly, gently and with conviction. In this
exercise you become the most harmonious conduit for the Creation to express itself as you exchange energy between Heaven
(*yang*) and Earth (*yin*). With this exercise, *chi* flows freely
through you, you empty your mind and you heal your body.

6. Do free-style Qigong according to your own intuition. At this
   point you have created enough openness in yourself that you
   will intuitively manipulate the *chi* according to your specific
   needs.

## Instructions for Part 6 (Rooting Down in Earth to Fill the Empty Vessel)

1.  Mountain pose (*tadasana*): The mountain pose (*tadasana*) (Picture 24) is not just standing up. It is an active pose wherein the body is symmetrically aligned along all its dimensions and strong with the participation of its major muscles. Here are some key points of this *asana*: feet may be touching each other or slightly separated, they must be parallel and strongly pressing down; all muscles in the legs are engaged, especially the quadriceps; the pelvis is aligned not tilting forward or backward; very importantly, the spine is long and erect; the upper chest is lifted without puffing out the lower ribs; shoulder blades are pressed into the body; shoulders are drawn away from the neck and aligned with the torso, not rounding forward

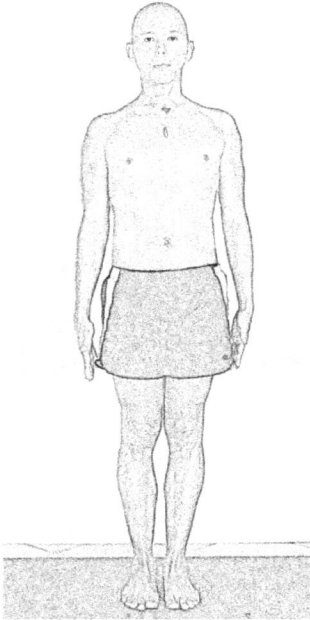

    Picture 24    or backward; neck is long, aligned with the torso, and crown of the head is reaching up; arms are engaged and extended alongside the torso and fingers are pointing to the ground. This pose constitutes a statement of your determination. (Hold the pose for at least five full breaths).

2.  Squat pose (*malasana*) with breath of fire (*agni prasana*): The breath of fire is a rapid breathing with deep but fast inhales and exhales while the abdominal muscles are relaxed following the breath in and out. The sound of the breath of fire resembles the sound of a locomotive engine in action. The squat pose (Picture 25a) has some key points: use the elbows to outwardly press the inner thighs as the thighs resist the elbows; keep the back long and straight as you bring your chest forward towards your hands; contract the urethral and anal

Picture 25a                    Picture 25b

sphincters and lift the muscles of the pelvic floor. (If the squat pose is challenging for you try to sit on a surface with a comfortable height as the soles of the feet are on the ground (Picture 25b)). The breath of fire is a cleansing and energetic breathing, and the squat pose brings your core closest to the ground while keeping the two feet firmly planted on Earth. The combination increases vitality and Earth awareness. (Hold the pose for at least one minute).

3. Seated cross-legged pose (*siddhasana, sukhasana* or any other similar pose) with breath retention (*kumbhaka*): As in all seated poses (Picture 26), keep your *tadasana* key points for the torso: back upright, chest lifted, shoulders away from ears, etc. Relax your arms and place your hands facing up on your thighs (In general, for all seated poses, consider sitting on a surface with the appropriate height for you if keeping

Picture 26

this pose becomes uncomfortable for you[3]). During this exercise, contract your sphincters and the pelvic floor as indicated in the previous exercise. In order to transition from the breath of fire, take several *ujjayi* (victorious) breaths once in the pose; then in your next *ujjayi* inhalation hold your breath for a few seconds (*antara kumbhaka*) followed by the respective *ujjayi* exhalation and again hold the breath for a few seconds (*bahya kumbhaka*). Repeat several times for at least two minutes. The duration of the breath retention depends on the practitioner. Starts first with a count of five or less and gradually increase the count as you get more experienced (ideally, inhalation, exhalation and both retentions should have the same duration but you can start with different durations for the retentions[4]). Return to the victorious breath at any time that the retention breath creates discomfort in you, and try again.

4.  Bound angle pose (*baddha konasana*): While still in a seated position, put the soles of your feet together (Picture 27a) and engage your pelvic floor again, as required in the previous two exercises, and while keeping your torso as in *tadasana*, flap

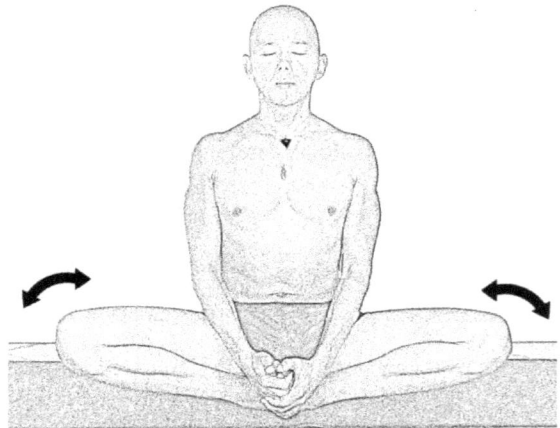

Picture 27a

your legs like imitating the wing flapping of a butterfly. Do it for five breaths. Then stop, inhale, lengthen your spine, and as you exhale lean forward as far down as you can go while

---

[3] You can always improvise a surface to sit, stacking up blankets or towels to the right height for you.

[4] The breath retention after exhalation is the most challenging. Initially, its duration can be zero count and then you can increase it gradually until it is long enough for you.

keeping the spine completely straight (see Picture 27b). Hold this pose for four breaths after which you inhale and bring your torso back to the upright position.

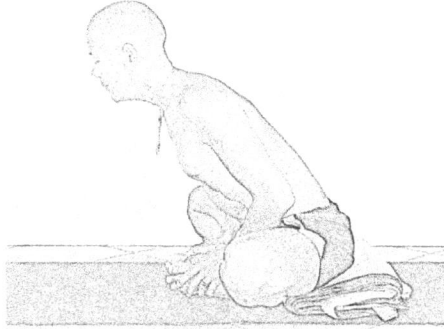

Picture 27b

5. <u>Twist in seated cross-legged pose</u>: In this pose, twist as indicated in Picture 28b.

Start twisting from the stomach holding the corresponding knee with two hands (see Picture. 28a) and engage your pelvic floor. When the twist is settled in the lower torso using the abdominal muscles, slowly start twisting the upper torso as you place the corresponding hand on the floor and hold the corresponding knee with the opposite hand (Picture 28b). Hold each twist for four breaths.

Picture 28a

Twists massage your internal core organs and are ideal for detoxification. (Important: Tailor this twist and any other twist according to your flexibility and do not do it if you are beyond the first trimester of pregnancy.)

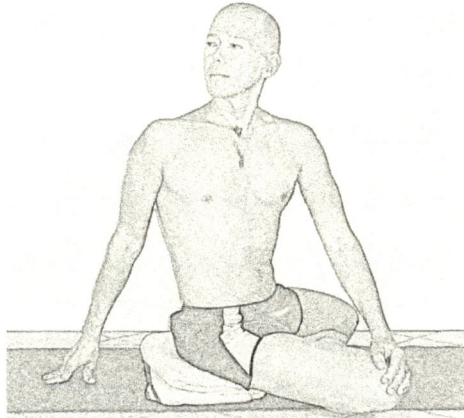

Picture 28b

6.  Cat/Cow (*marjaryasana/bidalasana*): In these poses, shoulders
    are directly above hands, hips are directly above ankles, and
    toenails and top of the feet are touching the ground (Picture
    29a). These two
    poses are not held
    but constantly mov-
    ing from one to the
    other. Start with a
    neutral back com-
    pletely horizontal
    and engage your
    lower abdominal
    muscles (Picture
    29a), in inhalation
    move into the cow
    pose (Picture 29b)
    and in exhalation

Picture 29a

    move to the cat pose (Picture 29c). Alternate between cow and
    cat for five breaths as you synchronize your breath with your
    motion.

Picture 29b

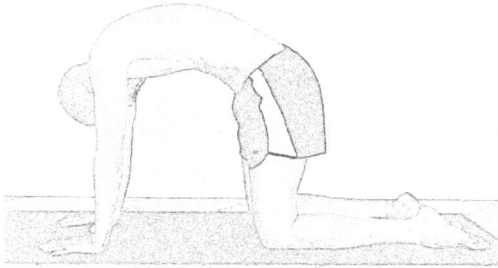

Picture 29c

7. Child's pose (*balasana*): At the end of the cat/cow exercise come into the child's pose (Picture 30a). Extend your arms in front of you with elbows off the floor and hands shoulder-

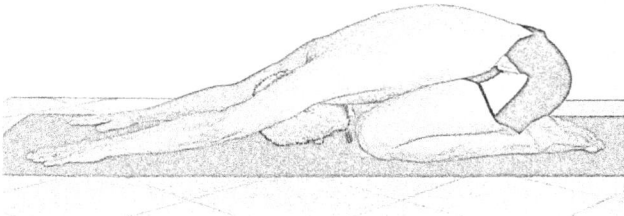

Picture 30a

width apart. Picture 30b shows a modification of the pose for people with sensitive knees and hips. Hold this pose for three breaths with the purpose of surrendering to Earth.

Picture 30b

8.  Downward facing dog pose (*adho mukha svanasana*): From the child's pose, walk your hands forward as far as you can and keeping them in place lift your pelvis up and back into the

Picture 31a

downward facing dog pose. In this pose (Picture 31a), hands are shoulder-distance apart and feet are hip-distance apart (you can separate hands and feet further apart to ease the pose) so that your body forms an upside-down V shape. Press firmly down with your hands to rebound and use that energy to press your tail bone away from your hands; keep your spine long and straight and aligned with the arms and head; straighten your legs and draw the heels towards the floor as much as you can. In this inversion pose, we use our hands and feet to hold strongly onto Earth for its nourishment. If you find this pose challenging, widen the distances between your hands and feet, or try using a wall as illustrated in Picture 31b. Hold this pose for five breaths and then walk your feet to your hands, bend your knees and slowly raise yourself to stand up to the mountain pose.

Picture 31b

9. Warrior I pose (*Vira-bhadrasana I*): This and the next three standing poses are strong grounding poses that free you from delusions. These poses express the power of your spiritual convictions. They state that you perceive reality as it is and that you are facing the delusions of this physical world with the serenity of a warrior unafraid to die. After all, the greatest battles are not the battles of war but

Picture 32a

the battles within, as we struggle to align our utmost pure

essence with our thoughts and actions. From the mountain pose of the previous exercise, step your left foot back as far as needed, the right leg is now in front. In warrior I (Picture 32a), the torso (from shoulders to pelvis) is meant to face forward maintaining the *tadasana* key points for the torso, the front leg is bent such that the front thigh is parallel to the floor and the front ankle is directly below the front knee, the back leg is straight and fully active and both feet are firmly pressing down into the floor. In this

Picture 32b

pose also, arms are firmly extended overhead keeping the shoulders away from neck and ears. Hold the pose for at least five breaths. Change legs and repeat (use *tadasana* as the transition pose). (To ease the pose, see Picture 32b.)

10. <u>Warrior II pose (*Virabhadrasna II*)</u>: In this pose (Picture 33a), the torso is meant to face sidewise keeping *tadasana* points. In order to come to the pose, make the transition from *tadasana* and step your feet parallel apart as wide as needed; then, turn the right leg (the front leg) out until the right toes are pointing straight ahead to the right with the second toe aligned

Picture 33a

with the kneecap. Turn the back foot slightly in. In warrior II (Picture 33a), the front leg is bent such that the front thigh is parallel to the floor and the front ankle is directly below the front knee, the back leg is straight and fully active and the feet are firmly pressing down into the floor. The arms are extended out to both sides at shoulder height and aligned with the front and back legs. Hands are

Picture 33b

facing down and the head turned in the direction of the front leg. Hold the pose for at least five breaths, after which you straighten you front leg and turn your legs until your feet are parallel and wide apart again. Change legs and do the other side by following the steps you did for the right side but now correspondingly for the left side.
(To ease the pose, see Picture 33b.)

11. Thunderbolt (or chair) pose (_utkatasana_): From the mountain pose, bend your knees and raise your arms to come to the thunderbolt pose (Picture 34a). In this pose, feet and knees are together and parallel, arms are firmly extended while shoulders are away from neck and ears, and sitting bones are drawn downward (not backward). Hold this pose for at least five breaths. (See Picture 34b for a variation at the wall).

Picture 34a

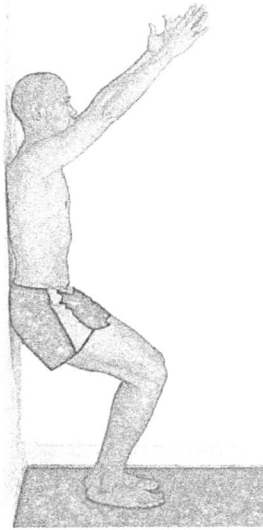

Picture 34b

12. <u>Tree pose (*vrksasana*)</u>: From *tadasana* come to the pose illustrated in Picture 35a. Press the lifted foot and the inner thigh of the standing leg against each other and keep the torso as in *tadasana*. Place the lifted foot above or below but not at the knee level of the standing leg. If the balance is difficult to maintain, try the variation illustrated in Picture 35b or use a wall. Hold the pose for at least five breaths and repeat for the other leg.

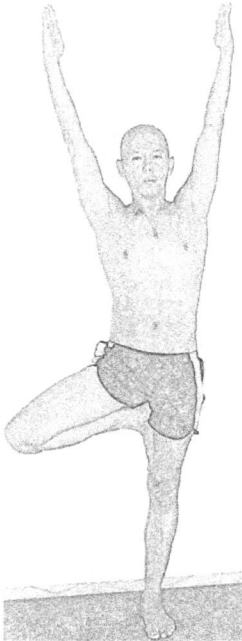

Picture 35a

Picture 35b

13. <u>Standing forward bend pose</u> (*uttanasana*): To get in this pose from *tadasana*, bend your knees and fold forward at the hips until you are able to get your chest in contact with your thighs (Picture 36a); then, start straightening your legs while keeping your chest as close as possible to your thighs, and let your head hang with its crown pointing to the floor (Picture 36b). Feet are parallel and together or at the most hip-distance apart. Stay for at least five breaths, after which you bend your knees, place your hands on the floor and step your feet back to the next pose.

Picture 36a

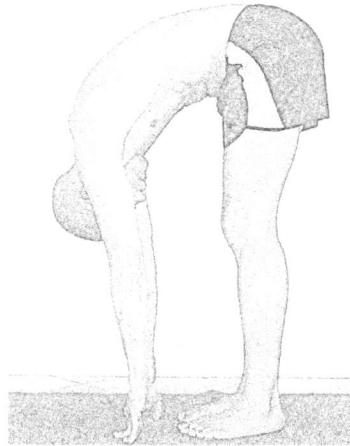

Picture 36b

14. <u>Planck pose</u> (*ardha chaturanga dandasana*): In this pose (Picture 37), put your hands on the floor and straighten up your

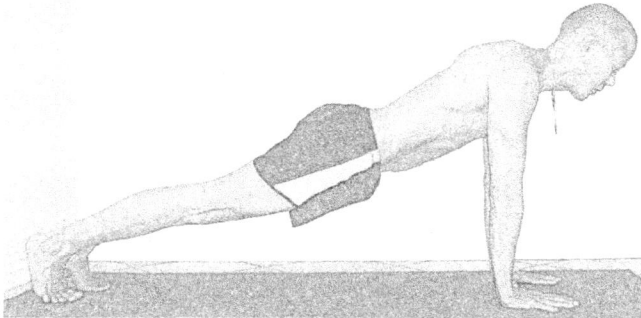

Picture 37

arms into push-up position. Make sure that your head, neck, torso, pelvis, legs and heels are aligned in one straight line. Firm your lower abdominal muscles and press your heels backward. Hold this pose as long as you can and place your knees on the floor to make a transition to the next pose.

15. Locust pose (*salabhasana*): Before engaging in this pose (Picture 38a), lie on your belly (prone position) with your arms alongside your torso. Turn your head to the left to allow your right cheek to rest on the floor for a moment. To come into the pose lift your legs, head, upper torso and arms (see Picture 38a). In the pose, to avoid lower back problems, press your tail

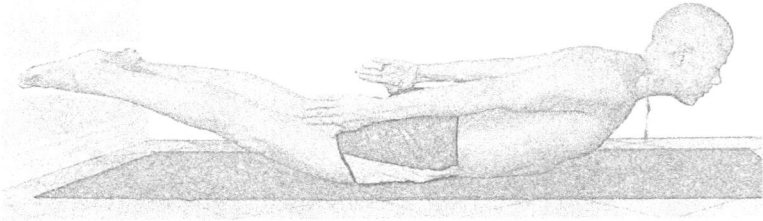

Picture 38a

bone towards the back of your knees and extend your feet as far as they can reach. Hold the pose for four breaths. Repeat again but now starting with your left cheek on the floor. (See Picture 38b for an alternative to this pose). This is an invigorating back bend that amplifies energy and stores it for moments of need.

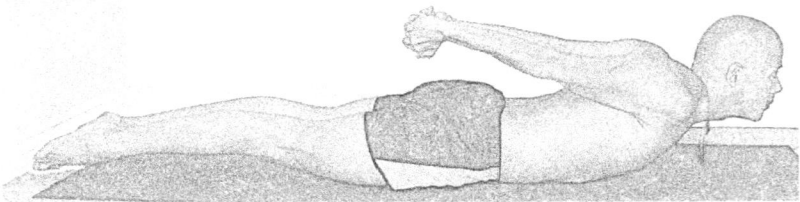

Picture 38b

16. Child's pose (*balasana*) (See Pictures 30a and 30b).

17. Stick pose (*dandasana*): This pose (Picture 39a) has the same key points as *tadasana* with the exception that you are sitting on the floor with the torso perpendicular to the legs. Legs are

active and toes are pointing to the ceiling; hands are not pressing down (the support for this pose originates in the back and abdominal muscles). Hold this pose for at least five breaths, then lean forward as far as you can while maintaining your back straight (no rounding of the back) (Picture 39b). Hold this extra forward bend for at least five breaths. This pose is to indicate that we abide by the natural order of the universe even though sometimes following the natural order does not seem to be an easy thing to do.

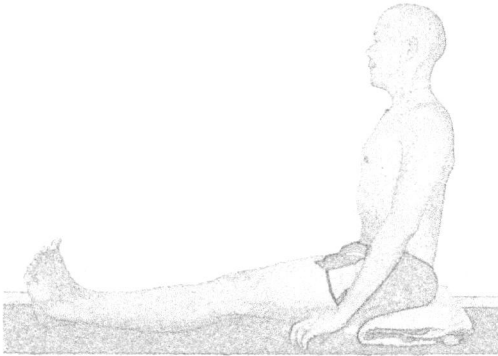

Picture 39a

Picture 39b

18. <u>Twist with one leg extended (modification of *Marichyasana*)</u>: The same general concepts of the twist explained previously

apply for this pose (see Picture 40a). (For each side, hold each twist for five breaths.) (See Picture 40b for a variation.)

Picture 40a

Picture 40b

19. <u>Bridge pose (*setu bandha sarvangasana*)</u>: To come into this pose, lie down on your back with the soles of your feet on the floor close to your sitting bones and arms alongside your torso; then press your feet firmly down and lift your hips. In the pose (Picture 41), use the strength of your feet and legs to keep your pelvis high off the floor. Do not compress your lower back and clench your buttocks; do lengthen them towards the back of the knees. Feet are parallel and hip-distance apart while the ankles are directly below the knees. (Hold this pose for five breaths minimum.)

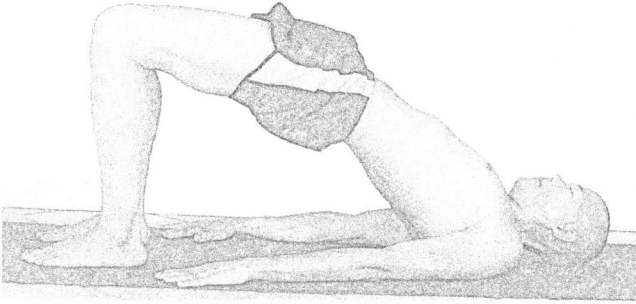

Picture 41

20. <u>Rock-the-baby pose with smooth, long deep breath</u>: Picture 42a illustrates this pose and Picture 42b illustrates a variation for the same pose. To come into this pose, start sitting on the floor in crossed-leg position and then with both of your arms lift a leg up and cradle it in your arms. In the pose, rock the lifted leg side to side from its hip connection. This pose will soothe the practitioner and prepare their hips for the final seated poses. (Rock each leg as long as needed while doing long, deep breathing, not *ujjayi* breath.)

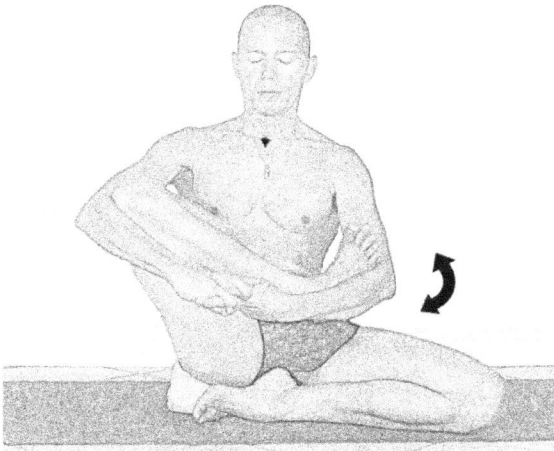

Picture 42a

Picture 42b

## Instructions for Part 7 (Reaching Beyond the Realm of Forms)

1. Alternate nostril breathing (*anuloma viloma*) in a cross-legged seated pose: With the right hand as indicated in Picture 43, use

Picture 43

the thumb to gently press the right nostril, and the ring and little fingers together to gently press the left nostril in order to alternately breathe through one nostril at a time. Exhale completely and start the alternate nostril breathing as follows: (a) press the right nostril with the thumb and breathe in through the left nostril, (b) press the left nostril with the ring and little fingers and breathe out through the right nostril, (c) keeping the left nostril pressed, breathe in through the right nostril, (d) press the right nostril, and breathe out through the left nostril, (e) repeat the cycle from (a) to (d). Do as many cycles as needed and remember that after breathing in you should switch nostrils. This exercise re-synchronizes both brain hemispheres and calms and balances the mind.

2. <u>Breath retention with the three locks (*bandhas*) in a cross-legged seated pose</u>: Breathe normally. Inhale deeply and hold your breath. Lift your pelvic floor contracting the urethral and anal sphincters (lock #1), press your stomach in towards the spine to create a depression in your abdominal area (lock #2), and bring your chin to your chest without straining your neck (lock #3, think as if you were bringing the sternum to the chin rather than the other way around, see Picture 44). Hold the breath as long as you can without releasing any of the locks. Then release only lock #3 by bringing your chin back up to the level position. Exhale completely and engage lock #3 again. Hold out the breath as long as you can without releasing any of the locks. Release lock #3 again, inhale and release lock#2, and then lock #1. This exercise seals the energy cultivated so far within the major energetic centers of the body.

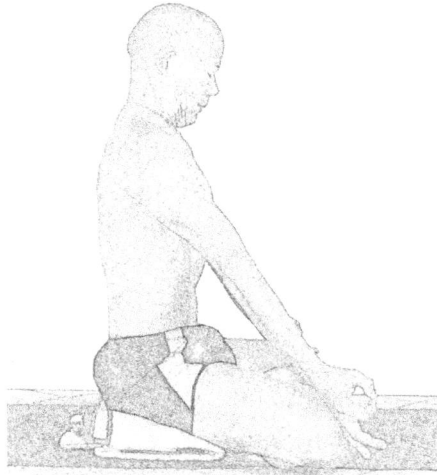

Picture 44

3. <u>Chanting</u>: Chant AUM (ah-oo-mm) seven times (or any multiple of seven). The mechanical vibration of this chanting will create electromagnetic vibrations at the cell level in your body to get you ready for meditation. The first sound A (ah) is made with the mouth wide open and directing the vibration towards the lower torso and pelvis. The second sound U ('oo') is made

with the mouth closed only midway (half closed) and directing the vibration to the heart area. Finally, the last sound M ('mm') is made with the mouth closed and directing the vibration to the nasal cavity and the crown of the head.

4. <u>Meditation</u>: The last element of the practice is a meditation while seated in a cross-legged position (modify the pose according to your comfort and remember to keep your torso as in *tadasana*). Close your eyes and start the meditation by concentrating on the air you breathe. Relax and take long and deep breaths. As you inhale, think you are directing the air (energy) to the lower abdomen and pelvic floor. In exhalation, think that you raise the air (energy) from the pelvic floor towards your heart and then towards the top of your head. Visualize that as the air travels upwards in your body, your energy is purified as your heart purifies your mind. From here, everything depends on your readiness. By narrowing your concentration to the mere essentiality of the air you breathe you will find out that the air is energy and energy is you; you will experience moments of profound connection and unity. Everything will occur at its due time, there is no rush but the peace and serenity of the moment we live. (Meditate as long as you can, the longer the better.)

Once you finish your meditation, rub your hands together briskly to activate them and cover your eyes with your hands for a few seconds. Then, use your hands to travel your body down in a Qigong fashion followed by a self-massage in your face, neck, head and ears.

*Contemplate Nature and you contemplate God.*
*Protect Mother Earth and you protect your soul.*
*Live within the harmony of the Creation*
*and you live in Happiness.*

# ABOUT THE AUTHOR

With a Bachelor's in Electronic Engineering and a Master's in Systems Engineering, José A. Luzardo (or JAL as he is also known) started his career as an academic, teaching at the Universidad Simón Bolívar in Caracas, Venezuela. In 1997, he obtained his Ph.D. degree in Engineering Mathematics from Claremont Graduate University and California State University, Long Beach. After his doctorate, he transitioned out of academia and started working full-time for industry in different high-tech companies in California.

With his technical skills and knowledge in high demand, Dr. Luzardo seemed to have complete control of his life until one day when he was about to lose everything he had ever really loved in his life—opening up a whole aspect of reality he never saw before. As a result, in February 2010 he and his wife, Ngoc Luzardo, founded Ardent Light to spread healing and peace, helping others to awake to this new realm of possibilities. In addition to his newfound gift and passion for writing, JAL is also a Reiki Master and a 500-Hr-certified Yoga instructor. He combines both disciplines, along with Qigong, in a unique and powerful way to free the body and the mind from blockages. JAL and Ngoc (a Holistic Health Practitioner and Divine Openings Giver and Healer) offer personalized holistic healing services through Ardent Light in Irvine, California. Learn more at www.ardentlight.com.

www.ingramcontent.com/pod-product-compliance
Lightning Source LLC
Chambersburg PA
CBHW032050080426
42733CB00006B/222